THE NOISE
OF CULTURE

THE NOISE
OF CULTURE

Literary Texts in a
World of Information

WILLIAM R. PAULSON

Cornell University Press

ITHACA AND LONDON

CORNELL UNIVERSITY PRESS GRATEFULLY ACKNOWLEDGES
A GRANT FROM THE ANDREW W. MELLON FOUNDATION
THAT AIDED IN BRINGING THIS BOOK TO PUBLICATION.

First published 1988 by Cornell University Press.

International Standard Book Number 0-8014-2102-0
Library of Congress Catalog Card Number 87-47822

Printed in the United States of America

Librarians: Library of Congress cataloging information appears on the last page of the book.

The paper in this book is acid-free and meets the guidelines for permanence and durability of the Committee on Production Guidelines for Book Longevity of the Council on Library Resources.

Contents

Preface

Literature and information make an uneasy pair. For seventy years formalist criticism has instilled in us the idea that literary texts are not primarily messages bearing information but, rather, autonomous objects that put into question our everyday view of language as communication and that must be investigated on their own terms. Humanistic scholars, meanwhile, are likely to see in the concept of information a kind of knowledge so external to the individual subject as to be barely worthy of the term *knowledge* and certainly inappropriate to describe the personal and ineffable experience of knowing literature. The world of information, in one sense, is the computerized society, the electronic global village in which anything not translatable into machine language can be at most a quaint relic, surely not a legitimate part of knowledge. Trying to understand the place of literary texts in this world may seem a perverse or self-defeating exercise, for it means speculating on the role of literature in a postliterary culture.

Yet this is by no means the only sense in which we may speak of a world of information. Gregory Bateson liked to define information as any difference that makes a difference, and in this sense information fills and indeed constructs the biological and social and cultural worlds. Departures from sameness and contexts in which these departures have effects are part of all systems that exhibit adaptive or cognitive behavior, be they thermostats, frogs, corporations, or scholarly disciplines. We now know how to read literary texts as systems of differences that make differences, and when Jacques Derrida, another strong theorist of difference, tells us that "there is no outside-the-text," he reminds us that the differential phenomena we know as textuality do not stop at the boundaries of works but extend throughout the cultural and mental contexts in which works are possible. Texts do not represent something outside of and unlike themselves, nor do they function as autonomous, self-referential monads; they are formed and informative objects that make differences in a formed and informative world.

This book began to take shape when I brought together two lines of thought that had been distracting me from more conventional literary studies. The first was a sense that literature's role in culture could best be thought of neither as a message nor as an object but rather as a source of differences. This approach implied abandoning—at least provisionally—the claim that literature is the vehicle of truths or teachings central to our culture and that the study of literature should thus have as its goal the successful reception of this central message that a civilization sends to itself over time. Displaced from the center to the margins of culture—a move that may in fact be inevitable in the information society—literature begins to look like a complex discursive form that can enrich thought and inspire new moves in the language games of society precisely because it differs from the communicative and instrumental modes of being-in-language that now seem culturally dominant. In other words, I came to think that in order to understand how important literature is and can be, it would be necessary to give up traditional assumptions about how important it is and has been.

While pursuing these reflections on what might somewhat grandiosely be called a "postmodern legitimation of literary studies," I discovered information theory and in particular the theory expounded by Henri Atlan of self-organization from noise. With its parallels to statistical thermodynamics, information theory suggests ways in which the structure and dynamics of communication and informational systems can be seen as linked to the relational properties of the physical world. In the writings of Michel Serres in particular, this link implies a structural basis for interdisciplinary approaches that bring together the study of texts and modern scientific thought. Atlan's formalism of self-organization from noise provides a framework for understanding how ordered complexity, information, even meaning, can arise from interaction with disorder. By *noise* is meant not loud or obnoxious sounds but anything that gets mixed up with messages as they are sent. Noise causes a loss of information in transmitted messages, but in organized systems in which message transmission is but a component function, the variety introduced by noise can come to be informative and meaningful in another, emergent context. The question of how there can be complex cultural meaning in spite of textual dissemination thus appears homologous to the question of how there can be complex natural structures in spite of the physical law of increasing entropy in a closed system.

Bringing together self-organization and the marginality of literature, I came to the assumptions that underlie the central arguments of this book: first, that literature is a noisy transmission channel that assumes its noise so as to become something other than a transmission channel, and second, that literature, so constituted, functions as the noise of culture, as a perturbation or source of variety in the circulation and production of discourses and ideas.

Only after working out the general form of these arguments did I realize that they were inseparable from the historical situation of literary studies. The idea that literature is an object of knowledge is a modern one; the academic disciplines devoted to its study are for the most part creations of the nineteenth century and can hardly be assumed to be immortal. Yet at the same time the study of literature can also be seen as a survivor of an earlier intellectual mode in which all study was essentially the study of texts, in which the written word was unquestionably taken to be a reservoir of knowledge. The discussion of literature's status as object or reservoir of knowledge, the attempt to bring insights from scientific disciplines to bear on cultural questions—these cannot be understood without reference to the history of literature's place in an increasingly divided world of knowledge.

What I am proposing here is not a method for the criticism or the interpretation of texts but a challenge to the idea that criticism and interpretation as traditionally understood are the only legitimate functions of literary studies. The kind of emergent meaning described here as self-organization from noise is not the same as received meaning; it is meaning constructed in a new context, situated at a different level within the overall cultural system. It is a kind of meaning that can be legitimately discussed only if we are willing to move away from the dead center of the literary disciplines, namely, from the implicit assumption that literature is an object of knowledge. In a sense I am proposing a new kind of argument for what Richard Rorty calls strong textualism, what Harold Bloom calls strong misreading. Beyond that, it is also an argument for interdisciplinarity, for using literature in processes of intellectual invention whose aim is other than to know the literary text.

Given these ambitions, it is probably inevitable that *The Noise of Culture* should itself contain and produce cultural noise, enacting the kind of emergence of meaning from disorder that it describes. In it I summarize and attempt to transmit to the reader a great deal of intellectual material that is not part of the current cultural baggage of the literary disciplines, and because of my own shortcomings and the nature of the task, there will be plenty of interference in the channel. What will be noise for some readers, however, will be new information for others, and indeed, were I a perfect expositor, I would have to be a completely unoriginal one. Moreover, it can be argued that such external concepts as information and self-organization, which function as information in their home fields, become noise and thus a risky and uncertain source of invention when they enter literary studies. The book contains many arguments, but its goal is not to refute any existing theories on their own terms; it is rather to provide some materials from which new levels of explanation may emerge.

I wrote the first draft of this book in Paris during the 1984–85 academic year. My leave of absence was made possible by a fellowship from the American Council of Learned Societies and by a faculty fellowship from Mount Holyoke College. My gratitude to both institutions is more than personal, for it reflects my admiration for their willingness to support a risky and unusual project.

It is impossible for me to thank all the teachers, colleagues, and students who in one way or the other have helped me to grasp and refine the ideas that make up this book. I owe a special intellectual debt to Michel Serres, whose writings were instrumental in convincing me that this was a book I should attempt to write. I have benefited greatly from conversations with Bruno Tritsmans and from Mary Cattani's perceptive comments on some of my drafts. Elizabeth MacArthur read the entire manuscript, filling its margins with questions and criticism and encouragement, and her insightful remarks suggested many ways in which I could make *The Noise of Culture* in revision more like the book I wanted to write in the first place. Bernhard Kendler and the staff of Cornell University Press have made the transition from manuscript to book easy and enjoyable. Finally, I thank my parents, Janet and Bill Paulson, not only for the many ways in which they helped me become the person who could write this book but for their intense interest in the project itself and for their help in ridding the manuscript of many typographical, grammatical, and logical errors.

All translations of quotations from foreign language sources are my own, except of course where I refer to a published translation. Words italicized in quotations were italicized in the original unless otherwise noted.

The quotations in Chapter 4 from "The Creations of Sound" are reprinted by permission of the publisher, Alfred A. Knopf, Inc., from *The Collected Poems of Wallace Stevens*, Copyright © 1954 by Wallace Stevens.

WILLIAM R. PAULSON

Ann Arbor, Michigan

THE NOISE
OF CULTURE

1 Literature and the Division of Knowledge

The study of literature now presents itself to us as an academic discipline. It was not always so. Our concept of a discipline, closely linked to our implicit and explicit representations of the university, implies that each discipline is but one among others, that the field of knowledge and inquiry is legitimately divided into discrete territories that have their own objects, methods, and institutional practices. We thus define literature as a particular object, susceptible to being approached in specific ways and in certain contexts. To know the text, to know the psyche, to know the organization of living beings: these are different tasks. Literature, as we now understand it, comes into being in the same movement that creates this division of cognitive labor. To some it may seem silly or tautological to observe that literature is literature because it is distinct from, among other things, psychology and biology, but the obvious is worth stating if it can help dislodge the prejudice that literature, as an object of study, has an almost natural existence.

The primacy accorded to the written verbal text distinguishes the literary disciplines from the scientific ones. Blake was a poet and Newton a physicist, but Newton is not read in the physics department in the way Blake is read in the English department. The reading of Newton's work as text would belong only to the history of science, not to science itself, whereas the reading of poetry from the past is a central activity of literary disciplines. This differing status of texts and reading seems quite natural to us, for we have grown up in a culture structured by such distinctions, in an intellectual universe split into what C. P. Snow called "the two cultures."

Snow denounced the consequences for intellectual life of the mutual ignorance of those who live by literature and those who live by science, two tribes barely able to communicate with each other. He reserved his sharpest criticism for the literati, who often seem to deny that science is of any cultural importance at all, or who are unaware of what the elements of a scientific culture might be. In perhaps the most famous sentence of his little book, he pronounced understanding of the second law of thermodynamics to be the scientific cultural equivalent of having read a work of Shakespeare's.[1] To a large extent, his argument is a protest, quite characteristic of the post-Sputnik era in which it was written, against the shortcomings of scientific education in institutions still dominated by the purveyors of literary culture. His identification of the "two cultures," however, has lost none of its pertinence and has consequences that run far deeper than problems of communication between academic tribes.

Richard Rorty has noted that the "two cultures" reflect a fundamental alternative in the relation between language and knowledge. Literary culture is the scene of competition between mortal vocabularies, whereas scientific culture is an attempt to add to eternal truth, to obtain agreement through argument about well-formulated propositions.[2] Science attempts to use a transparent language, the meaning of whose statements depends on universally accepted procedures and definitions. In literary culture, meaning cannot be separated from the particular language game being played by author and reader. Literary languages grow opportunistically, because they are of interest, and not because they refute other languages. They succeed each other over time, yet the languages of the past are not abolished; they remain a part of the literary cultural space. The reading of, say, Fielding and Joyce is a standard, central activity for students of English literature, but as Thomas Kuhn has observed, physics students have no reason to read Newton or Schrödinger when contemporary textbooks recapitulate their work in briefer and more precise form.[3]

[1]C. P. Snow, *The Two Cultures and the Scientific Revolution* (Cambridge, 1959), 16.
[2]Rorty, *Consequences of Pragmatism* (Minneapolis, 1982), xli and xlvii n. 50.
[3]Kuhn, *The Structure of Scientific Revolutions*, 2d ed. (Chicago, 1970), 165.

This division between the "two cultures" thus has philosophical roots that go back to Plato, but it takes on something like its current cultural importance only with romanticism, with our modern concept of the literary. If we examine the situation prior to 1800, we will find disciplinary divisions and differing relations of language to meaning and truth, but we will not find anything quite like the modern split between the literary and scientific cultures. The disciplinary landscape to which we are accustomed has a long and complex genealogy, one worth examining if we are to understand how literary studies now stand both as a component of the present-day division of knowledge and as a residue of past divisions.

"Our universities are an original creation of the Middle Ages," wrote Ernst Robert Curtius in his memorable *European Literature and the Latin Middle Ages*. The medieval universities, like the cathedral schools that preceded them, had their disciplines, but these could not be distinguished by whether or not they accorded the written word status as an object of study. In all fields, knowledge was sought in texts. An important twelfth-century guide to the arts, the *Didascalion* of Hugh of St. Victor, was subtitled *De Studio Legendi*, "on the study of reading." "The things by which every man advances in knowledge," wrote Hugh, "are principally two—namely, reading and meditation. Of these, reading holds first place in instruction."[4] The arts, and in particular the seven *artes liberales* deemed most essential to education, were in a real sense constituted by the texts that made up their curricula.[5]

The liberal arts, to be sure, were divided into groups that suggest a distinction between literature and science: the trivium (grammar, rhetoric, and logic) and the quadrivium (arithmetic, music, geometry, and astronomy). Although the arts of the trivium seem indeed the ancestors of modern studies in language, literature, and philosophy, they did not differ from the arts of the quadrivium in taking texts as an object of study, for the quadrivium arts did so as well. Astronomy, for example, was not an experimental science. To determine the cause of eclipses, it was necessary and sufficient to study the writings of Aristotle, Ptolemy, their commentators, and the other authors who had treated the sub-

---

[4]Hugh of St. Victor, *Didascalion*, trans. Jerome Taylor (New York, 1961), 44.
[5]Hugh wrote: "There are two kinds of writings. *The first kind comprises what are properly called the arts*; the second, those writings which are appendages of the arts" (*Didascalion*, 88; emphasis added).

ject. Just as in grammar and rhetoric the works of *auctores* (authors/ authorities) were studied to learn the principles of discourse, in astronomy the works of the auctores were read to determine the truth concerning the heavens.

Knowledge, in other words, was presumed to reside in the written works of those authors who, by their writings, had originated the arts and whom the institutions of learning thus recognized as authorities.[6] The function of the author was to guarantee the authority, the truth, of what was written. This is the opposite of modern scientific culture, which ostensibly claims that knowledge resides in a kind of statement whose truth depends not on authorship but on the procedures by which it is made. A valid scientific experiment can be, in principle, duplicated by anyone, and the writing of its results is a matter of impersonal transcription. The language of modern science disavows the authority of texts or authorship.[7] The edifice of medieval learning was, by contrast, a kind of textual formalism, in that inquiry did not extend beyond discourse, and a carefully limited field of discourse at that. "The respect inspired by the text sets the text in the place of the object," writes one historian of education; "it is not the book of nature that is read, but the book instead of nature; not the human body, but the *Canon* of Avicenna; no longer human language, but Priscian; not the universe, but Aristotle is read; not the sky, but Ptolemy."[8]

Of course, the Middle Ages were not without their disciplinary conflicts. Toward the end of the twelfth century, for example, the writings of Aristotle and especially his logic began to dominate university curricula, to the detriment of much of the traditional teaching of authors. This shift did not make studies any less dependent on texts and reading, for the curriculum of the thirteenth-century "Aristotelian" university consisted primarily of Aristotle's works. But the development of philosophical logic into a sophisticated discipline, spurred by the re-

[6]"We read that different persons were authors of these sciences. They originated the arts—some by beginning them, others by developing them, and others by perfecting them: and thus for the same art a number of authors are frequently cited" (Hugh of St. Victor, *Didascalion*, 83).

[7]It should be noted that generalizations concerning the objectivity or impersonality of scientific discourse cannot be regarded as absolutes. Recent work in the history of science has shown that questions of language, writing, authorship, and narrative are never as absent as the ideal—or perhaps myth—of scientific objectivity would have it.

[8]Eugenio Garin, *L'Education de l'homme moderne* (Paris, 1968), 67. Garin refers here to medieval education.

discovery of Aristotle, led many to claim that this logic was a powerful tool for arriving at truth without major recourse to the authority of tradition. Logic displaced grammar as the art most central to education. The beleaguered defenders of grammar protested that students were being encouraged to bypass a necessary foundation of their studies. On one side of the battle stood those who felt that truth could be reached through a single master language; on the other side, the defenders of familiarity with the multiple languages of the past. Already it seemed as if the study of a tradition and its languages, despite its importance in all fields of knowledge, was experienced as a kind of detour away from the present, a longer than necessary though perhaps richer path to intellectual and cultural competence.

The cultural moments designated as "renaissances"—that of Charlemagne in the ninth century, that of the twelfth century, and of course the Renaissance of the fifteenth and sixteenth centuries—all involved a turn to a more serious study of the written tradition, a longer and more profound detour through works from the past. Alcuin, the principal of Charlemagne's educational reformers, advocated the study of figures, and thus of classical authors, as necessary preparation for the study of the Bible and for preaching.[9] The turn to works from the past as a source of intellectual development cannot be separated from a sense of cultural belatedness, from a sense of coming after an earlier age of greater achievement than one's own. Here is how a French historian describes the twelfth-century renaissance: "man now sets out to encounter things equipped with an inherited capital, which increases his power ten-fold and assures his perspicacity, but which remains an inherited capital, inherited by books."[10]

The Renaissance humanists believed that the pedagogues and scholars of the Middle Ages had reduced the auctores to suppliers of sentences for handbooks and compilations and had, further, failed to distinguish, among auctores, between the truly important works of antiquity and second-rate commentators. They also denounced the neglect of original languages—Rabelais, for example, has Gargantua tell his son that the reestablishment of letters and disciplines coincides with the renewed study of Greek, Hebrew, and Chaldean. The humanists, in

[9]See Ernst Robert Curtius, *European Literature and the Latin Middle Ages*, trans. W. Trask (Princeton, 1953), 47–48.
[10]G. Paré, A. Brunet, P. Tremblay, *La Renaissance du douzième siècle: Les écoles et l'enseignement* (Paris, 1933), 145.

other words, criticized medieval education for not devoting a serious enough effort to the specificity of the tradition, for reducing it to a handy collection of accepted statements. As an alternative, they advocated the study of entire works and argued that authors be taken not as mere purveyors of accredited utterances but as examples of the finest human moral and intellectual achievement, bearers of a cultural spirit in which students must be encouraged to participate. With this concept of education, the written text from the past becomes less a direct source of truth (though this role is yet to disappear) than a means of initiation into the world of great minds who seek the truth. Renaissance humanism is a powerful move toward what we now call literary culture, although it does not entail a definition of literature per se anything like our own. More than in the Middle Ages, the study of texts begins to be identified with moral and aesthetic concerns.

Still, in the seventeenth and eighteenth centuries literature included not only the imaginative genres but also the writings of philosophers, moralists, and natural scientists. This usage survives today in the continued presence of such figures as Hooker, Descartes, Buffon, and Boswell in present-day literary curricula—although, significantly, there seem to be no canonical modern writers outside of poets, novelists, and dramatists, presumably because the definition of literature has changed. Thus the study of letters, although no longer the study of authorities, remained a broad category that included specifically rhetorical or linguistic studies and the study of great works and ideas concerning nature, man, and society. Literature was defined neither by subject matter nor in opposition to science but by its capacity to improve the reader by bringing him into contact with serious, universal culture.[11] If one consults a standard eighteenth-century work on the study of letters, such as Rector Charles Rollin's *Traité des études* (1726), one finds that the study of literature, principally the classical authors, teaches morality and good taste, multiplies and fortifies ideas in all domains, and prepares for both work and leisure.

Yet even in an era when writings on natural philosophy or natural history—disciplines that precede modern physics and biology—were considered part of literature, the rise of experimental science was changing the status of the text as a means to knowledge. Bacon and

[11]On the status of literature in the seventeenth and eighteenth centuries, see Lionel Gossman, "Literature and Education," *New Literary History* 13 (1982), 342–346.

Descartes were impatient with the vagaries of literary education, both the scholasticism that survived in universities and the belletristic concern of humanists with classical style. In his preface to the *Novum Organum*, Bacon stated that his new philosophy was sufficiently incompatible with traditional, textual knowledge that the two would simply remain separate: "Let there be therefore . . . two streams and two dispensations of knowledge, and in like manner two tribes or kindreds of students in philosophy . . . let there in short be one method for the cultivation, another for the invention, of knowledge."[12]

With the beginnings of observational and experimental science, the exclusive reliance on authorities from the past took on the aspect of a dogmatic textual formalism. In his *Dialogue Concerning the Two Chief World Systems*, Galileo has his Copernican confront his Ptolemaic adversary with the following demand: "So put forward the arguments and demonstrations, Simplicio—either yours or Aristotle's—but not just texts and bare authorities, because our discourses must relate to the sensible world and not to one on paper."[13] The practice of observation and experiment in the physical world implied that in certain domains the authority of precursors was insufficient. Experimental results and observations from such new instruments as the telescope inevitably consigned parts of the tradition to the domain of error and falsehood. The cultural strength of the tradition remained great, as Galileo's condemnation demonstrated; he was suspect not only because the results he proclaimed conflicted with church doctrine but also because his methods ran counter to the intellectual and institutional habits of those who judged him.

The problems that experimental science poses for the cultural authority of the ancients were put forth clearly by Pascal in his unfinished "Préface pour le traité du vide." Aristotle and his commentators had held that nature abhors a vacuum; modern experiments had shown that under certain conditions a vacuum could be made to exist. Pascal argues that for knowledge of the natural world, which is by definition subject to observation and experience, the ancients cannot be taken as authorities, since they themselves had attempted to go beyond their predecessors. But he distinguishes between this kind of knowledge and

---

[12]Francis Bacon, *The New Organon and Related Writings* (Indianapolis, 1960), 36.
[13]Galileo, *Dialogue Concerning the Two Chief World Systems—Ptolemaic and Copernican*, trans. S. Drake, 2d ed. (Berkeley, 1967), 113.

knowledge of the deeds, languages, and religions of the human race, which is entirely contained in what has been said and written. In particular, he condemns those who would change theology on the basis of reason and experience: theology is a matter revealed by God in sacred texts and henceforth to be sought in those texts alone. A similar distinction would be made by Vico, who argued that we could obtain certain knowledge only of those things that are of human institution and thus already in language—laws, history, myth, and religion—and not of nature, made by God. Vico thus stood on its head the still-emerging scientific view that certainty was to be found in the domain of natural science and of experimentation, whereas the historical disciplines would remain beset by errors, doubt, and opinion.

Vico's *New Science* would wait for the romantic era to have serious readers. The Enlightenment was more impressed with the new science of Newton. The principles of gravitation and the laws of motion were taken as proof that nature was subject to universal laws that could be given mathematical formulation. Physical events, thanks to the discovery of the eternal, objective rules that govern them, could become predictable, calculably regular. It was even believed by many that the explanatory power of the Newtonian paradigm was universal, that natural phenomena of all kinds could be reduced to the movement of particles and bodies in accordance with the laws of motion. Newton's laws were not simply perceived as better accounts of phenomena; they were explanations of an entirely new kind, unprecedented in their objectivity, generality, and predictive power. Throughout the eighteenth century, Newton's discoveries are celebrated in apocalyptic tones, of which Pope's proposed epitaph provides a fine example:

> Nature and nature's laws lay hid from sight.
> God said, "Let Newton be" and there was light.

Writing the "Discours préliminaire" of the *Encyclopédie*, the mathematician Jean d'Alembert was no less emphatic: "Newton . . . appeared at last, and gave to philosophy a form that it apparently will conserve."[14] By *philosophy*, d'Alembert means that part of human knowledge obtained by reason—as opposed to history or erudition, which comes from memory, and the fine arts, which come from imagination. Thus philosophy, now given its definitive form by Newton,

[14]d'Alembert, *Oeuvres* (Paris, 1821), I, 68.

amounts to nothing less than the investigation of nature, as well as including the more formal domains of logic, mathematics, and metaphysics. D'Alembert echoes eighteenth-century commonplaces in acknowledging that the success of philosophy, chiefly Newtonian philosophy, has discredited erudition and created an unfavorable climate for achievement in the arts of imagination.

According to d'Alembert, the discredit of erudition is unjust and unwise, for as useless as much historical research may seem, one can never be sure that everything has been done in any discipline, that the authors of antiquity can teach us nothing more. It is hardly a ringing defense of historical studies. The editor of the *Encyclopédie*, Diderot, displays a similar ambivalence concerning the study of writings from the past. He evokes the increasingly obvious distinction between those who seek new knowledge outside of the vast reservoir of printed books and those who search this archive seeking to rediscover or revalorize old knowledge:

> If we look ahead to the centuries to come, and imagine the face of literature, when the printing process, which does not rest, will have filled immense buildings with volumes, we shall see it once again divided into two classes of men. Some will read little and devote themselves to research which is new or considers itself new . . . ; the others, workers incapable of producing anything, will busy themselves leafing through these volumes day and night, separating out what they judge worthy of being gathered and preserved. Isn't this prediction starting to come true?[15]

It should be noted that Diderot, although drawing a distinction between the study of texts and the study of the world, does not oppose "literature" and "science." In fact, he makes it clear that he is talking about a division *within literature*, within the activity of producing serious writings. Literature is synonymous neither with erudition nor with imaginative writing.

It is true, however, that the rise of modern science profoundly altered the status of writing and language in the pursuit and dissemination of knowledge. Science changes qualitatively when it acquires what Thomas Kuhn has called *paradigms*, recognized scientific achievements that define acceptable problems and methods, providing a generally agreed to conceptual context for specialized work. In the

---

[15]Diderot, *Oeuvres complètes* (Paris: Hermann, 1976), VII, 235.

preparadigmatic phase of a science, its practitioners often hold incompatible, competing views about the nature of their object and the methods suitable for investigating it. They argue for these views by writing books addressed to one another and to a broad, cultivated audience. There is dialogue between the different schools of thought, not the experimental dialogue between the scientist and nature. As a scientific community adopts a given paradigm, the status of writing changes. Given the agreement on the nature of the problems to be solved and the general methods for doing so, there is no need for lengthy persuasive arguments on fundamentals. An exchange of information in technical and formalized language replaces the writing of treatises. Here is how Kuhn describes the transformation: "No longer will [the scientist's] researches usually be embodied in books addressed, like Franklin's *Experiments . . . on Electricity* or Darwin's *Origin of Species*, to anyone who might be interested in the subject matter of the field. Instead they will usually appear as brief articles addressed only to professional colleagues, the men whose knowledge of a shared paradigm can be assumed and who prove to be the only ones able to read the papers addressed to them."[16] Science, by becoming "paradigmatic" and thereby experimentally productive, becomes less literary, less written.

Newtonian science greatly accelerated the move away from treatise writing simply because it provided such a powerful and generally adopted paradigm. "By the early eighteenth century," writes Kuhn, "those scientists who found a paradigm in the *Principia* took the generality of its conclusions for granted, and they had every reason to do so. No other work known to the history of science has simultaneously permitted so large an increase in both the scope and precision of research."[17] With scientists in many fields agreeing that their task was to fill in the details of the Newtonian world picture, they had less reason to exchange narratives and rhetorical arguments. The highly wrought eloquence of the natural historian Buffon was even considered suspect, perhaps an indication that his work was not quite scientific. Modern science, at least insofar as it operates within generally agreed-to paradigms (what Kuhn calls "normal science"), shuns the traditional seductions of writing, the rhetorical powers of language.

Our modern notion of literature as imaginative, autonomous, non-

---

[16]Kuhn, *The Structure of Scientific Revolutions*, 20; see also 13.
[17]Kuhn, *The Structure of Scientific Revolutions*, 30.

utilitarian writing dates from the romantic era. It came about in part as a reaction against an economically and technologically modern society experienced as utilitarian and alienating.[18] As industrial revolution transformed the face of England and political revolution struck at the traditions of French society, literature came to be a voice for what the dominant, materialistic culture suppressed. In Blake's "Jerusalem," Newtonian and empiricist philosophy are part of a vision of mechanical and industrial horror:

> I turn my eyes to the Schools & Universities of Europe
> And there behold the Loom of Locke, whose Woof rages dire
> Wash'd by the Water-wheels of Newton: black the cloth
> In heavy wreathes folds over every Nation: cruel Works
> Of many Wheels I view, wheel without wheel, with cogs tyrannic
> Moving by compulsion each other.[19]

The poet's ways of knowing and speaking would soon be explicitly defined as opposing those of the scientist or political economist. Shelley, in *A Defense of Poetry*, contrasted the poetical faculty with the calculating faculty and denounced the consequences of their imbalance in modern culture: "The cultivation of those sciences which have enlarged the limits of the empire of man over the external world, has, for want of the poetical faculty, proportionally circumscribed those of the internal world; and man, having enslaved the elements, remains himself a slave."[20] The manipulative character of Newtonian science becomes equivalent, for Shelley, to the control exercised by a calculating society over the inner self of the individual. Life, history, human thought and emotion—these cannot be understood on the model of a mechanical system, a deterministic interaction of masses and forces. For the romantics—and there are modern scientists, such as Ilya Prigogine, who would agree with them—the universe of Newton and Laplace is an impersonal, disenchanted one, approached by science as

---

[18]For an argument in terms of the history of ideas that "Romanticism is, perhaps predominantly, a desperate rearguard action against the spirit and implications of modern science," see Hans Eichner, "The Rise of Modern Science and the Genesis of Romanticism," *PMLA* 98 (1982), 8–30. Eichner's negative conclusions concerning romanticism reflect both his traditional view of science and his failure to consider the autonomization of spheres of cultural activity characteristic of the romantic and modern period, but his historical account remains compelling.

[19]*The Portable Blake*, ed. Alfred Kazin (New York, 1976), 463.

[20]Percy Bysshe Shelley, *Shelley's Prose*, ed D. L. Clark (Albuquerque, 1954), 293.

by an external surveyor and manipulator. Romanticism was in part a protest against the cultural extension of the Newtonian paradigm of calculable, predictable trajectories.

It would of course be naive if not absurd to claim that romanticism was determined solely or even primarily by protest against science's disenchantment of the world. The specificity and autonomy of the literary also depended on the changed social status of the individual writer—a change of which Rousseau is both an early and spectacular manifestation—and on the evolution of aesthetics from the late eighteenth century to the followers of Kant. The autonomy of art and the mind's absolute freedom in aesthetic judgments had been theorized by Kant in his Third Critique. But Kant had at the same time devalued the reflective, aesthetic judgment vis-à-vis the determinate judgment of understanding: the latter, supported by rules and consensus, constituted real knowledge, the former merely the unregulated play of the mind. Kant had in effect ratified the Newtonian paradigm as the valid means of knowing the phenomenal world by installing Newtonian space and time as a priori categories of the transcendental subject. The aesthetic judgment, meanwhile, he considered noncognitive. The romantics took over the Kantian philosophical ratification of a split between science and art, but reversed their places. They claimed a cognitive status for what in Kant had been merely aesthetic judgment, thereby reversing Kant's valuation of the determinate over the reflective.[21]

Nowhere do the ideas of literature's autonomy and of its philosophical powers appear more clearly than in the group of writers associated with the *Athenaeum*, the short-lived review (1798–1800) in which the Schlegel brothers and their circle at Jena were among the first to articulate the romantic conception of literature. I shall return to them in Chapter 4 to discuss literary autonomy in the context of self-organizing, autopoietic systems; for now, I wish only to evoke the way in which they claimed the prerogatives of knowledge for the activity of writing and for the free play of subjectivity. For Friedrich Schlegel, the fusion of art and science, poetry and philosophy, was the raison d'être of modern poetry: "The whole history of modern poetry is a running commentary on the following brief philosophical text: all art should

[21]Concerning Kant's relation to Newtonian science and to romanticism, see Rorty, *Consequences of Pragmatism*, 141–150; Ilya Prigogine and Isabelle Stengers, *La Nouvelle Alliance* (Paris, 1979), 97–101; Philippe Lacoue-Labarthe and Jean-Luc Nancy, *L'Absolu littéraire* (Paris, 1978), 42–51.

become science and all science art; poetry and philosophy should be made one."[22] Philippe Lacoue-Labarthe and Jean-Luc Nancy entitled their anthology and study of the *Athenaeum* group's writings "The Literary Absolute," and the phrase fits the ambitions of the Jena group well. Literature was to be the genre of genres, creating itself by theorizing its own theorization of itself as creative. As Maurice Blanchot noted, writing itself, for the Schlegels, for Novalis, for Schelling, was to be an act of knowing: "It is the romantic writers themselves who, because they write, feel themselves to be the true philosophers, feeling themselves no longer called on to know how to write, but bound to the act of writing as to a new knowledge that they learn to recapture by becoming conscious of it."[23]

The cognitive and philosophical ambitions of literature did not, however, discourage romantic writers from drawing on science. Natural science had become an institution powerful enough to furnish models and metaphors for other cultural activities, and in the early nineteenth century those who rejected the Newtonian world view often turned instead to the metaphor of the organism. The nascent biological sciences had not yet advanced to a truly paradigmatic stage, to a point where arguments about the nature of life would be technical propositions accessible only to specialists. Those who sought to oppose mechanistic determinism could invoke vital forces and the intimate architecture of organic structure, thereby appropriating something of the modernity and authority of science without actually enrolling in scientific culture. Here is a fragment published in the *Athenaeum*: "Understanding is mechanical, wit is chemical, genius is organic spirit."[24] The explosive combinatorics of wit go beyond the repetitive ticking of understanding, and in turn are surpassed by the living productivity of genius. And for the *Athenaeum* group, wit and especially genius are the creative faculties that produce literature.

It is in the double context of an increasingly institutionalized, positivist science and a romantic literature claiming to be both aesthetically autonomous and rich in knowledge that we must consider the place of modern literary education. Literature with a capital *L* may have en-

[22]*Friedrich Schlegel's* Lucinde *and the Fragments*, trans. P. Firchow (Minneapolis, 1971), 157 (Critical Fragment 115).

[23]Blanchot, "L'Athenaeum," in *L'Entretien infini* (Paris, 1969), 519.

[24]*Friedrich Schlegel's* Lucinde *and the Fragments*, 221 (*Athenaem* Fragment 366).

tered the university, as Lacoue-Labarthe and Nancy claim, with the ambitious *Kunstlehre* of A. W. Schlegel, but for the most part the introduction of the modern literatures into curricula took place in the late nineteenth century and had nothing to do with the great figures of romanticism. Classical literature had never ceased to be a fundamental component of elite education; instruction in the modern literatures, primarily the national literature of each country, was a way of making literary study accessible to much larger numbers of students, those without the rigorous training in classical languages. But why was this extension of literary study deemed desirable? The justifications were generally political and ideological. In France, the teaching of the national literature went hand in hand with the teaching of the "national" language, with the attempt to acclimate the population to the linguistic and cultural centralism of the state. In England, Matthew Arnold and others saw English literature as a potential replacement for the waning moral authority of religion and thus as an emollient capable of reducing the tensions of class antagonism. Literature was felt to embody values that the nation-states and their rapidly developing capitalist economies were otherwise neglecting.[25]

There was quite naturally a tension between romanticism's protest against materialistic society and literary education's role as an ideological instrument of that same society. It is an opposition that can be felt in the vacillation between reform and repression in Arnold's pronouncements on literary education. At times Arnold seems convinced of the need to change society by means of the spiritual and human values associated with literature, and at other times he seems concerned only with protecting the social status quo by instilling some of these values in the lower orders. In France this tension was in part kept in check by what Roland Barthes called the "classico-centrism" of French literary pedagogy: with the age of Louis XIV at the apex of the curriculum, romantic and modern literature can be read as a fall away from classical perfection rather than as a discourse with something to say about modernity.[26]

By taking on literature as an object of study, the positivist university and the schools of the nation-state in effect placed themselves in the position of appropriating or domesticating a potentially opposi-

---

[25]See Gossman, "Literature and Education," 346–362, and Terry Eagleton, *Literary Theory: An Introduction* (Minneapolis, 1983), 17–30.
[26]Barthes, *The Rustle of Language*, trans. R. Howard (New York, 1986), 22–28.

tional discourse within their culture. The literary absolute was to be transformed into the *explication de texte*. The explication and other pedagogic devices were the compromise formations of an era when literary studies found themselves between the two poles of *Literaturwissenschaft* and edification. On the one hand, the study of literature had to be made into a respectable university research specialty, one discipline among many; on the other hand, it had to assume the function of providing a general cultural education. Scholars and teachers were supposed to make literature into the object of a positivist discipline, imitating the sciences if need be, and they were also supposed to transmit the contents of literature, which were to serve as a synecdoche for the lost cultural totality that once resided in the written tradition but that was now disappearing as science disqualified the authority of the merely written in a growing number of domains.

The modern history of literature's disciplinary status can in a sense be read as its reduction to an ever more circumscribed role. It was one thing that natural science ceased to be a matter of textual study; it was another when the study of human beings and culture ceased to be part of the literary domain. Before the advent of such social sciences as psychology and sociology, the sorts of things about which these disciplines now speak were, if they existed at all, thought to be the province of literature and its study. By reading and studying literature, one learned to understand human individuals, the historical moments of their culture, their life in society. The rise of the social sciences implied that if literary scholars continued to concern themselves with such matters, they would henceforth be doing so as unqualified amateurs. The study of literature was thus to fall back either onto aestheticism, literary history, or, most important, formalism.

A formalist approach to literature became deeply ingrained in the United States with the New Criticism of the 1930s and 1940s. The New Critics' emphasis on analyzing the internal dynamics of a single literary text seemed appropriate to the new status of literary studies as one professionalized discipline among others. Shunning both aesthetic dilettantism and the expounding of literary contents, the New Critics made the text into a spatial, iconic object of knowledge. The technical virtuosity of their readings did not, however, preclude a concern with values. Quite to the contrary: the New Critics had an ideological agenda, democratic or conservative or both, and the individual interpretations fostered by their brand of formalism left plenty of room for talking about the quasi-religious values associated with the poetic experience.

In 1926 the English critic I. A. Richards published a short book called *Science and Poetry* in which he derives a critical stance very close to that of New Criticism from the cultural situation of literature and science. Deeply impressed by the beginnings of experimental psychology, Richards attempts to de-idealize our thinking about poetry in light of the fact that the mind is becoming an object of science. We have traditionally assumed that our actions, and our response to poetry, depend on our knowledge and understanding. But our thought itself is a play of interests, he argues; the mind is a complex system of balances in which interests both conflict and seek equilibrium. Poetry acts upon this system of interests. Unlike science, poetry does not make statements that are true by force of logic and exact designation: "In its use of words poetry is just the reverse of science. Very definite thoughts do occur, but not because the words are so chosen as logically to bar out all possibilities but one. No. But because the manner, the tone of voice, the cadence and the rhythm play upon our interests and make *them* pick out from among an indefinite number of possibilities the precise particular thought which they need."[27] Rather than making statements to be understood as true or false by the mind, the poem acts on the mind, leading the reader to reproduce a play of interests similar to the one experienced by the poet. This view implies a psychological pole in the criticism of Richards but also a New Critical pole: "It is never what a poem *says* which matters, but what it *is*."[28]

What the poem is and how its being acts on the mind are, for Richards, particularly important in the cultural context of modern science. Science has provided a lot of reliable knowledge of how the world works—but also the knowledge that we do not really act on the basis of knowledge after all. We act on the basis of beliefs that are useful to believe because they enable us to act, but now science has made it impossible to believe in many of them. It has discredited our religions, our familiar and "magical" view of the world. This leaves us needing to preserve a whole raft of pseudostatements that we can no longer take seriously as statements. Here is where poetry comes in: it plays the role of substitute religion that Arnold, without sophisticated reference to

[27]Richards, *Science and Poetry* (New York, 1926), 33.
[28]Richards, *Science and Poetry*, 34–35.

science, had foreseen for it, for poetry is already the domain of pseudo-statement: "The remedy . . . is to cut our pseudo-statements free from belief, and yet retain them, in this released state, as the main instruments by which we order our attitudes to one another and to the world. Not so desperate a remedy as may appear, for poetry conclusively shows that even the most important among our attitudes can be aroused and maintained without any belief entering in at all."[29] The study of literature, in this view, cannot exactly be a study of contents or ideas, for poetry is a kind of being or process and not a communicative message. But this very quality gives us access to a world of beliefs and values, made palatable to our reason by their embodiment in poetry. Formalism and edification strike a compromise. We study the formal workings of the poem, but in so doing we therapeutically arouse and maintain attitudes. New Criticism, to a large extent, shares this perspective with Richards. The formal, technical interpretations of individual poems are also exercises in an exquisite preservation and savoring of the attitudes, or pseudobeliefs, that are ingredients of their being.

In France there was no movement comparable to the New Criticism in its power to satisfy the conflicting demands on literary studies. The arrival of formalism in the study of literature was both late and spectacular. Long after the New Criticism had become dominant in American universities, French university professors were defending Lansonian orthodoxy against the partisans of a *nouvelle critique* that flourished in nonuniversity institutions. In the mid-1960s, researchers grouped around Roland Barthes at the Ecole Pratique des Hautes Etudes were turning their backs on discussions of literary meaning and attempting to develop a literary semiology: a rigorous and formal account of how meaning is produced in literature out of the signs of language. To the horror of the university professors, Barthes and others working in the same vein were redefining the object of knowledge in literary studies. The semiologists refused to begin with the assumption that literature communicates something, that we can study it to learn the truth about something other than itself. Rather than examining the text as a meaningful document in an authorial life and a historical tradition, they approached it as a synchronic verbal structure, a machine producing meaning and not a vehicle of meaning. This structuralist or

[29]Richards, *Science and Poetry*, 72.

semiological project seemed to share with some of the early work of Richards and the New Critics the ambition of creating a scientific study of literature, a discipline devoted to elucidating what is intrinsic to literature as form rather than to the accumulation of knowledge concerning literature as tradition. But there were crucial differences: the antihumanistic stance of the structuralists and their refusal to grant any special, quasi-theological status to literary over nonliterary discourse.

Among the methods and concepts that critics have attempted to import into the study of literature, linguistic structuralism occupied a privileged position. Since literature exists in language, what could be more suitable to it than a theory that was already a theory of linguistic signification? Unlike models borrowed from biology or psychology, structuralism did not lead to treating the literary text as something it was not, such as a living organism or a mental state. It appeared that structuralism, while scientific, would still approach the verbal text as verbal text. In short, it offered the possibility of a study of literature, and of discourse in general, that could be rigorous without being reductive, that could be scientific without overlooking language.

Near the height of the "structuralist controversy," at the moment when the French works on literary semiology were first being widely diffused, Roland Barthes wrote a brief essay on structuralism, literature, and the disciplines called "De la science à la littérature." Published in English by the *Times Literary Supplement* in 1967, it remained unavailable in French until 1984, when it appeared in the posthumous collection *Le Bruissement de la langue*. In it, Barthes argues that science and literature can be distinguished, as discursive forms, by the status they accord to language and specifically to writing. Science uses language as an instrument for transmitting the contents of scientific messages; it assumes, in other words, that truth and meaning preexist the signs that serve as their vehicles. Literature, on the other hand, acknowledges its being-in-language and assumes the verbal density of language as part of its every act; in literature, there can be no appeal to a meaning outside signs. This opposition is a commonplace concerning literature and science, but Barthes gives it a polemical edge. Science hides what for Barthes is a fundamental truth of language, one that literature assumes: there is no meaning completely outside of language, no signified that transcends the realm of signs. And for Barthes and other members of the *Tel Quel* group, this privileging of the signified over the signifier has political consequences. By postulating the submission of expression to truth, scientific discourse is ultimately hierarchical and totalitarian, whereas the literary mode of writing points the way to deflating precisely these pretensions. Science, Barthes proposed, must become literature, become like literature in its use of language. He thus argues that structuralism provides more than the first real possibility of a science of literature, as distinct from a science of its history or the psychology of its authors. Structuralism assumes theoretically what literature assumes in practice and what other sciences hide: the productive dependence of meaning on language. A structuralist "science of literature" can thus avoid the totalitarian temptation of other scientific discourse, including the positivistic study of literature. Structuralism must consent to become *written*, it must partake of the adventure in language that is literature. Only in this way can the move from science to literature be a transformation and not a conquest; rather than submitting literature to a discourse of objectivity, science will come to acknowledge its own being-in-language.

Barthes's arguments point to, but do not develop, another and very different type of convergence between literature and science. By science, Barthes designates knowledge organized by society to assure the formation of specific individual and institutional competencies, as defined by institutions that teach and give diplomas. "Science," he writes, "is what is taught." His discussion alludes primarily to the social sciences, not because he distinguishes their discourse from that of the natural sciences, but because it is easier for him to see them in direct competition with literature at the level of content. The institutional privilege of science and scientific discourse hides a kind of identity between science and literature. The contents of literature are the same as those of science: literature has always *written* what science is now trying to *say*. Barthes the romantic accompanies Barthes the semiologist: in literature, writes the first, we encounter these contents in "that grand cosmogonic unity which so delighted the ancient Greeks but which the compartmentalized state of our sciences denies us today."[30] If literature has always written what the social sciences now say, then the latter are no more than "technical alibis" by which modern societies maintain the fiction of a knowledge that transcends language and

<hr>

[30]Barthes, *The Rustle of Language*, 3–4. On the "romanticism" of Barthe's critical work, see Tzvetan Todorov, *Critique de la critique* (Paris, 1984), 74–81.

signs. In this light, the project of a structuralist passage "from science to literature" (in which the "literarity" of science would be acknowledged) can be complemented by a symmetrically opposite passage from literature to science: an explicit recognition of the knowledge contained in literature. The latter project, scarcely developed by Barthes, was far less in resonance with the moment at which the essay was written, a moment of structuralist ascendancy in the intellectual world. It seemed more important to show that science represses the nature of language than to recall that literature plays with the truths of science. The two projects are nonetheless equivalent parts of the same operation of displacement, transgressing the separation between science and literature in opposite directions.

From the vantage point of institutional practice, the implicit second project of Barthes is not radical at all, for it is routinely and traditionally carried out. The place of literary studies in the university is linked to the notion that literature has something to say about human beings, their societies, their history. Even if authority and competence in these areas of knowledge now reside officially with the social sciences, literature is still assumed by many to have something to say about them as well. This is particularly obvious, almost embarrassingly so, in official statements advocating study in the humanities. But our most recent and prestigious critical formalisms do not enable us to say much about literary content, at least not explicitly.

We can now say, more than twenty years after the first controversies over structuralism in literary studies, that despite the great intellectual influence of Saussure, Jakobson, and Lévi-Strauss, criticism as actually practiced has rarely been structuralist in any strict sense. I suspect that this is so because the assumptions underlying structuralist analysis, and the kinds of results it can offer, differ radically from deeply held expectations concerning what critics do and are incompatible with the present institutional status of literary studies. As Jonathan Culler has noted, the dominant activity in American criticism, at least since the triumph of the New Critics, has been the production of interpretations of individual works. Culler argues convincingly that this prejudice in favor of interpretation has acted as a filter for the reception of new methods by American critics: approaches to literature that have become popular, such as deconstruction and psychoanalysis, are those that lend themselves to the "task" of interpretation, while those that have not taken hold strongly, such as Marxism and structuralism, cannot easily be put to use in the making of ever more interpretations. He quite sensibly suggests that we cease to consider interpretation as the only valid project for criticism: "One thing we do not need is more interpretations of literary works."[31] But the resistance to structuralism has a deeper cause, of which the rush to produce interpretations is only a symptom. This cause lies in the status of literary studies in institutions and society.

Even in a time of retrenchment, literature departments remain large and influential, at least in comparison to departments of linguistics. Viewed taxinomically, the structuralist analysis of literature is a part of the structural linguistics of discourse, itself a branch of linguistics. Yet rare are the institutions in which the entire linguistics faculty would outnumber the members of a single large literature department. The causes of this situation lie in traditions and curricula: we grant an institutional status to the study of literature that far exceeds its status as structuralism would define it: an important subfield of a major but still emerging branch of linguistics. Our institutions, in other words, operationally describe literature as something much larger than what structuralist theory, if pushed to its logical conclusions, would declare it to be.

The shape of institutions, such as universities, depends only partially on present-day determinations of their function; it is to a much greater extent the end product of a complex history of transformations. The size and status of literature departments depend not only on what we now think the study of literature is but also on the institutional and social consequences of earlier notions. Literature departments are in one sense the residues of a kind of university whose activity resided almost exclusively in the study of texts; in another sense, they are subinstitutions created to carry out particular pedagogical, cultural, and ideological aims. When government commissions or university presidents expound on "the importance of the humanities," they speak of shared moral or cultural values, of initiation into ethical thinking, of the development of the individual in a free society. They assume, in other words, an extralinguistic value to the study of literature. Similarly, the phenomenon of hundreds of critics writing interpretive articles on the same works suggests that the scholarly genre assuages creative impulses not identical with a rigorous program of

[31]Culler, *The Pursuit of Signs* (Ithaca, 1981), 6.

semiological research. Whatever the abstract merits of such a program, it simply does not account for what we actually do in literary studies. The methodologically vaguer and more humanistic formalism of the New Criticism left room for discreet participation in the speculative and nostalgic pleasures of romantic literary culture. Many scholars are doubtless comfortable with "humanistic" justifications of their disciplines; others would rather defend a program more like that of structuralism or the several poststructuralisms, and quite a number would surely prefer not to think about such matters so that they can get on with their interpretations. But one great merit of structuralism ought to have been to force us—by claiming that the proper study of literature is linguistic—to examine the special and clearly nonlinguistic place of literary studies in our institutions. But structuralism and other critical approaches that attempt to demystify traditional concepts of the value of literature have in general not been eager to think rigorously about their position as occupants of an institutional territory measured out under earlier assumptions. One question that might well be asked by literary theory is, how does it conceive of, and use, the status presently accorded by society and institutions to literary studies? As a noble heritage to be maintained and defended? As a *rente de situation*? As a myth to be debunked? As a temporary problem of no real consequence?

Eric Gans has suggested that the scientific aspect of literary structuralism failed to take hold in the United States because the people in the literary fields are precisely those who refuse the limited goals of the social sciences.[32] But even that refusal can have two faces: it can be the deed of adventurous minds who see research in the social sciences as too narrowly empirical, or of traditional souls who want to defend individual imagination, beauty, truth, morality, and order in the face of what they see to be "value-free" or "dehumanized" social sciences. If the literati are indeed a beleaguered collection of individuals unable or unwilling to find a place in any of the more systematized disciplines, this is but an extreme consequence of the increasingly circumscribed role of literature—and thus of the rhetorical dimension of language—in education and society.

Literary studies are one discipline among many, and at the same time a shrunken remnant of the form of study practiced before the

[32]Gans, "Differences," *MLN* 96 (1981), 805n.

modern disciplines became a reality. This double status, and the strange relation to the social sciences that goes with it, contribute to the ubiquity of what Gans has called a minor debate, an ill-formed debate, among practitioners of literary studies. It is the debate between the intuitive conception of literary texts as meaningful and the deconstructionist notion of the literary text as a demonstration of language's inability to designate anything outside of itself. For the participants in this debate, the two trajectories explicitly or implicitly proposed by Barthes—making social science literary, making literature a valid source of knowledge—appear mutually contradictory. If the truth of language is to deny the existence of truths preceding or external to language, and if literary discourse is in this respect the most rigorous manifestation of the possibilities (and thus the impossibilities) of language, then how could we possibly hope to extract nonlinguistic truths from inside the literary text? If the promise of the sciences is to provide us with knowledge free from the vicissitudes of individual opinion, emotion, and ideology, then how can a return to nonscientific, rhetorical language be anything but an abdication?

This state of affairs is doubtless related to a question that I mean to address, explicitly or implicitly, throughout this book: what are the implications of *taking the literary text to be an object of knowledge*, of subjecting it to the practices of scientific culture? In other words, should one try to have a discipline, a rigorous branch of intellectual inquiry, that takes literary texts as its objects, that endeavors *to know the text*? But at this point the question is premature. It will suffice for now to answer it tentatively in the context of the double project suggested by Barthes's essay. Literary structuralism claimed to be this kind of discipline, one that would produce knowledge of the text. But even if literary structuralism could have been reconciled with the actual practices and institutional position of the literary disciplines, it is not clear whether we would have gotten from it a discipline of literary study in the traditional sense. Barthes insisted that the only real advantage of a structuralist science of literature would be the contamination of the method by the object, the production of a structuralism no longer scientific but literary, at least in its rapport with language. In this case the literary discipline would be defined not only by its relation to an object (literature) but by the literary character of its discourse as a discipline. Literature would become a stance toward language, not an object. The other direction, the project of taking seriously the knowledge written in literature, likewise displaces the center of attention away from the literary text itself: literature becomes a source or reserve of knowledge, rather than being itself the object that we seek to know.

Almost everyone in literary studies knows by now the famous phrase of Jacques Derrida, generally taken as the most lapidary statement of a critical nihilism regarding meaning: "Il n'y a pas de hors-texte" (There is no outside-the-text). Language does not give us access to a thematic totality that precedes it, to a meaning shining through the verbal message. In *De la grammatologie* and "La Double Séance" (*La Dissémination*), Derrida shows how the metaphoric workings of language undo the attempts of even such brilliant thematic critics as Jean Starobinski and Jean-Pierre Richard to define the authorial imagination behind the writings of Rousseau or Mallarmé. Meaning cannot precede the system of differences that is language; it is itself within this system. We cannot get behind or outside of language to a meaning free from the vicissitudes of signs working on one another.[33]

This book is not the place to discuss Derrida as a philosopher. One can, however, doubt the extent to which his arguments are as pertinent to or as catastrophic for the practice of literary studies as some of his American followers and detractors have said they are. Derrida is engaged in displacing, undermining, or more precisely "announcing the closure" of what he calls Western metaphysics; specifically, he is attempting to show that certain assumptions concerning the priority of presence over difference, of speech over writing, of meaning over expression, are logically untenable if one analyzes rigorously the very texts in which these hierarchical claims are made. But this does not mean that all language is meaningless or that all attempts to use language in a clear and unambiguous manner are deluded and thus inferior to discourses that know themselves to be "blind." The fact that certain metaphysical concepts have been presented as foundations preceding language does not mean that all meanings require such foundations; Derrida's arguments, whatever their implications for a certain philosophical tradition, do not remove the possibility that there may be

[33]This, at any rate, is what Derrida says if we read him as a "philosopher of language." He may be no such thing. Rorty, in particular, argues persuasively that Derrida is making statements not about the nature of language, but about philosophy. See his "Philosophy as a Kind of Writing: An Essay on Derrida," in *Consequences of Pragmatism*, 90–109.

perfectly effective modes of signification that do not depend on this tradition. There are doubtless other ways of living and encountering the closure of Western metaphysics than those of Derrida's followers in the American critical establishment. Derrida's own texts do not seem to be part of a universe in which meaning has become impossible, although this is what some polemicists infer from his writings. He reminds us that we still live within the epoch of Western metaphysics, even as we perceive its limits, and cautions against the illusion of believing that we have simply escaped into something else. He takes seriously problems of literary history and textual criticism (in *De la grammatologie*, for example), makes frequent references to events in Freud's life and their relation to such writings as *Beyond the Pleasure Principle* (in *La Carte postale*), and lectures on the relation between nationalisms and philosophical idioms.

Why, then, have Derrida's arguments caused such fascination, such handwringing, and such tedious polemics in literary studies? He himself makes clear that the type of meaning he is calling into question is a particular representation of what it is to mean: the notion of a sense completely separable from language and signs, existing in the consciousness or imagination of the author before being "put into" words. The fact that this kind of argument has seemed decisive to polemicists on both sides of the fence should give us pause. Is it really the case that in the study of literature we assume that at some point we can arrive at a stable meaning beyond language? Unfortunately, to hear the debate (the little debate, as Gans calls it), it seems that we do, or that we should, or should not; in any case, that this is a central question. If literary studies are indeed the last bastion of those who want to talk about consciousness and meaning without situating themselves and their topics within the signs and systems by which consciousness and meaning are produced, then Derrida's writings are indeed unsettling.[34]

[34]It should be added—and even so harsh a critic as John Searle is aware of this, whereas not all literary followers of Derrida are—that Derrida's project is largely political in the broad sense: he seeks out instances of unstable language, of contradictions and double binds, to undermine certain types of ideological arguments that invoke transcendent, extralinguistic concepts. But in the United States, the deconstruction of the metaphysical basis of ideological utterances is replaced by the deconstruction of individual literary texts—a symptom of the American literary establishment's obsession with producing interpretations.

While the literary disciplines are divided and polarized over such questions as whether there is a subject or not, whether there is meaning or not, whether there is theme, or only endlessly self-deconstructing structure—in other words, over a highly traditional concept of human nature and its negation—other disciplines are moving in directions that may well make this question moot. Consider for a moment the situation in neuroscience or in artificial intelligence research. The things we call thought, consciousness, and imagination do not exist in some transcendent domain beyond all signifying systems; they are common language designations for states and functions in a highly complex informational network, that of the human brain. That we do not fully understand these systems and their workings is obvious, but changes nothing fundamental. We know enough about brain functioning—albeit at discrete levels not yet fully integrated into an overall account—to suppose that there is no need of recourse to some metaphysical entity other than the physiological reality of the brain to account for ordinary phenomena of mind. We also know that the brain functions by means of signals, that it is a hypercomplex system for the processing of information and perhaps for the transformation of phenomena that are not yet information into information. "Il n'y a pas de hors-texte," writes Derrida, but if by *text* we understood the domain of signs, signals, and information, then text extends into what we have previously designated by such metaphysically loaded terms as consciousness, mind, and imagination.[35] Biological science is becoming increasingly a science of information, a cybernetics of the living, a science of the codes, the order and disorder that interact to define autonomous living systems. The last concepts thought to be the special province of humanists are, in their turn, becoming a part of the discourse of science, even as the humanists squabble over them in a debate uninformed by science and dominated by positions of traditionalism and nihilism.

Need this become yet another disaster, perhaps the definitive disaster, for the modes of inquiry we now know as literary? The rest of this book will be devoted to arguing that it need not, that we are presented not with a fait accompli but with an opportunity. Scientific discourse itself is changing rapidly as it discovers the role of information, of

[35]Derrida himself states this in his most influential work: "Finally, whether it has essential limits or not, the entire field covered by the cybernetic *program* will be the field of writing" (*Of Grammatology*, trans. G. Spivak [Baltimore, 1976], 9).

codes, of the emergence of order from chaos. With quantum mechanics, nonequilibrium thermodynamics, neuroscience, and molecular biology, scientists realize that they no longer can claim to occupy the position of disembodied, objective observers, outside the reality they are investigating. At the same time, the history of science continues to demonstrate the immersion of science in culture, to refute the idea—to which I have often given voice in this chapter, because it is an important and influential idea—that science is a foreign body invading culture from without. Beyond the modest hopes of Roland Barthes, science is discovering itself to be inside, not outside, language. The Nobel laureate Ilya Prigogine and his philosopher coauthor Isabelle Stengers put it this way: "Scientific knowledge, awakened from the dreams of an inspired revelation, can now discover itself to be both a 'poetic listening' to nature and a natural process within nature, an open process of production and invention, in an open, productive and inventive world."[36] And if we remain intimidated concerning the prospects for extracting knowledge from a literary discourse that we all know how to deconstruct, we would do well to consider this remark by the theoretical biologist Francisco Varela: "Our knowledge, including science, can be accurately empirical and experimental, without requiring for it the claim of solidity or fixed reference."[37] This is the closure of Western metaphysics, understood in its productive rather than its deconstructive dimension. If knowledge, and scientific knowledge, can do without fixed reference, then the rigorous and justifiable questioning of the referentiality of literature's language need not lead us to view literary discourse as a formalism removed from the world—or as an object of study only for a group of specialists unable to decide if they are working in a branch of linguistics or if they are the last generalists, the last representatives of a prescientific mode of intellectual inquiry.

[36]Prigogine and Stengers, *La Nouvelle Alliance*, 296.
[37]Varela, *Principles of Biological Autonomy* (New York, 1979), 277.

2 Science at Work: The Writings of Michel Serres

"This is sad and true: we had lost the world."[1] Thus does Michel Serres—philosopher, essayist, historian of sciences—lament the separation of philosophy, and literary culture in general, from direct knowledge of the universe. For the cultivated but otherwise ignorant practitioners of the human sciences, he argues, reality has been reduced to the stakes of arguments or struggles, to fetishes sacred and profane, to merchandise, to signs. The world is replaced by a theater of representations produced by culture and language, a theater whose ultimate expression and consequence is the discourse of nuclear war strategists, in which mass destruction seems rational and plausible because the world's existence has already been bracketed.

No one, and least of all Serres, can expect philosophy, literature, or the social sciences to do without language, or even to reach a point "beyond formalism" where semiotic questions would be so well resolved that users of signs could proceed confidently to a rediscovery of the phenomenal world. Serres invites us, however, to consider to what extent it may be possible, without actually disregarding the theater of cultural representations, to enlarge our gaze and see something of the world as well. In less metaphoric terms, Can we, without sacrificing the insights and rigor that have come from treating literary works as

[1]Michel Serres, "Commencements," *Le Monde*, January 4, 1980, p. 13.

existing in language, write a criticism that acknowledges their immersion in a universe that is more than linguistic, more than semiotic?

I would never have written *The Noise of Culture* without the impetus of Serres's questions and ideas. To anyone who accepts that the present state of literary studies is something like what I have described in Chapter 1, his project of escaping the agoraphobic formalism of the human sciences is a compelling one. His work provides a unique example of the possibilities opened up by bringing literary culture and scientific thought into play with one another. In so doing, it provides something more specific: an introduction to the changes that the sciences of energy and information could bring to literary culture. These are the post-Newtonian sciences that literary culture, striving to become an autonomous enclave shielded from the expansion of paradigmatic thinking, has never really integrated. Reading Serres, we encounter in literary guise the sciences that will make it possible to discuss the role of literary texts in a world of information.

An outspoken critic of mutual ignorance among disciplines, Serres has in more than a dozen books produced a major critical and philosophical work that crosses over most of the customary boundaries between fields of knowledge.[2] He would probably deny being a literary critic, yet his studies of Emile Zola, Jules Verne, and Jacques Roumain are included in the bibliographies of literary scholarship and cited with respect by the specialists concerned. More important, almost all of Serres's essays present themselves as a commentary or exploration starting from a text. It soon becomes apparent to the reader, however, that Serres is not concerned with elucidating the sense of the text in the traditional manner, nor with formulating true descriptive statements about the work as such. He practices neither hermeneutics nor formalism. Reading Serres, one has the uncanny impression that theoretical concepts and models are not being applied to the text but instead are being drawn out of it. Like the Barthes of "De la science à la littérature," he claims that the texts normally read as productions of the imagination contain knowledge—and contain it in a form less alienating, less clumsy and heavy-handed, than the supposedly rigorous discourses of the sciences, social or natural. Literature, he writes in a discussion of La Fontaine's fables, "made clear, even for the blind, a kind of figural, instructive anthropology that was both accessible and pro-

---

[2] The best introduction to Serre's work is a review article by Ross Chambers, "Including the Excluded," *Degré Second*, July 1983, 185–193.

found, but without theory, without awkward weight, not boring but intelligent. Why do we have to pay nowadays with lead for what we used to get from a quill pen?"[3]

To understand the basis of this claim and of his dazzling readings, it is well to recall one of Serres's earliest articles, a 1961 manifesto for a lucid and clearly defined structuralism. Unlike Barthes and other major figures of the structuralist movement in literary criticism, Serres did not see linguistics, and the fact that literature exists in language, as the foundation of a structural analysis of texts. In fact, his definition of structure says nothing at all about texts or language:

> *A structure is an operational set of undefined meaning* (whereas an archetype is a concrete set whose meaning is overdetermined), *bringing together a certain number of elements, whose content is not specified*, and *a finite number of relations of unspecified nature*, but whose function, and certain results concerning the elements, are defined. Suppose now that the content of the elements and the nature of the relations are specified in a determined manner; one then obtains a model (a paradigm) of this structure: *this latter is now the formal analogon of all the concrete models that it organizes.*[4]

An abstraction from specific contents, a formal invariant, structure as defined here does not have any particular kinship with linguistics or semiology or anthropology. Specific realizations of invariant formal systems, of structures, might thus be found at many different levels of a literary text—in linguistic features or in conventions such as versification, to be sure, but also in the vocabulary of colors or in exchanges carried out between characters or in descriptions of time, weather, space. We might call it a *structuralism of contents*, as opposed to a linguistic structuralism, but in fact the banal distinction between form and content plays no role in the work of Serres.

Serres's early analysis of Molière's *Dom Juan* exemplifies this kind of structuralism and provides a good example of its importance to his strategy of reading the literary text as a source of knowledge. The invariant in question is the structure of gift and exchange, the act of giving and rendering in kind as an elementary link in the structure of social relations. The structure is presented in a small-scale model by Sga-

[3]Serres, *The Parasite*, trans. L. R. Schehr (Baltimore, 1982), 6. Cf. *Le Parasite* (Paris, 1980), 13.

[4]Serres, "Structure et importation: des mathématiques aux mythes," in *Hermès I: La Communication* (Paris, 1968), 32.

narelle's opening monologue on the social virtues of tobacco, then realized in scene after scene as Dom Juan confronts society, violating its most fundamental forms of behavior. Dom Juan can be defined structurally as the transgressor of this elementary invariant of social relations; instead of rendering payment in kind, he rewards Pierrot for saving his life by seducing his fiancée; he pays Monsieur Dimanche, his creditor, with words and embraces instead of cash; he gives alms only in exchange for blasphemy (not, as he first desires, the beggar's, but his own, which he forces the beggar to hear). The Commander, of course, finally submits Dom Juan to the structure of exchange, giving him death for death, but even in death he violates the contract, for he has left the wages of Sganarelle, his servant, unpaid. These are but a few of the models of gift and exchange in the play, but there is no need to summarize the entire reading here. Of greater interest than Serres's dexterity in accumulating textual examples is the fact that this structure is to be found not only in the play but in the anthropological work of Marcel Mauss (*Essai sur le don*). Molière, in other words, has already modeled the structure identified by the anthropologist—and has done so some three hundred years earlier and in an entertaining form. Why go to the Pacific, then, why spend years observing archaic societies, to learn slowly what we can see some evening at the Comédie Française or the Bouffes du Nord? That is the question Serres would ask of those who do not see in literature a reserve of knowledge, but he also knows that this reserve must often be activated by something outside itself: "But could we ever have read Molière without Mauss?"[5]

A cynic might argue that Serres has done no more than apply, reductively, a structure discovered by twentieth-century anthropology to Molière's play, producing an anachronistic interpretation that teaches us nothing new about Molière or the seventeenth century, and nothing new about anthropology. How is the cynic to be answered? In the first place, it should be of no small interest concerning the seventeenth century that its comedy provides a model of what has been proposed in our own time as a fundamental anthropological structure, a model as rigorously complete as any other. As far as the *text* is concerned, Serres's readings invariably account for minute or seemingly puzzling details: his structuralism of contents, far from being limited to ex-

[5]Serres, *Hermes: Literature, Science, Philosophy*, ed. J. V. Harari and D. F. Bell (Baltimore, 1982), 13. Cf. Serres, *Hermès I: La Communication*, 245.

tracting or abstracting grand lines of a work, seems to lay bare levels of coherence that other readings have had to leave aside. According to Mauss, exchange is always associated with eating together: Serres points out that Monsieur Dimanche's refusal of Dom Juan's dinner invitation corresponds to the lack of exchange between them. Moreover, if the entire play is about exchange, then it must itself be a meal, and its subtitle, *Le Festin de pierre*, says that it is. For Dom Juan, submission to the law of exchange and thus to death comes with his acceptance of the Commander's dinner invitation. And so forth. But to return to our hypothetical indictment of Serres, on one count he has pleaded no contest. His reading of *Dom Juan* depends on modern anthropology—and so much the better. Here is how he put it in a 1982 interview:

> Each generation should, at a certain point, devote itself to a great reread-
> ing of the tradition that preceded it. . . . Today, we're witnessing the
> birth of a new kind of culture—a scientifically based culture in which
> the science-culture link appears as a totally new articulation. . . . When
> people know a little more genetics—as they inevitably will—they'll read
> Zola as I read him. When they know what a "turbulent state" is in phys-
> ics, they'll read the poem of Lucretius as I read it. So what am I doing?
> I'm using the culture that I see emerging to reread the tradition.
>   In these circumstances, why reread Molière's *Dom Juan* the way it
> used to be read? Dom Juan, a seducer, a ladies' man? Given the evolu-
> tion of mores, not too many people would be interested in that anymore.
> On the other hand, read it starting out from what anthropology has
> taught us and you'll find an admirable description of exchange, of obli-
> gation and of the "Gift."[6]

In acknowledging the modernity of his reading, Serres becomes the advocate of an interdisciplinary culture, one that would unite the latest discoveries of the exact sciences with the accumulated tradition that has gone before them. There is nothing surprising about this plea, and given its journalistic context, we could just assume that this is the point Serres is making and let it go at that.

The argument's implications for literary studies, however, go beyond the almost obvious desirability of improved contact with scientific culture. If literature were really an object of research, if we were concerned with discovering and stating *what literary texts are* (in all

---

[6]Serres, "A quoi sert la philosophie?" *Le Nouvel Observateur*, édition internationale, February 6, 1982, p. 15.

the ramifications of such a general project), then how could we plan to decide every generation that they are something different? Two representations of the uses and abuses of literature are at issue here, one scientific, the other romantic. On the one hand, literature may be an object that we try to understand, albeit with techniques and concepts that change over time; on the other hand, literature may be an input to a wider cultural reflection, or to new literary creation, or to a project that is not itself strictly literary. The two representations do not really contradict each other, but they correspond to divergent strategies for studying and reading. The first characterizes literary studies as an academic discipline; after all, no discipline likes to admit that it exists so that its object will make useful reading for others, who are free to redefine it every thirty years. In the second alternative, literature and its traditions appear as a resource in the continual elaboration of new cultural works and configurations. Literature, in this context, need not be defined as a specific type of writing to be investigated and understood, but becomes instead that body of writing upon which we draw: a cultural and discursive reservoir. Serres has little use for the disciplinary pseudo-objectivity of *Literaturwissenschaft*, and he places himself clearly in the tradition of what Rorty calls modern literary culture, the culture of mortal vocabularies, of meanings that succeed one another in time. But by including the sciences within this culture, he advocates a use of literature that recalls the era when literature was synonymous with written culture, when literary education was not a specialty but was nearly identical to education in general. He does so not nostalgically, in the manner of Barthes and his longing for the cosmogonic unity of the Greeks, but with an eye to scientific modernity and to a kind of inquiry consisting of local and multiple passages rather than general or totalizing knowledge.

For much of his career Serres has endeavored to show that any global rationalism is a cultural disaster. He constantly emphasizes the connection between, on the one hand, the ambition of global, universal knowledge and, on the other hand, force and violence. In a memorable essay on La Fontaine and Descartes, he shows that the philosopher's strategy in the *Rules for the Direcion of the Mind* is isomorphic to the predator's strategy in the fable "The Wolf and the Lamb." Wolf and philosopher both try to occupy the extremum in a series of positions, the point from which Descartes will have maximum certitude, minimum doubt, from which the lamb will lose every argument with

the wolf. The project of Cartesian rationalism, of a knowledge committed to maximal clarity and maximal efficacy, is the method of the
strong, a project of violent domination.[7] The real is only rarely rational; the zones to which maximally ordered schemas of understanding
can be applied are isolated pockets of order, islands distributed in a sea
of chaos. We are constituted as subjects of knowledge by our fear of
the immense disorder, the immense background noise of chaos, and
our predilection for the extrema of order and universal method is the
violent consequence of our fear. But if we wish truly to know the real,
Serres argues, or to escape the hell of political and military violence
that modern rationalism has helped to create, we must shift to ways of
knowing that negotiate with complexity, uncertainty, and disorder.
"Science is not necessarily a matter of unity or of order; multiplicity
and noise are not necessarily on the irrational side."[8]

At the beginning of this chapter I quoted from the review Serres
wrote of *La Nouvelle Alliance* by Prigogine and Stengers. In the "metamorphosis of science" that they describe, Serres sees the possible dawn
of a scientific culture less dependent on ahistorical, universal laws, less
committed to the exclusion of the circumstantial, the random, the bi-
furcation leading to irreversible change. Such a science would be less
totalitarian in and of itself and less radically separated from the historical and human disciplines that study the cultural change within which
they exist: "There is as much unexpected as one wants, at least for us
who are not omniscient. But we are all there is and omniscience has
fled. What will happen tomorrow, at the threshold of my locality, will
be of rule and of chance. Science and history speak with a single
voice."[9]

The vision of a future culture at once literary and scientific compels
us to take seriously the question of intellectual relations between literature and the sciences, to suspend our habitual practices of disciplinary
autonomy. But that does not mean seeking global paradigms, universal
ways of ordering, that can join the literary and the scientific. Serres
contends that there are no such paradigms or methods, that what must
be sought are not general correspondences, not totalizing, abstracting
schemas for integrating different fields of inquiry, but *passages* from
one domain to the other, route that may be as difficult, as complex,

[7]Serres, "Le Jeu du loup," in *Hermès IV: La Distribution* (Paris, 1977), 89–104.
Cf. Serres, *Détachement* (Paris, 1983), 152–155.
[8]Serres, *Genèse* (Paris, 1982), 211.
[9]Serres, "Commencements," 13.

as problematic as the Northwest Passage sought by French explorers from Cartier to Chateaubriand. Such passages, he argues, are rare, complex, and local; they have partial applications and are not steps on a hypothetical pathway to generalized knowledge or universal method.[10]

The remainder of *The Noise of Culture* will be devoted to what Serres would call passages between science and literature, in particular to the group of related passages offered by the theories of information, self-organization, and autonomous systems. As a first step in our exploration of these passages, let's turn to a somewhat abstract character devised by Serres as a means of passage between thermodynamics and information theory. In *Le Parasite* (1980), he forges an "intellectual operator" from the triple semantic field of his title and the invariant structures associated with the three related domains. The word *parasite* in French denotes not only the organism that lives in or off another, not only the sponger who is always inviting himself to dinner, but also the static or noise that interrupts and muddles electronic communications. The word thus brings together biology, the anthropology of human relations, and communications theory, and this is no mere accident of language but a conceptual invariant: the parasite always *interrupts*, be it the circulation of nutritive elements, the service of food, or the transmission of signals. All three kinds of parasites have a parallel relation to order and disorder: they place themselves in relation to order that they have not produced, and their presence brings disorder to the systems in which they appear. The triple meaning of *parasite* enables Serres to translate stories and fables into a commentary that is in turn biological, anthropological, economic, and informational. He begins with a translation or retelling of La Fontaine's "Le Rat de ville et le rat des champs":

> The city rat invites the country rat onto the Persian rug. They gnaw and chew leftover bits of ortolan. Scraps, bits and pieces, left-overs: their royal feast is only a meal after a meal among the dirty dishes of a table that has not been cleared. The city rat has produced nothing and his dinner invitation costs him almost nothing. Boursault says this in his *Fables d'Esope*, where the city rat lives in the house of a big tax farmer. Oil, butter, ham, bacon, cheese—everything is available. It is easy to invite the country cousin and to regale oneself at the expense of another.

[10]See Serres, *Hermès V: Le Passage du Nord-Ouest* (Paris, 1980), especially 15–24.

The tax farmer produced neither oil nor ham nor cheese; in fact, he produced nothing. But using power or the law, he can profit from these products. Likewise for the city rat who takes the farmer's left-overs. And the last to profit is the country rat. But we know that the feast is cut short. The two companions scurry off when they hear a noise at the door. It was only noise, but it was also a message, a bit of information producing panic: an interruption, a corruption, a rupture of communication. Was the noise really a message? Wasn't it, rather, static, a parasite? A parasite who has the last word, who produces disorder and who generates a different order.[11]

The parasitic relations form a cascading chain: from the place of production, rich and rare, energy and information fall through a series of diversions and interceptions, toward their eventual dissipation into disorder, their dissolution into background noise.

Although my intention in this book is not to propose critical methods or offer examples of readings, it seems useful at this point to look at what Serres's parasite can enable us to do with a particular literary text. My aim in so doing is not to provide a model of practical criticism but to introduce some of the concepts used by Serres in an idiom with which literary scholars will be comfortable. So let's turn the rats into poor relations. Balzac wrote two great novels about such unwanted and dangerous family appendages: *La Cousine Bette* and *Le Cousin Pons*. Old Bette complains about her parasitic status: "With a poor relation, people act as they would toward rats to whom they're giving a bit of fat. . . . I've had all their left-overs for twenty-six years."[12] The poor relation seems to be a parasite by definition, and in the case of Cousin Pons, Balzac left no doubt. He even considered calling his novel *Le Parasite*. (Had he done so, Serres would surely have had to write about it.) In the widely used *Petit Robert* dictionary, the entry *pique-assiette* (moocher) contains a phrase from Balzac's description of Pons. The novel provides an ideal setting for exploring the workings of parasites and introducing some of the concepts invoked by Serres to form his intellectual operator.

Pons has two manias, both of which depend on his being a parasite. He loves food and he collects decorative and artistic objects. What does the perpetual guest, the moocher, offer his hosts in exchange for

---

[11]Serres, *The Parasite*, 3; translation modified. Cf. *Le Parasite*, 9.
[12]Balzac, *La Comédie humaine*, ed. Castex (Paris, 1976–81), VII, 150, 147. Subsequent references given in parentheses in the text.

his dinners? Nothing tangible or solid: words of thanks, even of flattery at times, perhaps witty conversation. The parasitic bargain sets up a one-way flow of goods or energies: from livestock to farmer, from farmer to tax farmer, tax farmer to city rat, city rat to country rat, rich relatives to poor Cousin Pons. "A pecking bird, flitting off with a full gullet, and warbling a tune as his sole thanks, Pons felt a certain pleasure in living well at the expense of society, which demanded what of him? Make-believe money" (VII, 493). Pons places himself at the end of a long chain, getting himself invited by the hosts of the hosts of his hosts. "And Pons would come along at the tail of the Camusots and the Cardots to the Chiffrevilles, and thence to the Popinots, always as the cousin of the cousins" (VII, 504).

For years, despite a slow decline from honored guest to sponger, Pons remains comfortably and firmly in his place at the end of this parasitic chain, but one day he tries to offer something in return for his dinners, and disaster strikes. Using his talents as a collector, he finds and gives a fan painted by Watteau to Madame Camusot, his cousin's wife. Offended at the idea of owing anything to their despised parasite, the Camusots throw him out for good, cutting him off from all his tables. "He's a done-for rat," exclaims their old cook. Back at the apartment he shares with his old friend Schmucke, Pons finds himself condemned to modest dinners; worse yet, to paying for them himself out of the meager funds he was used to putting into collecting.

Pons has thrown nearly all his life's resources into building his collection. He acquired the core of it while in Italy, ostensibly studying musical composition as the young recipient of the Rome Prize. His collecting makes use of energy otherwise destined to other activities: music, to which Pons never devotes enough time to become a great composer, and love, denied him by his physical ugliness. Right from the start, his collecting lives parasitically off the rest of his life. More important, Pons the collector obeys a particular principle, "the axiom of Chenevard, the learned collector of precious engravings, who claims that one can only take pleasure in looking at a Ruysdaël, a Hobbema, a Holbein, a Raphaël, a Murillo, a Greuze, a Sebastiano del Piombo, a Giorgione, an Albert Dürer, insofar as the painting has only cost fifty francs. Pons admitted no acquisition above a hundred francs; and for him to pay fifty francs for something, the object had to be worth three thousand" (VII, 489–490). The method works only because Pons has so much time to look: he waits in ambush for the rare and precious item lost in the chaos of thousands and thousands of objects for sale in Paris. "Rare had been the occasions," writes Balzac, but Pons had what was needed to seize them: legs, time, and patience. He runs, waits, and stays on the lookout, thereby obtaining an astounding return on investment: "After having spent, since his return from Rome, around two thousand francs a year, Pons had hidden away a collection of masterpieces in every genre whose catalogue reached the fabulous number 1,907. From 1811 to 1816, during his meanderings through Paris, he had found for ten francs what now costs a thousand to twelve hundred francs. Paintings, culled from the forty-five thousand paintings shown every year in Parisian sales" (VII, 490). Pons the collector could be defined as an animated eye that places itself at the right spots to sort and select. His astronomical profits are of the same order of magnitude as the number of items he sorts through for each find.

Now this system is unique neither to Pons nor to Balzac nor even to collectors. Suppose we turn the art objects and knickknacks into fast-moving molecules, randomly distributed among others, more or less slower moving. To do so, we need only read a justly famous passage from James Clerk Maxwell's *Theory of Heat*:

> One of the best established facts in thermodynamics is that it is impossible in a system enclosed in an envelope which permits neither change of volume nor passage of heat, and in which both the temperature and the pressure are everywhere the same, to produce any inequality of temperature or pressure without the expenditure of work. This is the second law of thermodynamics, and it is undoubtedly true as long as we deal with bodies only in mass, and have no power of perceiving and handling the separate molecules of which they are made up. But if we conceive a being whose faculties are so sharpened that he can follow every molecule in its course, such a being, whose attributes are still as essentially finite as our own, would be able to do what is at present impossible to us. For we have seen that the molecules in a vessel full of air at uniform temperature are moving with velocities by no means uniform, though the mean velocity of any great number of them, arbitrarily selected, is almost uniform. Now let us suppose that such a vessel is divided into two portions, A and B, by a division in which there is a small hole, and that a being, who can see the individual molecules, opens and closes this hole, so as to allow only the swifter molecules to pass from A to B, and only the slower ones to pass from B to A. He will thus, without expenditure of work, raise the temperature of B and lower that of A, in contradiction to the second law of thermodynamics.[13]

13Maxwell, *Theory of Heat* (New York, 1872), 308.

This of course is "Maxwell's Demon," the little being who produces an improbable molecular distribution through microscopic sorting. If we replace the energy corresponding to molecular velocity by exchange value (a metaphor quite familiar to the nineteenth century), we find once again the method by which Pons extracts, from a vast and varied set, a subset made homogeneous by the rarity and value of its members. In both cases, the act of sorting itself establishes the improbable concentration and thus the value or usable potential energy.

To some this abrupt translation between literary and scientific discourse may seem arbitrary, even absurd. It is a structuralist move in the sense developed by Serres, the identification of an invariant model. But to those who find this type of structural parallel unconvincing in itself, we can add that in this apparent detour through physics, we remain in fact entirely within the space of nineteenth-century cultural production, the age of motors and reservoirs. It was Sadi Carnot of the Ecole Polytechnique who first concluded that motive power of fire comes not from heat in and of itself but from a difference of temperature. Motors required a heat source and a heat sink. But in a closed system, differences disappear with time, so that in the end there remains only a homogeneous state from which no more work can be obtained.

The concept of entropy was introduced by Rudolf Clausius as a scientific measure of a system's inability to yield usable energy. The second law of thermodynamics states that in a closed system, entropy will increase to a maximum. Ludwig Boltzmann and Maxwell proposed a statistical interpretation of the second law that brings us to an identification of order with difference, disorder with homogeneity. Temperature is a function of the average velocity of billions and billions of molecules; a hot zone is a zone where there is a relative concentration of rapid molecules and thus a high average molecular velocity. Over time, the molecules drift toward a maximally probable distribution, that is, toward a homogeneous mixture in which no particular local concentration remains. Local concentration, differentiated from the rest of a system, is a kind of order, improbable. As the molecules are fully mixed, entropy tends toward its maximum; no more work can be obtained from the system because no more differences remain. Unless . . . And here is the literally fantastic challenge of Maxwell's Demon. The Demon is a serious intellectual construct that has played a nonnegligible conceptual role in the natural sciences. But is it not also a theorization of nineteenth-century fantasies—perpetual motion, energy without expenditure, the production of a generalized reservoir? The Demon holds out the promise of reversing the irreversible time that accompanies and haunts an industrial civilization founded on heat engines. The pleasure felt by Pons in acquiring, by sorting, the elements of a fine collection at a price almost infinitely below their value, seems to be a particular case of a fantasy whose highest conceptual expression would be none other than Maxwell's Demon.

Twentieth-century science has "exorcized" the Demon by showing that the conditions required by Maxwell are unrealizable in the real world of energy and information. According to a theorem of Leon Brillouin, the information needed by this microscopic gatekeeper turns out to have a cost in negative entropy that will prevent the extraction of usable energy from a truly closed system. In the system put forward by Maxwell, the Demon will in fact be unable to see or otherwise detect the molecules. If one adds, say, a source of light, then the system is no longer thermodynamically closed. In this case the Demon can indeed diminish the entropy of the vessel divided into A and B by sorting, but the light source "pours negative entropy into the system" at an even faster rate, so that the second law is not violated.[14] Entropy may diminish locally, but addition of a nonequilibrium source of radiation to the system implies that outside the vessel, entropy is increasing. The creation of order, of improbable distributions, is of necessity a local activity in an open subsystem of a larger, closed system in which entropy is increasing. The second law implies that a local decrease in entropy must be accompanied by its increase somewhere else. If we apply this restriction to Balzac's novel, it becomes clear that Pons the Demon must also have his source of energy somewhere so as to be able to sort.

To return to the rats of Serres: the parasite captures energy, information, and rarity from "upstream" and lives off them, discharging them "downstream" in diminished form. Parasites are links in the chains of relations through which order and usable energy are spent, diffused toward the chaos of maximum entropy. As such, they are the operators of irreversible time: the time of burning reservoirs, of dissipation, expenditure, death.

This kind of time dominates in *Le Cousin Pons*, for in spite of his life as a gourmand moocher, the old musician is less a parasite than an

---

[14]Brillouin, *Science and Information Theory*, 2d ed. (New York, 1962), 164.

unwilling host. For once his collection has been assembled, once the 1,907 items are in place and catalogued, it falls prey to a swarm of parasites. The novel, after explaining how this stockpile was amassed (biography of Pons, axiom of Chenevard), recounts at length the maneuvers of this parasitic troop as its members place themselves to collect a little something, or something big. It makes a fabulous tale, for the characters, like the rats, monkeys, and cats of La Fontaine, line up behind each other, the better to steal from one and all. Little parasites like Madame Cibot the concierge and Rémonencq the junkmonger are supplanted by bigger ones like Doctor Poulain and Attorney Fraisier. The latter in turn have to give way to the Camusots, parasites on a grand scale. Minor parasites, content to get a pair of ermine gloves or an order for a cemetery monument, place themselves along the path of major parasites to try for their share. And as Serres conjectures, all these parasites make a lot of noise: Madame Cibot lulls the suspicions of Pons with endless chatter that garbles the old musician's thoughts, only to be interrupted herself—persuaded to drop her prey, just like La Fontaine's crow—by the grating and diabolical voice of Fraisier.

Pons, then, can be found in turn on both ends of the parasitic relation. This double position is essential to our translation between the novel and statistical thermodynamics. The parasitic life of Pons during his collecting years allows us to say that the second law holds true in the novel; its hero is Maxwell's Demon as corrected by Brillouin. Parasitism provides the energy that gives the Demon the time, mobility, and fine perception needed for his lifelong selection. The generosity of Schmucke underscores this necessary link between collecting and sponging: when Pons is forced to pay for his own dinners, his friend offers to join him (financially) in collecting, so as to compensate for the loss of revenue brought on by expulsion from his cousins' tables.

The collector-Demon must be someone else's parasite, but locally he produces, he works. He works on behalf of his parasites, bringing order and value out of disorder, like the cat Raton in La Fontaine's "Le Singe et le chat," which Serres retells: "The producer promotes rarity out of the common, when rarity is absent; he turns it over to the parasite. The fire cooks the chestnuts; with a prudent and careful paw, Raton parts the ashes and grabs the best-cooked ones; behind him, Bertrand munches them. . . . Raton chooses, but Raton doesn't eat; Raton is parasited, Raton at the gate: here is Maxwell's Demon. Everything is there: fire, the chestnuts/particles, the choice, and behind, the one who believes in perpetual paradise."[15] Raton's work, like that of Pons, produces local order out of surrounding disorder. For Serres, this kind of work characterizes above all the living organism, itself an island of ordered complexity in a universe governed by the second law:

> What is work? Undoubtedly, it is a struggle against noise. . . . To work is to sort. Maxwell's Demon is inevitable, just like the parasite. Alas, they are twins perhaps. . . . Men are not the only ones who work. . . . Animals work, as do living organisms. What I mean by that is that life itself works—that it is life through its struggle against the tendency to death, through sorting, through the activity of Maxwell's Demon. The organism gets order and energy, chews them up, sorts them, classifies them, and re-forms its own order and its own energy, eliminating the waste-products. Does a miller do otherwise?[16]

Serres the philosopher speaks here in the voice of modern biology. And in the link between thermodynamics and biology, we have a conceptual tool with which to connect the Pons collection to other figures of creative activity in Balzac's earlier works, for the author of *La Comédie humaine*, as is well known, often took the biological science of his time as a model.

From its beginnings about 1800, biology has attempted to explain the principle, force, or mechanism by which organisms resist death, resist the degradation of order and energy that seems to be universal. The primacy of this question, in fact, largely distinguishes biology from the natural history that had preceded it. Among the earliest explanations to which biologists turned was vitalism: each organism, in this view, would begin life with a reserve of vital force enabling it to maintain its organization. Death would come with the exhaustion of the reservoir. In his history of biology, François Jacob explains how the seemingly unscientific notion of vital force did in fact function as an "operator of knowledge": "If vital force became a concept of such importance at the beginning of the nineteenth century, it was because it then played a role subsequently assumed by two new concepts. Today, living organisms are seen as the site of a triple flow of matter, energy and information. In its early days, biology was able to recognize the flow of matter; but, lacking the two other concepts, it had to postulate a special force."[17]

[15]Serres, *The Parasite*, 152; translation modified. Cf. *Le Parasite*, 202.

[16]Serres, *The Parasite*, 86. Cf. *Le Parasite*, 117.

[17]Jacob, *The Logic of Life*, trans. B. E. Spillmann (New York, 1973), 95; see also 88–100, 192–196.

In other words, the notion of vital force stands proleptically for the work of sorting and ordering energy and matter that is necessary for life in a universe governed by the second law, the tendency toward maximal entropy.

Jacob's remark enables us to link Balzac's vitalism to the "thermo-dynamic" analysis of *Le Cousin Pons* made possible by Serres and his parasite. Critics have already noted that the collection seems to be a form of artistic creation on the part of Pons. Now the earlier models of artistic creation in Balzac's work were generally and explicitly vitalis-tic. The Pons collection, then, retrospectively translates into a new lan-guage (which would soon become that of science) the vitalistic models and figures that are so well known in the first works of Balzac's matu-rity. It can thus be argued that with *Pons*, Balzac's text anticipates de-velopments in the natural sciences, but perhaps it is more prudent to note simply that with statistical thermodynamics, science called on a conceptual configuration that was already well established culturally and integrated by Balzac into novelistic writing, namely, a certain the-ory and practice of parasitism, of selection and collection.[18]

The kind of reading that *Le Parasite* opens up for *Le Cousin Pons* will not surprise readers of Serres. In fact, among literary critics at least, his name and work are closely linked with thermodynamics, en-ergy, entropy, and information. These sciences and concepts entered the writings of Serres with *Hermès III: La Traduction* (1974), notably in the far-reaching essay on Jacques Monod, "Vie, information, deu-xième principe." They remain central and explicit in the books that followed—the studies of Zola, Verne, and Lucretius, above all *La Distribution*—and implicitly central in *Le Parasite* and *Genèse*. What has interested Serres are not the kinds of statements that specialists in the disciplines of thermodynamics or information theory could make but, rather, the kinds of translations or passages opened up by the common formalisms of these fields. "It is possible," Serres wrote in the preface to *La Traduction*, "that science is the set of messages that are optimally invariant for any translation strategy."[19] Scientific state-ments about energy and information are important to Serres because of the translations they make possible.

---

[18]I develop the implications of this reading for Balzac studies in "Le Cousin Par-asite: Balzac, Serres et le démon de Maxwell," *Stanford French Review* 9 (1985), 397–414.

[19]Serres, *Hermès III: La Traduction* (Paris, 1974), 11.

The mathematical theory of information, worked out by Claude Shannon in the 1940s, defines information as a quantity, a particular probability function. The more improbable the arrival of a given message element, the more uncertainty its actual arrival resolves in its receiver, the more information it conveys. A single letter in our twenty-six-letter alphabet can convey more information than a single binary digit, which must be either 0 or 1. Information is defined as an inverse function—actually, the negative logarithm—of the probability that a given specified or meaningful outcome will be selected from a more or less large distribution of possibilities. Shannon's formula for information has the same form as the formula by which Boltzmann defined entropy as a function of the probabilities of microscopic molecular arrangements in a physical system. Shannon in fact often referred to his information function as "message entropy"; others have noted that the concept of entropy corresponds more precisely to information that we lack when we have not received a message, so that information actually received should be considered negative entropy, or "negentropy." The interpretation of this formal identity between the definitions of entropy and information is not a problem that can be resolved by experimentation, for it is a matter of convention, of choice between competing heuristics: do we identify information with the ordered specificity of messages sent or with the uncertainty in which a receiver awaits a possible message?

Serres is not interested in laying to rest this problem of convention. He wants to put the problem to work, to use the possible interpretations of the entropy-information isomorphism as an intellectual operator. "That entropy is linked to information," he wrote in *La Traduction*, "is the greatest discovery in history, in the theory of knowledge and in the theory of matter."[20] The structural identity of Boltzmann's and Shannon's formulae—one describing the organization of matter, the other describing the organization of transmitted information—provides a terrain for passages between the "exact" and the "human" sciences. It is a mathematical counterpart (albeit a debatable one) to the link between the appropriation of substance and the interruption of communication suggested by the semantic field of the French word *parasite*. If Serres shows enthusiasm, it is not because he hopes to reduce the theory of knowledge to the theory of matter (or vice versa) but

[20]Serres, *Hermès III: La Traduction*, 71.

because a translation has been found between the two. We can now think of communications in a physical, impersonal way, as we would think of collections of molecules, and thus begin to understand how our messages interact with the background noise of the spaces in which they travel. We can now think of thermodynamic systems in an observer-oriented way, as though distributions of molecules contained possible messages. The isomorphic role of order and disorder in thermodynamics and information theory points to a continuity of relational properties between matter, energy, and information; between, in other words, the world and the means we have of making statements about the world.

In a brief and powerful essay in *La Distribution*, Serres uses the work of the theoretical biologist Henri Atlan to explore the mediation between matter and information that takes place in the living organism.[21] Organisms are systems, he notes, and have long been understood according to models provided by nonliving systems. In the age of Newton, the living being was a mechanism, a representation that by the romantic era seemed reductive and irrelevant. Criticizing a classical treatise on animal movement, Balzac denounced its treatment of the organism as a system of pulleys and cords, levers and counterweights.[22] In the nineteenth century, as I noted with respect to *Le Cousin Pons* and Balzac's early vitalism, the organism became a thermal machine, possessing a stock or reservoir of energy that permits it, for a time, growth, activity, and the maintenance of its organization. As François Jacob noted, we can now consider the concept of vital force to have been a way of designating the energy and information derived by an organism from interaction with its environment. We can, in other words, translate the language of nineteenth-century science into that of twentieth-century science. Living beings are not subject to entropy increase predicted by the second law of thermodynamics, we now say, because they are open systems, receiving energy from without. The earth itself is an open system, receiving a constant flow of energy from the sun.

[21]Serres, "Origine du langage," *Hermès IV: La Distribution*, 259–272. The essay originally appeared under the title "Le Point de vue de la biophysique" in an issue of *Critique* (no. 346, March 1976) devoted to psychoanalysis. It has been translated into English as "The Origin of Language: Biology, Information Theory, and Thermodynamics," in *Hermes*, 71–83.

[22]Balzac, *Théorie de la démarche*, in *La Comédie humaine*, XII, 273.

The role of information in the structure and function of organisms is the contribution of twentieth-century biology, which has modeled life on transmitted signals, codes, even computer programs, just as the eighteenth and nineteenth centuries modeled it on mechanisms and motors. The preservation, modification, and transmission of information now provide models for understanding the processes by which organisms function, maintain their organization, and even increase in complexity through learning or evolution. Genetics and molecular biology provide the best-known examples of this informational modeling, but they describe only the first levels of the hierarchically organized systems we call living beings. According to Jacob, the living thing is a hypercomplex system integrating many subsystems, themselves integrating subsystems, and so on down to the molecular level, like nested Russian dolls.

Now at each level of such a system, Serres proposes, there is information and transmission of information, and there is noise—from the environment, to be sure, but also from the activity of the subsystems, from the imperfections of internal communications. The noise produced by one level must be converted, at least in part, into information at the next level, so that the system is not overwhelmed and disorganized by its own noise. At a given level of the system there is transmission of information and generation of noise. The next level acts as an observer of the preceding one, and for this observer, the ambiguity resulting from noise in the first transmission of information becomes a source of new information, of added organizational complexity. "In a certain sense, the next level functions as a rectifier, in particular, as a rectifier of noise. What was once an obstacle to all messages is reversed and added to the information."[23]

Serres is in fact offering a speculative interpretation of the "formalism of self-organization from noise." Atlan proposed this theory, which is based on Shannon's theory of information, as an explanatory mechanism for phenomena of biological complexity and evolution. Serres supposes that Atlan's formalism functions at every change of level in a hierarchical system, at every site where an observer distinct from the receiver of transmitted information observes the entire process of sending, transmission, and reception that is part of the next level down. What we call language, then, may simply be the informa-

[23]Serres, *Hermes*, 78.

tion at the last level of this process, the singular instance at one end of the body's organizational tree.[24] "The body is an extraordinarily complex system that creates language from information and noise, with as many mediations as there are integrating levels."[25] In other words, what we call knowing, perceiving, speaking, are all activities that imply, and take place through, the integration of information and noise. These activities are not necessarily different in form from the organization of matter into organic molecules and living cells, or even into nonliving ordered structures such as crystals or whirlpools. Between the signals in our brain that we call thought, and the relations of organization in the natural universe, we can describe a continuum. From objects to human language, noise and information circulate and are integrated by successive "observers," notably by the subsystems of our own organisms. We do not know the details of this process nor can we even identify all its levels, but Serres—in effect speculating on a scientific future—argues that a process of integration must take place in something like this manner. Knowing, then, would be the culmination of a process that takes place at every level, not just in the conscious mind. "The observer, like the object, the subject, like the observed, are wrought by a shared division more stable and potent than their antique separation: they are, together, order and disorder. . . . *It is no longer incomprehensible that the world is comprehensible.*"[26]

The link between language and the world passes through the body, the physical system in which perception and thought and speech take place. To make this kind of argument is to accept a cognitive role not only for linguistic and cultural structures but for biological and physical structures as well. In this view, we are capable of knowing what is around us not because we are separated from it, subjects facing objects, but because we are part of it, order amid disorder. What is noise, what is information depends on the position of the observer: information theory recognizes that it is itself caught up in systems of information. Only thematic distinctions separate the sciences of nature and the sci-

---

[24]In one of his fascinating but unprovable asides, Serres suggests that we already have a theory about what happens in the conversion of noise and information between the top two levels: psychoanalysis. What we call the unconscious, a source of potentially information-producing noise (slips, dreams, neurotic symptoms) for our consciousness, is simply what is going on one level down.

[25]Serres, *Hermes*, 82.

[26]Serres, *Hermes*, 82–83; translation modified.

ences of man: the latter are part of the former, because man is a being in nature, and the former are part of the latter, for there is not a single statement of natural science that is not part of the culture produced by human beings.

I have summarized Serres's essay on Atlan here for two reasons. For one thing, it provides a foretaste of concepts indispensable to a study of the relations between literature, knowledge, information, and noise. If literary texts appear as paradoxical objects in a world of information, it is because of the ways in which they both complicate information with noise and bring meaning and order out of disorder and play. The formalism of self-organization from noise will be at or near the center of my arguments throughout this book, and I will take up Atlan's work and its possible implications for textual studies in some detail in the next chapter.

More important, "Origine du langage" provides an example of the speculative interest and audacity of Serres's writings, to which too little serious attention has been paid. It is a striking—and perhaps overly ambitious—demonstration of how the categories, codes, and perhaps even algorithms of science can be used to speak of something of which we have always spoken in terms that come from our philosophical and literary traditions: the relation of mind to matter, subject to object, speech to inarticulate sensation and feeling. But the remainder of this book will not be a commentary on Serres. His work calls not for discipleship but for the formation of what he calls *tiers-instruits*, persons capable of navigating the passages between the constraining estates of sciences and letters. If I have chosen to explore some problems that he has treated, I do so neither to reproduce his work nor to improve on it but rather to set off in new directions, and, as I begin, perhaps to make some of his work accessible to a different audience. For Serres writes elliptically and allusively, conducting serious arguments in a style not always appreciated by American scholars. Some of those who do appreciate Serres are in all likelihood so convinced of the metaphoricity of all texts as to miss, or refuse, much of what is most radical in his thought. That radical message is: we cannot continue to do the humanities, or the human sciences, alone, unless we are willing to turn them into more or less fashionable museum pieces. Nor can we stand by while natural science is done, not alone, but in communication only with power, wealth, and arms.

A few paragraphs back I wrote that Serres "supposes" the functioning of Atlan's organization from noise formalism. This is precisely what Serres has said he does with science: he *supposes* it. At the conclusion of his latest book, *Les Cinq Sens,* he explains that he is not interested in copying science or in judging it but in placing science in the position of the subject of his discourse. That is what he means by supposing it. Rather than treating science as an object to be examined or a space to be delimited, he assumes that it is not only known but digested, now as much a part of our subjectivity as language long has been:

> I do not therefore work on science; in my texts science works. It could work on science: it does so in scientific texts, which philosophy can recopy, which it can also judge useless to recopy, for reasons of redundancy or honesty. In my texts, it is active, it works on something not itself.
>
> A very secret revolution, which bears no name: objective knowledge, supposed, has taken the place of the subject. This transformation gives rise to a new world, to new texts, to another kind of thought.[27]

This should not be read, I believe, as an advertisement for the singularity of texts written by Serres. His project is not to write idiosyncratically, though some would say that that is what he has achieved. He wishes to anticipate, to make palpable in his texts, a transformation that affects all of us, that changes our relationship to language, thought, and the world. Science is replacing language as the mediation between us and the world, the medium in which we exercise our subjectivity. It is beginning to think within us, to work in our texts. Every domain of experience has its corresponding scientific discourse, and this discourse changes the meaning of our words, restructures our experience in something like the way in which language must have restructured the experience of the first generations to speak. This process, I have suggested, is already happening in Balzac; it is happening far more explicitly in Serres, who sees it as our common future.

Serres argues that language is now in crisis because of its disqualification by science. He does not mean by language the faculty of the subject to speak; he means rather the fact that we have always spoken and thought in languages not based on true algorithms, not "based" on anything in fact except our use of them, the traditions and stories and figures that accompany them. Serres is in effect generalizing the dis-

---

[27]Serres, *Les Cinq Sens* (Paris, 1985), 371.

qualification of rhetoric and narrative by paradigmatic science, arguing that this shift now affects every speaker of language. As science disqualifies the medium through which we have experienced and spoken the world, language and culture as we have known them are swept away at an astonishing rate. This may be a disaster, or it may be an opportunity, a chance to create a new culture whose language will be of science as well as of tradition, whose science will be of the subject as well as of the object. If we want to preserve something of our subjectivity, our traditional and rhetorical and literary ways of living our subjectivity, then we must open our texts to the new codes and messages and noises of science, begin to place science in the place of the cultural subject. Such is the program of Serres—and a possible future for what we still call the humanities.

3 Self-Organizing Systems: Information and Noise

> Chance and chance alone has a message for us. Every-
> thing that occurs out of necessity, everything ex-
> pected, repeated day in and day out, is mute. Only
> chance can speak to us.
>
> MILAN KUNDERA,
> *The Unbearable Lightness of Being*

To place science in the role of the subject, according to Michel Serres, one must forget science. If we remember it, then we write about it as an object, we work on it rather than enable it to work through our texts. In the new kind of scientific culture that Serres sees emerging, the statements and algorithms of science will become as much a part of our subjective makeup as any other aspect of the personal and cultural past that remains forgotten within the individual.

This stance creates a temporary problem for readers of Serres, one that is especially apparent in his most recent books. To forget implies having learned. The science "forgotten" by Serres and now at work in his texts has never been learned by most of us on the literary side of the aisle. He is not writing *about* science, yet he is writing for readers who need to learn about science if they are to forget it with him as they read.

In this respect my approach is the opposite of that of Serres. I cannot and do not claim to have forgotten science, nor do I posit a reader who is in a position to do so. Exposition and equations will abound in the present chapter, for my goal is to present as explicitly as possible the formalism of self-organization from noise and its relevance to our understanding of literature and literary studies. Conceptually central, it is the most technical chapter of the book, for in the final chapters I will be moving out from this particular passage between science and literature to its broader critical and cultural implications. Readers uncomfortable with mathematical formulae need not worry or skip ahead: everything essential is also explained in words, and the equations, I am tempted to say, are here only so as to be forgotten.

The theory of self-organizing systems offers a new vocabulary and a new set of concepts with which to describe what goes on in texts and discuss problems in literary theory. Its concepts and terms may at first seem strange or ill-suited to literary studies precisely because of their simplicity. It will be necessary, in order to describe in a new way the impossibility of treating literary texts as simply messages, to suppose that messages are indeed what they are. In other words, we will often have to treat literature as an instrument of communication in order to prepare a theory of its autonomy. Conversely, we will begin to argue the importance of literary contents by defining literature exclusively in terms of its form. Such paradoxical moments in the exposition are no accident; they are entailed by the nature of self-organization as an explanatory schema. The theory of self-organization from noise offers a framework for the qualitative understanding of complex and emergent phenomena, but it does so by beginning with the quantitative and seemingly reductive concepts of mathematical information theory.

Information Theory

The mathematical theory of information is not initially a theory of language or of human communication, although it may very well have implications for our understanding of how we speak and write to one another. It is, rather, a theory concerned with quantitative problems in the transmission of signals, problems such as: can we minimize the number of signals needed to transmit a given quantity of information? what are the effects of transmission error on the information we send? can we encode information in a manner that resists degradation through transmission errors? can we do so efficiently? It is thus not immediately obvious that information theory can say anything pertinent about human language and, specifically, about literature. The power of information theory derives from its generality: it begins by supposing merely that there are alphabets, that there are codes, that strings of characters from alphabets can be formed, then transmitted from one site to another. Its statements thus concern the formal conditions of transmitting messages and not the eventual meaning or significance of messages that might actually be sent. The information theorist cares no more about the meaning or significance of transmitted messages than an expert in postal efficiency does about the meaning of the letters people write to each other.

To define information independently of meaning or significance, Shannon employed the notion of the receiver's uncertainty as to the content of the message to be received. Obviously, if the receiver already knows what the message will be, the message conveys no information at all. If there are two possible messages that might be received, then the actual reception of one and not the other amounts to a decrease in incertitude, or a gain in information: the receiver now knows that what could have been A or B is in fact A. The arrival of the message can thus be considered an event for the receiver; the amount of information received is the degree to which the receiver's uncertainty concerning that event has been diminished. Quantities of information are generally counted in *bits*, the number of elements needed to encode the number of possible messages in a binary alphabet. In the above example, an event or message with two possible states, we count one bit of information, since the transmission of a single o or 1 will end the receiver's uncertainty. If there are four ($= 2^2$) possibilities, we will need two bits, which can be combined into the possible messages oo, o1, 1o, 11. In general, the quantity (H) of information in bits is the base-two logarithm of the number (N) of possible states of the message, $H = \log_2 N$. Written as a function of the probability ($p = 1/N$) associated with each possible state or letter, this equation becomes $H = -\log_2 p$. This is the simplest case, since we have assumed that all states, or letters of an alphabet, are equally probable, a situation rarely found in the transmission of real messages. This type of measurement, however, can be generalized to include cases in which the events, or symbols of an alphabet, are not equally probable. In this case the quantity of information is given by the sum of the base-two logarithms of the probability of each individual outcome or character, with the probabilities themselves used as coefficients: $H = -\Sigma p_i \log_2 p_i$.

The generality of these formulae, the fact that they take into account neither the physical means of transmission nor the qualitative nature of information, makes it possible to take seriously their analogy with Boltzmann's formula for entropy, $S = -k \Sigma p_i \log p_i$. Boltzmann's constant, k, expresses the relation between the macroscopic quantity, entropy, and the determination of this quantity solely by the probabilities associated with its microstates. To return for a moment to our exposition of statistical thermodynamics from the last chapter, in the simple case of a gas in two halves of a container, the entropy is greatest when the respective temperatures are equal, that is, when the distribution of fast- and slow-moving molecules is approximately the same in both halves. From a statistical perspective, this state is the most probable because there are the most possible ways to produce it, the greatest number of distinct microstates all of which have the same macroscopic consequences. There are far fewer combinations of microstates in which, for example, almost all the fast molecules are on one side of the barrier, just as if we toss a coin 100 times, there are billions of distinct sequences that will lead to 50 heads and 50 tails, each as improbable in itself as the one and only sequence that will lead to 100 heads.

The parallel equations of Boltzmann and Shannon make it possible to treat both energetic and informational systems in terms of distributions and probabilities. The notion of uncertainty, or of information not possessed by an observer or receiver, can be linked to this kind of analysis of probabilities: if we know that 100 heads were obtained in 100 coin tosses, then we know the sequence of the tosses as well, whereas if we know that the outcome is 50 heads and 50 tails, we would need a great deal more information to know in what sequence this combination was produced. Similarly, if we go back to our divided vessel of gas, we lack an enormous amount of information concerning the microstates of the evenly distributed system, whereas only a relatively small number of microstates can produce the maximally uneven distribution, so that our uncertainty concerning the actual microstate is correspondingly much less. Shannon, consequently, sometimes called his function H the "entropy of the message," since the function measures the number of possibilities and thus the receiver's uncertainty concerning the message's contents, just as entropy is in a sense a measure of the uncertainty of an observer concerning the state of a system she is observing. But if we want to equate the entropy of a message with disorder, the disorder in question must be the uncertainty in which the message's receiver is maintained as long as he has not yet received the message. It is the fact that the specific outcome or symbol he is about to receive is, for the moment, "lost" among a more or less large number of possible outcomes or symbols he could be about to receive, just as the actual microstate is "lost" for the observer among an enormous number of possible microstates compatible with the observed macrostate.

Our qualitative intuition of "information" is just the opposite; we consider only what is uniquely defined, in a sense expected, as information, whereas unexpected and random sequences of events appear to be confusing and uninformative. By information, in other words, we want to mean the message actually sent, its specified order, and not a chaos of possibilities. Both thermodynamic and information systems contain patterns that may be characterized as orders or disorders, depending on the viewpoint of the observer. When we speak of problems in the transmission of information, we assume that there exist given, specified messages to be sent and received, so we are using the word *information* not in the sense of "quantity of information" ("entropy of message") but in the sense of a *specific message of given quantity, sent by a sender, but not neccessarily integrally received.*

The transmission of information from sender to receiver plays the same role as the passage of time in a closed vessel of gas: the "received" state is what has happened to the initial state over time, in one case, or during its transmission through some kind of physical space, in the other. To be very explicit, let's see what might happen when we send a message whose information can be evaluated at 100 bits. Suppose that 10 bits are lost, that is, replaced by random bits, in the course of the transmission. Now in one sense, the receiver still gets 100 bits of something—perhaps information. But given a context, given the fact that 10 of these bits are not informative for the receiver— that is, they cannot reduce the receiver's uncertainty concerning the events symbolized by the message—then in fact only 90 bits of information have been received. By comparison with a perfect transmission of all 100 bits, entropy has increased in that the receiver's uncertainty, his ignorance of the message sent, is greater than it would have been had he received it all without the introduction of any disorder. What happens when information is transmitted is well described by Derrida's well-known phrase, "Une lettre n'arrive *pas toujours* à destination" (a letter does not always arrive at its destination).[1] Entropy may have increased, but specified information has been degraded because it has failed to arrive. In other words, information, like energy thermodynamically available to perform mechanical work, can only be degraded in a closed system. We have thus constructed a parallel between the transmission of a message and the thermodynamic evolution over time of a closed system as described by the second law. In both cases, en-

[1]Jacques Derrida, "Le Facteur de la vérité," in *La Carte postale* (Paris, 1980), 517.

tropy increases, thus increasing the observer's uncertainty concerning the initial state. The quantity of information received is less than or equal to the quantity transmitted. This is a more intuitively satisfying intepretation of the second law as it applies to information than the purely quantitative "entropy of message," since significant information does not simply consist of a quantity of symbols; it must be a specified, highly improbable sequence of symbols in order to function.

If information is inevitably degraded in transmission, one might wonder how a modern society increasingly based on electronic communication between computers manages to function at all. How is it that we can have confidence in telephones or electronic banking, despite the second law of thermodynamics? The answer to this question lies in one of the most important concepts of information theory, that of *redundancy*. We tend to deplore redundancy in writing, considering it to be a sign of muddled thinking, or the refuge of those who have little original thought to express. And yet almost all our utterances are filled with   , as for example this sentence, whose context and syntax would enable the reader to supply the missing word *redundancy* if by some collusion of author and printer it should be missing. In this particular example, redundancy is realized in two ways: first, the sequence "deplore redundancy. . . . And yet . . . filled with   " leads the reader to expect a particular word, which would thus be partially redundant if and when it appeared; second, and more heavy-handedly, there is what one might call a very crude error-correcting code at work in the second part of the sentence, an explanatory statement to the effect that "in case there was a word missing back there, it was *redundancy*." We can relate this example of redundancy directly to the concept of information as a message that resolves, for its receiver, an uncertainty: since the reader can expect to find the word *redundancy* in what turns out to be a blank space, its presence there would have resolved very little uncertainty and provided very little information—less, certainly, than the word *sex* ("our utterances are filled with sex"), which would have signaled a surprising change in the thematics of the chapter. In the mathematical theory of information, redundancy is a ratio denoting, in effect, the portion of a message given over to the repetition of what is already found somewhere else in the message. If we encode 70 bits of information in 100 bits, using the remaining 30 bits to repeat part of that information in some form, we have a message that is 30 percent redundant. The redundancy R of a message is given by $R = (H_{max} - H)/H_{max} =$

$1 - H/H_{max}$, where H is the quantity of information of the message, and H_{max} is the quantity of information that the message would carry if it contained no redundancy. To explain this, and also to understand how it can be related to our informal example taken from natural language, we need to go back to the definition of H, the quantity of information. In this definition, no mention was made of the length of message as a consituent of the quantity of information. This is because the function H is normally defined as the quantity of information conveyed *by a single character of the alphabet* of a given system. For example, the arrival of a o or 1 in a binary alphabet resolves our uncertainty between two possibilities; if we assume these to be equally probable, its information quantity is $H = \log_2 2 = 1$ (bit). As we have noted, this equation can also be written in terms of the probability (here, 0.5) of each letter rather than the number of letters: $H = -\log_2 (0.5) = 1$.

If we assume that the 27 characters of the English alphabet (including the blank space) are equally probable (a false assumption for natural languages), the mean information per letter would be $H = \log_2 (27) = -\log_2 (1/27) = 4.76$. We can generalize this calculation to the case in which the letters are not equally probable by using the equation $H = -\Sigma\, p_i \log_2 p_i$. The actual frequency distribution of English gives approximately $H = 4$. But even this "corrected" value of H gives the mean information per letter of a message if and only if there is no redundancy, which is equivalent to saying if and only if the frequency of each letter in the message is completely independent of its position vis-à-vis other letters. But since, for example, the probability of finding a U following a Q is greater than $1/26$, the letters cannot be said to be independent, and our computation of H has to be thrown out and redone. This statistical dependence of one letter in a message on its environment is precisely what we mean by redundancy in a linguistic sense: in English or French, a U following a Q is so probable that its presence provides us with almost no additional information, and we can say that it is largely redundant. Approximate calculations of the redundancy of natural languages can be carried out; that of French has been estimated at 55 percent. "In other words, if 55% of the units of meaning were randomly suppressed, a message could still be understood."[2]
U le tr   n' r   v   p   o j   r   à d s   a io .

[2]Group μ, *A General Rhetoric*, trans. P. Burrell and E. Slotkin (Baltimore, 1981), 34.

Redundancy can be realized in a number of ways, of which plain repetition is the simplest and least interesting. It is not without its uses, however, as people trying to speak through a bad telephone connection know well. More typical of both natural languages and the error-correcting codes of communications engineers is a contextual redundancy such as the one we observe in English with Q and U, the nonindependence of successive letters implying that certain significant units of the message are coded in more than one way. In languages, this type of redunancy is not limited to letters but can be found in spoken phonemes and at various syntactic and grammatical levels: the agreement of subject and verb endings provides redundancy in French, as does the use of two words (*ne . . . pas*) in negation. It is redundancy, in the form of error-correcting codes, that makes computers and other instruments of electronic communication reliable: Shannon's theorems establish the existence of codes that can provide arbitrarily good protection against degradation of the message without becoming arbitrarily cumbersome or expensive through the simple multiplication of copies transmitted. In general, this is accomplished by the introduction of redundancy that is not repetitive but is instead like linguistic redundancy in that it involves relations of structure, correlations between different elements or features of the message.

The theory of information has not gone unnoticed by literary researchers. Because of the obvious, if incomplete, analogies between machine languages and natural languages, attempts were made very soon after Shannon's formulation of the theory to apply it to the analysis of language. Shannon himself attempted to calculate the "entropy of printed English" using statistical analyses of frequencies of letters and combinations of letters.[3] This kind of computation does not reveal much about language, and even less about meaning. In the years following the publication of Shannon's work, however, other researchers began to note that the statistical approach to problems of signal transmission may be but one interpretation of a more general calculus of information that also has implications at the level of semantic information.

Shannon's initial exclusion of meaning from his mathematical theory of communication was methodological, not ontological. He made

---

[3]*Bell System Technical Journal* 30 (1951), 50–64; see also Claude E. Shannon and Warren Weaver, *The Mathematical Theory of Communication* (Urbana, 1949), 10–26.

no claims to having dealt with meaning, but he did not say that the theory had no relevance to questions of meaning. As Roman Jakobson noted, Shannon's exclusion of meaning paralleled the temporary exclusion of semantics by structural linguistics.[4] One of the first researchers to consider the relevance of Shannon's work to semantics, Yehoshua Bar-Hillel, proposed distinguishing between "the (statistical) Theory of Signal Transmission" and the "Theory of Semantical Content" and noted that whereas the theories are by no means equivalent, they share underlying formal characteristics: "both of these theories can be regarded as different interpretations of a common formal system, the Calculus of Information."[5] Donald MacKay, who had worked independently of Shannon on his own version of a quantitative information theory, pointed out that units of semantic information and transmitted signals might eventually be treated as particular cases of a general concept of information.[6] Such a concept would depend on treating information as that which can resolve uncertainty and on measuring uncertainty by calculating the probabilities associated with ranges of possible outcomes or messages. This approach, MacKay notes, would correspond to the receiver's sense of what information is at a semantic level: "I get more information from that which makes a bigger change in what I know"—from that which resolves, in other words, a greater degree of uncertainty.[7] According to MacKay's hypothesis, a received message in effect performs a selective operation among possible states of awareness or readiness or action in the receiver; richness of meaning corresponds to the complexity of the selective operation. "The concept of the meaning of a message," writes MacKay, "can be defined as its selective function in relation to the 'adaptive-response-space' of the human receiver."[8] This amounts to an interpretation in human terms of the notion that meaning in nonhuman information systems can be defined as the effect of the message on the receiver. The concept of selec-

[4]Jakobson, "Linguistics and Communication Theory," in *Selected Writings* (The Hague, 1971), II, 577.

[5]Bar-Hillel, *Language and Information: Selected Essays on Their Theory and Application* (Reading, Mass., 1964), 291.

[6]MacKay writes that "while the connection between statistical and semantic features of information cannot but be indirect, these are features of one and the same central concept, which admits of a single universally applicable operational definition" (*Information, Mechanism, and Meaning* [Cambridge, Mass., 1969], 58).

[7]MacKay, *Information, Mechanism, and Meaning*, 59.

[8]MacKay, *Information, Mechanism, and Meaning*, 76.

tive function or effect on the receiver both offers the possibility of reintroducing meaning into information theory and ensures that meaning cannot be simply equated with quantity of information.

Any linguistic application of information theory (or of what Bar-Hillel would prefer to call the "calculus of information") must be situated at one or more of the hierarchic levels that make up language. The role of information theory in Jurij Lotman's *The Structure of the Artistic Text* is a case in point. The heir of the Russian formalist school of metrics, of theorists like Boris Tomasevskij, who used statistical methods in the analysis of verse, Lotman summarizes the work of A. Kolmogorov and others who attempted to calculate the entropy of an artistic language. He begins by pointing out that since language is a hierarchic system, whose structures are in effect nested in one another, there is no interest in attempting to calculate an absolutely general entropy function by taking, say, printed letters or phonemes as fundamental units. We can only calculate, indeed only conceive of, information *within* hierarchic levels, at whatever level we are interested in or find significant. Kolmogorov and his school distinguish between two kinds of entropy (or quantity of information) in the artistic text: h_1, the capacity of a language to express different signifieds (per unit length of message), and h_2, the capacity of a language to express a single signified in more than one way (per unit length of message). In each case, what is measured is a variety of possibilities, that is, the number of *possible* messages among which a single *actual* message will "decide," and hence the quantity of information of a single message in the system. Lotman can thus distinguish two kinds of entropy (or quantity of information): the entropy of the message and the specifically artistic entropy of its expression. In general, the total entropy is the sum of these two, $H = h_1 + h_2$, but for languages with no suppleness of expression, such as certain artificial languages, $h_2 = 0$ and there is no "artistic information" possible, $H = h_1$.

In natural languages, the situation is further complicated by what we know about specific discursive subsets such as verse or classical eloquence. In general, literary conventions impose restrictions on what may be done with a language: certain words may be excluded from literary discourse, rules of meter and rhyme are introduced that greatly restrict word choice and thus reduce the entropy of the language. Kolmogorov and Lotman label this "using up" of linguistic entropy by artistic conventions β and conjecture that $β < h_2$ is a necessary condition for poetic creation; in other words, that conventions can use up part of, but not exhaust, the expressive suppleness of the language in which they function.[9]

As Lotman is quick to point out, this distinction between two kinds of information in an artistic text poses some problems, notably concerning the relation of author and reader. For the author, it may very well be that up to a point there is a certain message for which she then chooses words (Lotman cites the existence of manuscript variants of poems), but for the reader, each word on the printed page has become a necessity, inseparable from the message, since the reader does not consider the possibility that another word might have been selected in its place. What was artistic information, as distinct from semantic information, for the author, becomes simply information for the reader. "The reader, sensing the necessity of poetry, sees it not as the means for saying in verse what might be communicated in prose [this is the sense of h_2], but as a manner of setting forth a particular truth unformed outside the poetic text."[10] This statement suggests that what we call literature is in fact a strategy for using the synonymic capacity of a language in such a way as to augment its informational power, a system for converting varieties of expression into subtlety of expression. But it could also suggest that there is an element of artificiality or heuristic convention in making the distinction between "variety of message" and "variety of expression" in the first place. Such distinctions arise, however, in every attempt to apply information theory to the study of language and literature, and we shall have to return to them in a number of ways. Anyone trained in deconstruction could challenge the distinction with a by now familiar argument: since there is no signified preceding, and exterior to, its production by signifiers, all language is always already literary, since no variation in signifiers can be said to

[9]One could perhaps argue that for $\beta > h_2$, poetic creation could still exist, but at the price of a restriction in contents or messages that could be transmitted, since $H = h_1 + h_2 - \beta < h_1$. An example of this might be an extremely complicated and restrictive verse form in which, quite simply, fewer things could be said than in the natural language in which the verses are written.

[10]Jurij Lotman, *The Structure of the Artistic Text*, trans. G. Lenhoff and R. Vroon, Michigan Slavic Contributions, no. 7 (Ann Arbor, Mich., 1977), 28. Cf. Jakobson: "for speech perception the message is *first* a stochastic process. . . . For the receiver, the message presents many ambiguities which were unequivocal for the sender. The ambiguities of pun and poetry utilize this input property for the output" ("Linguistics and Communication Theory," 575–576).

leave the "message" expressed unchanged. Theoretically, therefore, we are dealing with an ultimately untenable distinction. But the very ease of this deconstruction is an index of how little it would actually tell us. Heuristically, the distinction is both necessary and useful, in that it provides a hypothetical "degree zero" of nonpoetic language against which literary language can be measured—not measured in terms of absolute quantities but differentially, so that literature could be described tendentially. What we must deal with are an ensemble of properties that enable us to speak of texts as more or less rhetorical, more or less poetic, without claiming that such a thing as a nonrhetorical or completely unpoetic text exists in natural language.

This notion of a degree zero or nonrhetorical language is central to the use of information-theoretic concepts by the Belgian Groupe μ in their *Rhétorique générale*. A rhetorical device, they argue, must be defined as a departure from a degree zero, which can be considered intuitively as "a 'naive' discourse without artifice, without connotations, for which 'a hole is a hole.'"[11] The limit of this degree zero would be the univocity ostensibly sought in scientific language, and as such would exist not in actual utterances but as a limit outside language, which under certain conditions language may closely approach but not attain.

The redundancy of ordinary language implies a certain degree of expectability or predictability built into its structure. If we recognize enough of a word we can supply a letter or two that may be missing; after the verb *to drink* we can expect a noun designating a liquid; associated with a feminine noun, in Romance languages, we can expect a feminine adjective, if any. Such redundancy is even present in our idealized degree zero language without artifice or connotation. Rhetorical devices, local departures from the degree zero, imply a reduction of predictability: the rhetorical deviation (*écart*) diminishes redundancy. A rhetorical figure such as "When I had drunk all my shame" (Villon) takes away the redundant relation between drink and a liquid object. Redundancy, which in general provides language with a capacity for self-correction (in the face of misprints, loud noises, sloppy grammar, inattention, and the like), provides the margin of intelligibility by which we manage to understand rhetorical figures. If language, without rhetorical departures from a norm of direct simplicity, were al-

[11]Group μ, *A General Rhetoric*, 30.

ready without redundancy and therefore already on the very limit of intelligibility, demanding of us that we receive and interpret correctly its every feature, then an unexpected departure from such expectations as we had, from such codes as we possessed, would push the message over the line of unintelligibility. The impossibility of such a situation is pointed to by my strange phrase, "such expectations as we had," since in the absence of *all* redundancy, with every linguistic element functioning so as to represent a statistical maximum of possibilities, it is difficult to see how we would have, in any local context, any "expectations" that a rhetorical departure from the norm could then frustrate. The rhetorical device, then, goes against the usual rules of predictability, but does so in an environment where sufficient redundancy remains so that the departure from the norm is nonetheless intelligible. In this sense, the rhetorical device is part of Lotman's h_2 function: an increase in entropy (unpredictability) and hence a decrease in redundancy by virtue of a language's capacity to say something in more than one way. But like Lotman and Kolmogorov, the linguists of Groupe μ recognize that literary language is also an affair of increased redundancy and decreased quantity of information. They distinguish between rhetorical *deviations* (écarts) and rhetorical *conventions*; the latter, shared by sender and receiver, decrease the unpredictability of the message and thus increase redundancy.[12]

The use of information theory by Lotman and the Groupe μ is sufficiently schematic and abstract as to suggest that we are not dealing with the direct application of a working scientific theory to a new empirical doman: the literary text cannot simply be placed in the position of electronic signals and analyzed quantitatively. What we have instead is the conceptual use of terms such as *foreseeability* and *redundancy*, which have acquired specific meanings in information theory and now enter the field of textual studies with these meanings. In other words a concept such as redundancy that is not inherently limited to the theory of information becomes at once more specific and more complex as a result of its articulation within that theory, and can retain something of this meaning when returned to its original field or imported into yet

---

[12]This is essentially Lotman's β function: "In broad terms, therefore, poetry operates in two opposite ways on the messages it expresses. First, there is a lowering of redundancy (deviations); and second, a reinforcement of it (conventions). It is tempting to see here a play of compensations whose goal is the maintenance of the overall intelligibility of messages" (Group μ, *A General Rhetoric*, 38).

another territory. This process may in turn lead to new kinds of conceptual thought concerning the literary text, but it certainly does not amount to a method that promises or offers immediate results.[13] And although one of my principal goals in this book is to explore further the contribution that information theory may make to the study of literature and to our understanding of that study, I do not intend to go beyond this kind of heuristic use: I do not propose to make the literary text the object of a quantitative study along Shannonian lines, although I cannot claim to exclude such a possibility in the future, since versions of the theory of information sufficiently adapted to natural language and textual studies might one day be developed.

Self-Organization from Noise

To designate a rhetorical device or figure in general, the members of Groupe μ adopted an unusual term: *métabole*. A departure from the norm at any linguistic level can create a métabole: it can be of the signifier or the signified, within a word or within a sentence. The first and longest part of the *Rhétorique générale* is a typology of métaboles, or rather of what the authors call, self-consciously, "the metabolic system" (*le système métabolique*). The identity of expression with the biological concept of metabolic system seems startling and fortuitous: what, besides an etymology, could a rhetorical system and a system of biochemical regulation have in common? And yet this double inscription of the word *metabolism* may be taken as the epigraph for what follows in our attempt to link information theory to the study of literature: a major excursion into theoretical biology. The theory of information, as it has been adapted to the task of understanding the complexity, adaptability, and evolution of living beings, is not the same as the theory of information developed by communications engineers. It is in information theory as it has been adapted to the study of living structures that we will find concepts suited to exploring the interferences between literature and information.

The second law of thermodynamics, understood statistically and

---

[13]The theory of information "offers not only properly new results, but a new method of presentation, a synthesis of known facts in a new structure, making evident the gaps, destined to be filled, in our knowledge. It may be classed, with the great scientific theories, among the *heuristic methods*" (Abraham Moles, *Information Theory and Esthetic Perception*, trans. J. Cohen [Urbana, Ill., 1966], 32).

thereby translatable into the theory of information, states that in a closed system consisting of sender, channel, and receiver, information transmitted can lose, but not gain, specificity. The transmitted message, in other words, if modified at all during its passage through the channel, will be modified in the direction of taking on a more probable state. Whatever random modifications a message undergoes, these tend to muddle it up, to reduce its initial specificity and thus to reduce the degree to which that specificity could resolve the uncertainty of the receiver. A message degraded in transmission contains less information than a message transmitted intact because it resolves, for the receiver, less uncertainty than it might have: the receiver remains uncertain concerning those parts of the message that have been muddled.[14]

The causes of muddled transmission are collectively designated in the theory of information as *noise*, a usage that derives from the theory's early preoccupation with radio transmission and thus with the problems of atmospheric noise, static, jamming. But noise need not be sonorous: anything that arrives as part of a message, but that was not part of the message when sent out, can be considered as noise introduced in transmission. Noise may thus be the interruption of a signal, the pure and simple suppression of elements of a message, or it may be the introduction of elements of an extraneous message, like the ghostly voices often heard on long-distance telephone lines, or it may be the introduction of elements that are purely random. There is, in practice, a strong tendency to assume the latter hypothesis, to treat noise as a random disturbance in the transmission channel, but it must be remembered that a probabilistic term such as *random* has a relative, not an absolute, meaning: the noise is random with respect to the message it muddles, although it may have a perfectly defined and determinate cause in another system. One person's intelligent conversation becomes random noise when introduced into another person's idle gossip on the phone lines.

Although the noise that confounds a message may be said to have a source external to the transmission channel, the noise itself is said to be part of the channel for the purposes of defining a system of communication. When we speak of such a system as closed, then, we do not

[14]See Moles, *Information Theory*, 86: "The general theorem about entropy, 'disorder can only increase in an isolated system,' amounts to saying that noise can only degrade the orderliness of the message; it cannot increase the particularized information; it *destorys intent*."

exclude noise as something exterior; we include whatever noise is actually present in the channel and thus inseparable from its function as a channel. To exclude noise from a closed communication system would be equivalent to excluding molecular movement from a closed system as defined in thermodynamics; it would be equivalent to excluding time. The transmission of a message through a channel is homologous to the passage of a closed system from one state to another over time. It is thus appropriate to consider a given kind or magnitude of noise as specific to a given channel or means of transmission.

In the analysis of *Le Cousin Pons* in the last chapter, it was noted that the "vital force" by which early nineteenth-century biologists explained the capacity of organisms to resist disorganization and death was a scientific "fiction" occupying the place of what would later be understood as the role of energy and information in the organization of living beings. Organisms are open systems, constantly drawing energy from their environment and thus escaping the energetic implications of the second law. They are also systems which preserve and transmit information concerning their own structure: this information permits the individual to resist death by regenerating cells, and the species to resist extinction by reproducing individuals. Information in organisms, however, is not confined to the so-called genetic code but is present in such systems as the immune system and the nervous system as well. It is reasonable to relate the complexity of an organism to the quantity of information it contains, although attempts at global calculation of the informational content of organisms have not proved too useful or satisfying—probably because, like similar reckonings for language, they fail to account for the different kinds of information involved in a complex system, the specific functions of information and different hierarchical levels.[15]

The attempt to use information theoretic concepts in biology is part of the long history of the liquidation of vitalism. The belief that living matter had to possess some unique properties beyond those of a highly organized physicochemical system remained scientifically respectable until the Watson-Crick discoveries concerning DNA, the so-called genetic code. The patterns of DNA revealed that species can maintain their organization because organisms store information and transmit it

---

[15]See Henri Atlan, *L'Organisation biologique et la théorie de l'information* (Paris, 1972), 65–70.

to their offspring. It was at first assumed, by those attempting to understand such phenomena as evolution and adaptation in terms of information theory, that organisms do for information what they do for energy, namely, that they take it from their environment, preserving and transmitting their acquisitions through such mechanisms as memory and the genetic code. The physicist Schrödinger proposed that "what an organism feeds upon is negative entropy"; it increases the entropy of its environment to maintain its own order.[16] But to say that order comes only from order does not explain the increasing complexity observable in living systems: emergence, evolution, adaptation, learning. Heinz Von Foerster, writing in 1960, added something new: the idea that "self-organizing systems do not only feed upon order, they will also find noise on the menu."[17] If a system is *self*-organizing, if it is autonomous, then it cannot simply be the receiver of organizational information. What is outside it can be considered a source of variety but not of information. Henri Atlan gave Von Foerster's conjecture on self-organizing systems a mathematical formalization using Shannon's information theory; more recently, Atlan has worked on the development of computer simulations that exhibit self-organizing properties.[18]

What does it mean to say, instead of "organism" or "life," "self-organizing system"? The term refers us to a considerable domain of research situated at the intersection of cybernetics, theoretical biology, and, more recently, physics and chemistry. Historically, the concept first appears systematically in the writings of Von Foerster and his colleagues at the Biological Computer Laboratory of the University of Illinois about 1960, but its beginnings can be traced back to the Macy's conferences on cybernetics of the late 1940s and early 1950s, which assembled John Von Neumann, Gregory Bateson, Norbert Wiener, Warren McCulloch, and others. Von Neumann's *Theory of Self-Reproducing Automata*, published in 1966, constituted an attempt to found a formal, mathematical theory of systems having properties normally associated with living organisms: not automata produced by a

[16]Erwin Schrödinger, *What Is Life?* (New York, 1945), 72.
[17]Von Foerster, "On Self-Organizing Systems and Their Environments," in *Self-Organizing Systems*, ed. M. C. Yovits and S. Cameron (New York, 1960), 43.
[18]On the history of "self-organization," see *Généalogies de l'auto-organisation*, Cahiers du C.R.E.A., 8 (Paris, 1985), especially the article by Isabelle Stengers (7–104) and the interviews of Atlan (243–254) and Von Foerster (255–273).

maker, but automata that reproduce themselves, that do not appear to result from or obey any finality outside themselves. To speak of the organism as a self-organizing system is to speak of it as a machine, but a kind of machine no longer conceptually opposed to the living being. The nineteenth century saw in the machine the antithesis of the organism, because the machine had been constructed according to a plan or organization external to itself. It had no autonomy. The autonomous, self-programming machine is a problematic but not impossible metaphor, for the concept of machine has now changed to include informational machines, cybernetic regulators that make use, via feedback, of their own output as one of their inputs.

As Atlan has pointed out, to say that organisms are physicochemical machines that construct themselves does not constitute a reduction of biology to physics and chemistry but an enlargement of physics and chemistry into a "biophysics of organized systems."[19] Here is how he describes the importance of the shift from "organisms" to "self-organizing systems" in view of the empirical fact that the only *known* self-organizing systems in the physical space are, at present, organisms:

> When one uses this terminology, one implies that the most extraordinary performances of living organisms are the result of *particular cybernetic* principles that must be discovered and specified. As *particular* principles, they should account for the characteristics proper to the living organisms that present these properties. But as *cybernetic* principles, they are postulated in a continuum with other domains of cybernetics, the best known, those that apply to artificial automata. The consequences of this postulate are twofold: a) the specificity of living organisms is linked to principles of organization rather than to irreducible vital properties; b) once these principles are discovered, nothing should prevent their application to artificial automata, whose performances would thus equal those of living organisms.[20]

The second claim may seem unsettling, suggestive of the artificial production of life or of intelligent robots: it must be noted that this is a limit, a stage that could be reached only if *all* the appropriate particular cybernetic principles were both fully elucidated and susceptible of artificial realization. What is far more likely, and what certainly characterizes the present state of research, is that *some* small portion of the

---

[19]Henri Atlan, *Entre le cristal et la fumée: Essai sur l'organisation du vivant* (Paris, 1979), 23–24.
[20]Atlan, *Entre le cristal et la fumée*, 24.

particular cybernetic principles can be elucidated, perhaps in a very general form, and these used not to produce imitations of life but to identify how certain systems, not themselves living organisms, may exhibit *some* of the properties of living organisms. For example, it is known that living organisms are highly reliable, as wholes, in comparison with the reliability of their constituent parts. The brain goes on functioning when brain cells die. Computers are far less reliable, depending in general on the near-perfect functioning of all their components. There are, however, ways of organizing computers so as to make them somewhat more reliable, at least partially able to continue their functions in the face of a failure somewhere within them. There may be analogies between the kind of organization that increases the reliability of artificial automata and the kind of organization that, in a more fully realized and far more complex form, provides living organisms with such a high degree of reliability. In fact, in both cases reliability can be related to organizational redundancy, to the fact that a loss of information somewhere in the system can be self-corrected by the system as a whole. This is a far cry from saying that if you build a sufficiently redundant machine you will have created life, or artificial intelligence. It is only a matter of recognizing, on a general and intuitive level, a systemic property common to living systems and to nonliving systems certain of whose performances resemble those of living systems.

It is this kind of structural or systemic analogy, and no other kind, between living organisms and other systems that I will be exploring in making use of what might be called "biological information theory." In other words, there is no vitalism involved, no appeal to an intuited "livingness" or even "organicity" of language or literature. In recent generations many humanists and social scientists have quite legitimately been wary of "biologism," of arguments that would account for cultural phenomena by means of a biologically determined nature or through a mystical appeal to a prerational force of life. Dangers and mystifications often inhabit such arguments, and there is every reason to suspect such mystification in the very places where the biological metaphors seem most familiar—in the "organic unity of the text" or the "organic society" of the New Critics, for example. But the cybernetic approach to biological entities need not lend itself to such misleading applications, because in its formalization it carries with it the conditions of its own extensions or limitations. In other words, a cybernetic characterization of an organism is still a cybernetic characterization, not an appeal to an intrinsic essence of life. As such it may or may not be found to be a valid formal model for nonliving systems, but it is at most just that: a formal model. As Atlan has written, "the political and logical dangers of organicism are today well enough known so that one can avoid falling into its traps, yet without rejecting what the study of natural systems can teach us, in terms of logical possibilities, concerning organization in general."[21]

We must now return to the question of noise and information in self-organizing systems. In a very general sense, the theory of self-organizing systems attempts to give a nontheological answer to the old question, Why is there something rather than nothing? The form of the question that it addresses would be better stated, Why are there highly complex things and not just generalized chaos? If highly complex organized systems such as organisms have evolved from less complex entities, and ultimately from a primordial chaos, then there must be processes by which order and complexity emerge from disorder or simpler states. The terms *order* and *complexity* may lead to confusion, especially in the context of information theory. We can imagine two completely different types of organized states, both of which would be intuitively opposed to chaos or random disorder. The first, which may be appropriately called "ordered," is characterized by a high degree of redundancy and thus a low level of information; the message AAAAAAAAA would be an example, since it is both very much unlike a random sequence of letters of the alphabet and very low in information. The second, which would be better called "complex" or "varied," is characterized by a low level of redundancy and a high degree of information. The complex state may be formally identical to the chaotic state but with the following crucial difference: its particular arrangement is meaningful or important in some context. It might be very difficult to distinguish on a purely statistical basis between "JH ch. JF 18-26 pr. sor. et + si aff." and "JQ 93 st. ap. ex. RS 1941 ÷ or pos," but to readers of the personals section of *Le Nouvel Observateur*, one would be a significant message and the other a nonsensical foul-up of typography.

Almost every kind of system in which students of self-organization are interested involves both order and complexity, repetition and variety, redundancy and information. If by *system* we mean an entity com-

[21]Atlan, *Entre le cristal et la fumée*, 6.

plicated enough to contain within it subsystems of communication, each with an emitter, a channel, and a receiver, some redundancy in the form of codes shared by emitter and receiver is necessary if the communication is to have any function at all within the system. Information cannot inform in a system devoid of redundancy, and redundancy remains the pointless repetition of the same in a system devoid of variety. The kind of organization that emerges from disorder, and that can be contrasted in significant ways with disorder, cannot be described by a single concept from information theory, such as redundancy or information, but must contain within itself structures that exhibit both redundant order and informational complexity.

A transmitted message can arrive either intact or degraded by noise. From the point of view of a receiver whose uncertainty can be resolved only by the specific message transmitted, for whom "information" is identical with "transmitted message," the introduction of noise in the message means a loss of information. If we consider an organized system to be such a receiver of information from its environment, it is impossible for it to receive more information than the environment "emits." But organized systems are not simply receivers; in fact, as noted above, they contain within themselves instances of internal communication, of emitters, channels, and receivers. Environmental noise in fact intercepts and confounds internal communication. But this is not its only effect, nor is it the only kind of noise in an organized system, for there is also the noise associated with internal transmission channels. Under the right circumstances, noise—from whatever source—can create complexity, can *augment* the total information of a system: this is the lesson of Atlan's formalization of Von Foerster's speculations on order from noise. "Randomness is a kind of order, if it can be made meaningful," writes Atlan; "the task of making meaning out of randomness is what self-organization is all about."[22]

Suppose that in a system there is a transmission of information between two subsystems, A and B. For the sake of simplification, suppose that what is sent is the state of subsystem A, the information needed to describe or reproduce A. If the transmission is accomplished without noise, B then obtains a copy of A, has the same information as A. But if there is noise in the channel, the information received at B is dimin-

---

[22]Henri Atlan, "Disorder, Complexity and Meaning," in *Disorder and Order*, ed. P. Livingston (Stanford, 1984), 110. Atlan defines meaning as "the effect of some information transmitted by any channel of communication."

ished by a function known as the ambiguity of the message, the quantity of information coming *from* the channel that is independent of the information that entered the channel—or, in other words, the informational quantity of that part of the original message lost in transmission. From the viewpoint of B—that of the pure and simple receiver of the message from A—there has been a loss of information. To the extent that the system's function depends on communication between its subsystems, its function may be compromised. But consider now the point of view of an *observer* of the combined subsystems A and B (and the channel). Such an observer might be a scientist exterior to the system, but more significantly it might be a higher level subsystem within the hierarchical organization of the system, a subsystem related to (A → B) as B was to A. It goes without saying that this observer will also receive information through some kind of transmission channel, but for the moment the important fact is that the emitter for this channel is constituted by the system (A → B). What is the quantity of information emitted by (A → B)? It is the information received by B *plus* the ambiguity: the modification of the message from A to B implies that B is no longer a copy of A but contains information independent of A. Atlan calls the two effects of ambiguity "destructive ambiguity" (B's copy of A is poor) and "autonomy-ambiguity" (B is now more than a mere copy of A). The system (A → B) is more complex, contains more information, if B has an imperfect copy of A than if it has a perfect copy. In other words, the partial destruction of a transmitted message within one level of a hierarchy leads to an increase in the complexity of the message that this level in turn transmits to another part of the system.

Atlan theorized that this mechanism of informational recuperation, by which an organization converts a loss of specificity in communication into a gain in overall complexity, could only function in certain kinds of systems, specifically those that Von Neumann, attempting to develop a formal characterization of self-reproducing automata, called "extremely highly complicated." Here is why. In such a highly complicated system there would be not a few subsystems but millions or more, millions of transmission channels linking different subsystems to one another in enormously many ways. The information of subsystem A would not simply be sent to B; it would be constantly being sent out to many other destinations, which in turn would communicate with B by other paths, and it would itself be constructed out of information received from many other subsystems. In this kind of system, if information is lost in transmission from A to B, the system as a whole may very well compensate for this loss through other channels; in other words, enough near-perfect copies of A circulate in the system as to make the imperfections of the particular copy transmitted to B a negligible threat to the system's function and organizational viability. At the same time, the "creation of information" in the channel between A and B, from the viewpoint of whatever subsystems receive copies of (A → B), may be of real benefit to the system, increasing its complexity and hence, perhaps, its adaptability.[23]

This kind of system, with its multiple copies of information, must have a high degree of redundancy. Without initial redundancy, every degradation of information through noise would have a disorganizing effect on the system so strong as to exceed any possible organizational gain from the increase in information that noise might imply for another level of the system. Consider a system with no redundancy, in which the ratio of information to maximum possible information is already 1. It is clearly impossible to increase the quantity of information of such a system by any means other than simply increasing its size, so that the only effect of noise can be to diminish the specificity of the information present and thus impair the system's organization and function.

All this implies that a certain degree of initial redundancy is a necessary condition for the production of complexity from noise or disorder in a self-organizing system. Atlan describes this mechanism as "self-organization by diminution of redundancy."[24] The definitions of information (H), maximal information (H_{max}), and the redundancy ratio (R) imply that $H = H_{max} (1 - R)$. If we are interested in the organizational effects of noise, or of perturbations from the environment, over time, a good function to look at would be the derivative of H, dH/dt, the variation of the quantity of information with respect to time. Note that by considering the derivative, or variation, we are moving away from an approach that would depend on the quantitative estimation of total information, and toward one that uses the parameter of information to determine whether a system is moving toward greater or lesser complexity. By differentiation of the expression $H = H_{max}$

[23]Atlan, *Entre le cristal et la fumée*, 48–49.
[24]Atlan, *Entre le cristal et la fumée*, 49–51; Atlan, *L'Organisation biologique et la théorie de l'information*, 264–270.

$(1 - R)$, we obtain $dH/dt = -H_{max}(dR/dt) + (1 - R)(dH_{max}/dt)$. The two additive terms of the right-hand side of this equation correspond to two effects of ambiguity on the variation of information, one positive and the other negative. As noise is introduced, redundancy is diminished, so the change in redundancy with respect to time is negative, $dR/dt < 0$, and so the first term of this expression for dH/dt is positive; it corresponds to an increase in information or complexity, Atlan's "autonomy-ambiguity." The other effect of noise, however, is to decrease the maximum quantity of information that can be transmitted in the system. This diminution of H_{max} can be written as $dH_{max}/dt < 0$, making the second term of the equation negative. This negative term corresponds to a loss of information, "destructive ambiguity."

It must be emphasized that this entire discussion of noise, information, and comlexity refers only to systems concerning which we do not have complete knowledge: if we have a complete structural and operational description of a system, our uncertainty concerning its state is nil, and while the system may be very complicated, it is not complex, since complexity measures our uncertainty concerning its precise state. If we already understand completely the mechanism by which, at a given level, the presence of noise becomes a positive factor in the organization of a system, then "the 'organizing noise' would not appear to us as noise but as signals."[25] If we know all the principles or constraints that generate a message, then the message holds no surprises for us; it is not informative but simply redundant.

To consider the organizational effects of noise (positive or negative) is to reintroduce the problem of signification, which was explicitly absent from Shannon's theory concerning signal transmission. When we say that the introduction of noise has a destructive effect at the level at which the transmission is taking place, but can have a constructive effect at a higher level that "observes" the former, we necessarily understand that the same noise-modified message has different signification at the two levels. The problem of information's signification for a given observer or site is of central importance in considering cultural information systems in terms of self-organization from noise. The observer's perspective is crucial, for example, in Atlan's discussion of an ordinary library as an illustration of the concepts of information and redundancy:

[25] Atlan, *Entre le cristal et la fumée*, 87.

The organized system and the observer can be compared to a library containing elements through which are transported the knowledge, or even the culture, of the observer (supposing, obviously, a knowledge that is only bookish). One must distinguish between the information transmitted to the observer through each book, and that which is transmitted from one book to another, in the form of diverse forms of citation, from literal quotation to summary allusion. If there is no transmission between the books, one is dealing with N books, each of which contains a complete system, closed on itself, without any reference to anything whatsoever contained in another book. For the observer, that will not constitute knowledge [un savoir], still less a culture (unless by his own genius, he should himself establish relations between the books, in which case the question arises of real or imaginary character of these relations; and in any case, we are leaving behind the context of the comparison, for the organization would at this point be assumed to be located in the observer himself and not in the organized system). Similarly if there is transmission [between the books] without ambiguity or equivocation, the system, in its limiting case, will be the same book repeated N times and knowledge will be reduced to the content of this book alone: one could hardly speak of culture. In fact, culture corresponds to the existence of different books, having relations between them, but which have room for ambiguity or equivocation, if one considers these relations themselves. But it is this ambiguity, a consequence of the differences between the books, that constitutes the surplus of information received by the observer, so that we speak of culture and not of mere juxtaposition or repetition.[26]

A library that consists only of transmitted copies of a single book would be ideal for a hypothetical observer (reader) who by definition could receive as information only the contents of that book. For the human reader, however, the ambiguity between books entails no loss of information but rather a kind of gain associated with the experience of culture.

Atlan's library is considerably more banal than that of Borges's Babel; it is the kind of library with which we are all familiar, containing enough redundancy to be intelligible and enough information to be worth consulting.[27] The analogy offers no new insights into culture,

---

[26]Atlan, L'Organisation biologique et la théorie de l'information, 259.

[27]The "Library of Babel," whose volumes contain random sequences of printed characters, contains a maximum of variety, a maximum of information in the Shannonian sense of uncertainty to be resolved. But since there are no codes for understanding these random characters, their informational value to actual readers is virtually nil. This does not stop the librarians from pursuing their searches for the pockets of intelligibility that many believe must be there somewhere (Borges, Ficciones [New York, 1962], 79–88).

and its model is rather simplistic. What is noteworthy is the fact that the concepts of redundancy, transmission of information, ambiguity, and equivocation can be used to describe, not quantitatively but qualitatively, certain features of a system of information far more familiar and interesting to us than the calculation of information quantities in arbitarily selected alphabets. If we push Atlan's comparison a little further, we may see whether the notions of complexity from noise, of destructive ambiguity and autonomy-ambiguity, can be made a part of it. Suppose that there is a subset of the library consisting of a book A and copies or subsequent editions or imitations of it, A_1, A_2, A_3, and so forth. In other words, all the books in the subset that are not A are transmitted copies of A, copies that have not passed unchanged through the transmission channel. Perhaps the printing press has not yet been invented and we have a series of manuscript copies, $A \rightarrow A_1 \rightarrow A_2 \ldots$, with new errors or lessons introduced at each copying; perhaps the author himself has revised his work and had it reprinted; perhaps its contents are sufficiently important that others have deemed it worthy of being paraphrased or condensed or annotated or translated. Whatever the causes, the message has been modified in transmission, which is to say in a formal sense that its transmission channel has contained noise. The term *noise* seems just right for errors of scribes and printers, but we may wonder at its use to designate changes made by an author or a translator. The formal justification for its use, however, lies in the fact that the changes are external to, and independent of, the exact words in A. In effect, we are giving to the term *noise* a formal definition somewhat removed from our intuition of it, since we now consider as noise anything received that is not part of what was transmitted. Now let us consider the effects of this modification of the message. To a reader whose sole aim is to recover the original message in A, for whom the specificity of A and nothing else is significant, the copies and imitations are nothing but degraded versions of A, containing less specific information than the original.

Suppose that A is a manual of shipbuilding techniques published in Hamburg in 1635.[28] This hypothetical book was revised and reissued by its author in 1654 and again by his successor in the trade in 1678; it was translated into Dutch and reprinted several times in Rotterdam

---

[28]I have no idea whether such manuals ever existed, or if so in what era, or whether and how they referred to one another.

between 1660 and 1710; much of it was copied, with modifications appropriate to different regional traditions of construction, by the authors of English and Spanish shipbuilding manuals of the eighteenth century. Suppose now a reader who is writing a history of naval construction in the German Baltic cities from 1610 to 1640. If such a reader uses any of the aforementioned reeditions, translations, or rewritings of this manual, she will derive from them less information than she would from A, since for her only the original message in A is significant. If A itself has been lost and she is forced to rely on A_1 ... A_n, she will experience their difference as noise, as a disorder reducing information, and her uncertainty concerning shipbuilding in the Hanseatic cities in 1640 will be less fully resolved by the modified copies than it would have been by A, since she will not know for sure either what was modified in the 1654 edition and the Dutch translations or to what extent the techniques she reads about in these editions were present in the text of 1635. For this reader, whose position is strictly that of receiver of the original message, there is only destructive ambiguity. But suppose another reader, this one concerned with the evolution of shipbuilding techniques in seventeenth- and eighteenth-century Europe, or perhaps with the history of trade and technical treatises and their publishers during the same period. To such a reader, the modifications of the message in A, the ambiguity between A, A_1 ... A_n, will generally constitute a gain in information, an autonomous surplus of information provided by each "faulty" transmission of the message; in other words, what Atlan calls autonomy-ambiguity. Obviously this occurs because the second reader is positioned differently with respect to the system (A, A_1 ... A_n). The first reader is but the receiver of A, linked to A by a single transmission channel. In that context, more information was transmitted through the channel (A $\rightarrow$ reader) than through, say, the channel (A $\rightarrow$ A_1 $\rightarrow$ A_4 $\rightarrow$ reader). For this reader, there can be only "destructive ambiguity." But the second reader is positioned so as to observe the system, through what might be called a metachannel, so that the situation is something like this:

$$\begin{bmatrix} A \rightarrow A_1 \underset{\searrow}{\rightarrow} A_2 \\ \quad\quad A_3 \underset{\searrow}{\rightarrow} A_4 \\ \quad\quad\quad A_5 \end{bmatrix} \rightarrow \text{reader}$$

For this reader, the system can contain more information than A alone, because to her the noises in the various transmission channels are significant. "Autonomy-ambiguity" is present and may well outweigh "destructive ambiguity." Clearly the problem of the signification of information is present here and is related to the position of the observer or reader. In a strictly formal sense, the system (A . . . A_n) contains a greater quantity of information than A, whereas the subsystem (A_1 . . . A_n) contains less of the specifically defined information that makes up A than does A itself. Which of these quantitative relations is pertinent depends on the position of the observer, in other words, on the qualitative relation of the observer to the information in question.

Literature, Noise, Organization

The simple examples at the end of the last section suggest that the use of informational concepts does not entail the reduction of the cultural to the physical or biological or mathematical, but they tell us nothing about why the extension of these concepts to problems of literary theory and interpretation would be an interesting or worthwhile move in the critical game. Neither an abstract library nor a putative series of technical books has much to do with the specificity of literature. But what is the specificity of literature? Or rather, given the enormity and uncertainty of that question, does literature have *some* specificity that makes for a more controlled and pertinent application of the concepts of self-organization? Can information theory help us see what the specificity of literature is?

As was noted in Chapter 1, "literature" as we know it is a modern, specifically romantic concept, and literature's status as the object of study in an academic discipline is likewise a development that can be situated in recent history. The most prestigious and widely accepted modern views of literature, all more or less derivatives of romanticism, deny that literature is simply communication. For the romantics, literature could be separated from other instances of culturally significant writing by its freedom and autonomy, its nonutilitarian use of language. The artistic text exists in and for itself, not as the communicative instrument of some project outside of it, though it may communicate as well. The commonplace analogy of literary text to organism arises from this insistence on autonomy: the literary work is opposed to the utilitarian use of language as the living creature is opposed to the machine or artifact.

It might seem that the pertinence of information theory to literature is disqualified by our doubt as to whether the literary act really is a transmission of information, an act of communication. But this equivocation is in fact what makes the information-theoretic approach pertinent—problematically pertinent, but so much the better. The romantic definition of literature survives today in an intuitive form—the assumption that literature is made up of the imaginative genres of fiction, poetry, and theater—and in a more sophisticated form known as formalism. The critics known as the Russian formalists gave a linguistic turn to the romantic definition by identifying literature's autonomy with the primacy of its language, of signifiers, of the message itself in its material specificity. This primacy of the sounds, structures, and internal relations of an artistic text was given its canonical formulation by Roman Jakobson: "the set (*Einstellung*) toward the message as such, focus on the message for its own sake, is the poetic function of language."[29] In the work of the formalists, this emphasis on the set toward the message produced the project of a serious, disciplinary study of the specificity of literary discourse, its techniques and devices. This kind of study, as Paul de Man wrote in one of his last essays, gives rise to what we now know as literary theory, a discipline by no means identical with that of literary studies.[30] As noted in Chapter 1, the study of literature owes its place in the university, in large measure, to expectations and assumptions that precede the modern project of literary theory and that are not necessarily compatible with it. Nonetheless, the romantic-formalist definition of literature corresponds to at least one defining characteristic of literary studies: the status of language in the objects of the discipline. A poem, read in the English department, has a status different from that of any work read in the departments of sociology or physics, for in the latter case one reads not to know the text but to know its referent, to know something extratextual. Such was once the ambition of literary history as well, as formulated by Hippolyte Taine and his followers, but now even in the most traditional departments, where the greatest stress is laid on the author's life and milieu, the relations between the work and its context are studied as part of the project of understanding and knowing the work.

[29]Jakobson, "Closing Statement: Linguistics and Poetics," in *Style and Language*, ed. T. Sebeok (Cambridge, Mass., 1960), 356.
[30]de Man, "The Resistance to Theory," *Yale French Studies* 63 (1982), 7. See also Group μ, *A General Rhetoric*, concerning the continued pertinence of the formalist program.

The definition of the poetic function as a set toward the message, of literature as a discourse in which the poetic function assumes a preeminent role, has been given a counterpart in the theory of information. The French communications specialist Abraham Moles argued that any use of the notion of information in dealing with works of art must take into consideration the difference between "semantic information" and "esthetic information." The former corresponds to our interrogation concerning the state of the world, and is thus, for Moles, universal and *translatable*; the latter is specific to the natural or aesthetic language which conveys it and "cannot be translated into any other 'language' or system of logical symbols because this other language does not exist."[31] One can argue about the appropriateness of the terms *semantic* and *aesthetic*, or question whether translatability could ever serve as a pragmatic criterion for distinguishing the two, but Moles's definition of the aesthetic remains fundamentally identical to the romantic-formalist concept of the poetic or literary: both differ from the utilitarian use of language to describe reality and both postulate a privileged relation between the message and the language in which it is transmitted. "Esthetic information is specific to the *channel* which transmits it; it is profoundly changed by being transferred from one channel to another."[32] Semantic information, on the other hand, is what can be captured by an observer who takes signals at their source and translates them into a universal metalanguage. This gives the following diagram:[33]

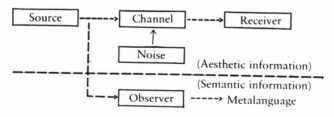

For *channel*, in literary works, we could substitute *language*—and we must remember that as always every channel has its inherent noise. Readers familiar with Jakobson's diagram of linguistic communication should remember that the term *channel* refers to the ensemble of means

[31]Moles, *Information Theory*, 129.
[32]Moles, *Information Theory*, 131.
[33]Adapted from Moles, *Information Theory*, 129.

of transmission between sender and receiver; it cannot be equated with the Jakobsonian *contact* but includes the *message* and *code* as well. The source strictly speaking would have to be located within the sender's brain, since once a message in language has been produced, the channel has already been entered. I claim only heuristic value for this model and have no intention of proving that it could ever give rise to an empirical procedure for distinguishing semantic and aesthetic information. Both kinds of information are conceptual limits. Derrida's "Il n'y a pas de hors-texte" becomes, in this schema, "All information is aesthetic." It is worth noting, however, that specialists in the treatment of linguistic material by computer have developed universal metalanguages, for purposes such as indexing, that are capable of translating *part* of the information contained in texts. Machine translations are neither exact nor subtle nor elegant, but they are, in certain contexts, usuable.

For our purposes, Moles's concept of aesthetic information has the interest of identifying the poetic function with a specific kind of transmission channel and thus with the inevitability of noise. A language used as a pure instrument of efficient communication should be as free from noise as possible; thus if literature is to deviate from the utilitarian task of communication, it must be an imperfect process of communication, an act of communication in which what is received is not exactly what was sent. Rather than attempting to reduce noise to a minimum, literary communication *assumes* its noise as a constitutive factor of itself. This quite naturally raises doubts as to whether it is an act of communication at all, since it deliberately sacrifices the aim of communicative efficiency. These doubts do not arise from the attempt to understand literature in terms of information theory, but are a canonical feature of romantic-formalist definitions of literature. For Lev Jakubinskij, the language of poetry acquires an autonomous value when the practical, communicative purpose of language moves to the background.[34] The members of Groupe μ go further: "The final consequence of this distortion of language is that the poetic word is disqualified as an act of communication. In fact, it communicates nothing, or rather, it communicates nothing but itself. We can also say that it communicates with itself, and this intracommunication is nothing

[34]Quoted by Tzvetan Todorov, *Critique de la critique: Un roman d'apprentisage* (Paris, 1984), 18.

other than the very principle of form. By inserting at each level of discourse, and between levels, the constraint of multiple correspondences, the poet closes discourse on itself. It is precisely this closure that we call the opus."[35]

Paul de Man's longstanding insistence on the rhetorical dimension of language, its an autonomous potential to create effects that have no counterpart in reference and cannot be resolved by grammatical reading, asserts a similar opposition between literariness and communicativity: "This gives the language considerable freedom from referential restraint, but it makes it epistemologically highly suspect and volatile. . . . Whenever this autonomous potential of language can be revealed by analysis, we are dealing with literariness and, in fact, with literature as the place where this negative knowledge about the reliability of linguistic utterance is made available."[36] De Man's view of literariness, though clearly situated in the romantic-formalist tradition, has a radicality not found in much contemporary literary theory, a radicality due in large part to his rejection of the romantic notion that literature and nonliterature can be opposed to one another and clearly separated, and also to his suspicion of the view that the work is a harmonious totality. If literary theory begins, for de Man, with the decision to treat literary language linguistically, it must subsequently encounter the impossibility of completing this task; it discovers that the literariness of language produces a residue that cannot be analyzed by grammatical means, by the procedures of linguistics extended beyond the sentence to all of discourse. "The resistance to theory is a resistance to the rhetorical or tropological dimension of language."[37] The most subtle resistance to theory thus resides in the most sophisticated of the literary theories that are committed to the resolution of textual uncertainties through grammatical or hermeneutic models. These theories aim, in effect, at an eventual reduction of the noise in the literary channel by ever more sophisticated understanding of codes and formation rules. As useful as this task may be, its considerable successes tend to mask what is most irreducibly literary about certain linguistic messages: the fact that what is received cannot coincide with what is sent, that there is, in other words, noise in the channel.

[35]Group μ, *A General Rhetoric*, 12.
[36]de Man, "The Resistance to Theory," 10.
[37]de Man, "The Resistance to Theory," 17.

The foregoing considerations that the notion of self-organization from noise may have something to tell us about how literary texts, in spite of everything, manage to signify, how poetry can be valued as an intense, exquisite communication rather than dismissed as poor communication. All theorists of literature are aware of the seeming paradox in defining poetic function by means of its departure from the norms of communicative prose: something occurs in the poetic use of language that escapes completely the notion of "prose complicated by devices," so that the poet produces new kinds of effects not found in mere "rhetorical prose." Lotman called it the conversion of multiple ways of saying the same thing (h_1) into ways of saying multiple new things (h_2). Like Atlan's formalism of self-organization from noise, Lotman's description of this conversion takes into account the position of the observer. Lotman's h_1 existed from the author's standpoint, before transmission, and amounted to the possibility of encoding the same thing in more than one way in a given channel; his h_2 was on the side of the reader and represented an increase in information resulting from the particular form of message chosen. What is aesthetic variety from the author's perspective becomes semantic information from the reader's.

In another section of his book Lotman writes explicitly of "noise" and literary or artistic information. Here his conclusions echo almost exactly Atlan's notion of the production of information from noise: "Art—and here it manifests its structural kinship to life—is capable of transforming noise into information. It complicates its own structure owing to its correlation with its environment (in all other systems the clash with the environment can only lead to the fade-out of information)."[38] It must be noted that Lotman does not define noise in a literary context as residing within poetic language itself, as I have been suggesting in the last few pages. Rather, he refers to instances of external interference with the work of art: the missing arms of the Venus de Milo, the fading of paintings, a foreign word on a manuscript. In the relatively narrow context of Lotman's implied definition of noise, the work of art is nevertheless precisely the system in which noise can be converted into information. This fact stems, for Lotman, from the organizational nature of works of art, in other words, from a particular type of play between redundant order and informative surprise. The

---

[38]Lotman, *The Structure of the Artistic Text*, 75.

poetic text begins as an attempt to go beyond the usual system of a language—in which the word is a conventional sign—to a specifically artistic system, in which sounds, rhythms, and positional relations between elements will signify in new ways. The poetic text, in other words, demands of its reader that she create new codes, that she semanticize elements normally unsemanticized.[39] Aspects of language that in nonartistic communication would be extraneous to the message become elements that enter into secondary or tertiary signifying systems. Such new systems, in order to be systems, must be made of regularities and must therefore imply a degree of predictability, of redundancy. A system of versification provides an example of this: it puts in place a new system, new ways in which linguistic elements can signify, and at the same time it increases the foreseeability of certain textual features.

This would suggest that artistic texts are always more predictable than nonartistic ones, and yet the opposite seems truer to experience. Artistic texts do not become predictable, because their systems are continually disrupted by new unpredictabilities—out of which, in their turn, new systems of regularity are posited by the reader. Whereas in nonartistic communication there can be *extrasystemic* facts, aspects which are simply ignored or discarded because they are not dealt with by the code being used to interpret the message, in an artistic text there are only *polysystemic* facts, since whatever is extrasystemic at a given level, and thus destructive of regularity or predictability at that level, must be taken on as a possible index of another level, of another textual system. The multiplication of codes, or rather the creation of new and specific codes for a given genre, a given text, is the essence of the artistic text. Here is how Lotman sums up this process: "Any 'individual' fact, any thing that is 'a near miss' in an artistic text comes into being when the basic structure is complicated by additional structures. It arises as the intersection of at least two systems and takes on a special meaning within the context of each one. The greater the number of regular features intersecting at a given structural point, the greater the number of meanings this element will acquire, the more individual and extrasystemic it will seem. What is extrasystemic in life is represented as polysystemic in art."[40] For the reader, one might say that where the

[39]Lotman, *The Structure of the Artistic Text*, 55, 59.
[40]Lotman, *The Structure of the Artistic Text*, 72.

seemingly individual fact was, there the intersection of systems shall be. What appears to be a perturbation in a given system turns out to be the intersection of a new system with the first. This is the case with many events that we call random, but what matters is that in an artistic text the random is not the gratuitous. *The principle of constructing a pattern out of what interrupts patterns is inherent in artistic communication, because this kind of communication arises by deviating from the regularities of nonartistic communication, and this deviation must be the source of whatever advantage or specificity artistic communication possesses.* In the language of the Groupe μ (and of Jean Cohen), the poetic function implies departures from norms and then the production of new kinds of relations and meaning from these departures.

The artistic text's capacity, then, to enter into correlation with external noise as into correlation with yet another system, depends simply on the properties that it already must possess to be an artistic text. If "irregularities" within the text can and must be interpreted as part of multiple systems of coherence and signification, the same can be said for "noise" arising outside the text: the already multiple layers of textual coherence are augmented by another level, this one located in the system (text + environment). "A statue tossed in the grass can create a new artistic effect if a *relation* arises between the grass and the marble." Moreover, this type of relation depends on the observer: the beholder of the fallen statue may not be able to make the needed correlations, so that "the question of whether 'noise' is transformed into artistic communication always presupposes a description of the type of culture which we take as the observer."[41] Lotman restricts the term *noise* to external disturbances of the artistic text, but his argument for what amounts to a theory of textual "complexity from noise" depends on the existence of a similar productive mechanism for dealing with internal unpredictables. The encounter of text and external noise can be productive because of the way that texts already articulate their internal noise. External noise can contribute to complexity because it does not differ fundamentally from internal noise. If the beholder can make a superior artistic work out the toppled statue, this is precisely because he was already capable of making an artistic work out of the sculpted figure when it was still standing—in spite of the irregularities in its

---

[41]Lotman, *The Structure of the Artistic Text*, 75.

marble, the singular position of its right arm, the fact that it was different from any statue or model he had seen before. Lotman's theorization of the role of external noise presupposes that something like noise already plays an internal role in the artistic text.

All this, however, should remind us that we are far from having settled the question of what, in literary works, may be considered noise. The concept of noise, as it arrives from the mathematical theory of information, is not entirely satisfactory for use in talking about language and literature. This puts us in the position of both needing to have the concept and needing not to have it. The difficulty arises from two definitions of noise, essentially compatible or complementary in mathematical information theory and not so elsewhere. On the one hand, noise is defined as whatever enters a message in transmission and alters it, so that whenever messages do not arrive as sent, we can speak of noise in the channel. This definition allows for a fairly reasonable extension to the ambiguities of natural and, especially, poetic language. On the other hand, noise is defined as aleatory, randomly distributed, having no rapport with the message it confuses. The two sides of the definition are compatible, even identical, in Shannon's theory: between an input and an output there is a statistical correlation, expressed as a number, X, between 0 and 1, which corresponds to the transmission of information that has been accomplished; what is not correlated, $1 - X$, is precisely what is aleatory. But in language, whereas we may accept that ambiguity is present, even ubiquitous, we find it harder to accept that this ambiguity residing in language could be without correlation to the message in which it appears. In fact, in language we have no sure way of distinguishing between message and noise, since the notion of noise as something contained in the text requires the postulation of a message existing prior to its being conveyed in language, and it is impossible in general to guarantee the existence of such a message.[42] And so we are left with a model of language, and especially poetic language, as a noisy transmission channel, but we have no way of separating exactly the noise from what is transmitted. Does this mean

[42]Here is how de Man describes the inextricable relation between message and indetermination in literature: "Literature is not a transparent message in which it can be taken for granted that the distinction between the message and the means of communication is clearly established. . . . the grammatical decoding of a text leaves a residue of indetermination that has to be, but cannot be, resolved by grammatical means, however extensively conceived" ("The Resistance to Theory," 15).

that any and all speculation concerning self-organization from noise and literary interpretation comes down like a house of cards? Only if such speculation depends on the ability to distinguish, *unambiguously*, between message and noise; only, in other words, if we require that our interpretive or theoretical observation of the message-noise-transmission system be itself accomplished via a channel free from noise, something like the metachannel in Moles's diagram. We can accept from the outset, however, that a noiseless metachannel does not exist. The schema of "complexity from noise" awaits us, inside and outside the text, in the reduction of the humblest rhetorical deviation as in the interpretation of the most irreducible undecidable.

If we cannot found a general distinction between message and noise, we may nonetheless be able to decide whether—for any specific step of the process of literary "communication," for any specific receiver—there are effects that can best be described by message and noise. Noise is aleatory, but what does this mean? We are thrown back on the definition of the random as the intersection of independent causal series. In Lotman's view, the artistic text arises when its reader encounters elements for which the ordinary codes of language possessed by him are not adequate, elements, in other words, which are foreign to his reading process as determinism, as reception of signs according to rules already possessed. Of course the appearance of phenomena that cannot be accounted for by existing schemas of understanding is not unique to art or literature, so that what really constitutes the artistic text is the reader's decision to consider the elements hitherto unencountered as part of a new level of signifying structure. This strategy quite literally complicates the reader, who ceases to be comparable to a single receiver of information in a communicative situation (as defined in the theory of information—this parenthetical remark being necessary because the strategy in question is so universal in reading as to *seem* almost a natural part of receiving a message). The reader must in effect shift position, and consider both an ambiguity and the entire process of communication that has produced it. This shift may involve an attempt to construct a new context (referent or intertext), or to recognize a second-order signifying system at work in the text (at the level of imagery, rhythm, assonance, etc.). Why can this process be called a shift in position? If we suppose for a moment that a competent user of a natural language can decode messages received in that language according to fixed and known rules, then it is reasonable to assume, initially, that such a reader occupies the position of a receiver in a simple communicative situation:

If the reader has no supppleness, no capacity for adaptation or for learning new codes, then whatever ambiguity is introduced in the channel can only diminish the information he receives; it is perceived as destructive noise. (In this case, for the sake of argument, we are assuming that the language itself can be used unambiguously, an idealization whose untenability reminds us that the phenomenon of literarity is not confined to literature.) Such an unadaptive reader remains precisely in the position of a receiver of transmitted information. The example, far from being unrealistic, calls to mind a student who has no experience reading poetry, no idea of "how does a poem mean," in John Ciardi's phrase, and who accordingly considers whatever is specific to the *poetic* text as such to be simply an impediment to its understanding. Such a student will either abandon the attempt to read the poem or wish for a technique by which the noise can be filtered out so as to permit the reception of a nonpoetic message. Fortunately, however, human beings are not decoding machines, and the student will either adapt or will not join the community of literary readers. Once the reader assumes the task of integrating elements that ordinary codes of reading do not account for, then she is no longer simply a receiver: this reader *includes* within herself the receiver of linguistic messages, but adds to it an instance of receiving or understanding which takes as its input both the first communication and the ambiguity affecting it.

Does this really mean that simple operations of understanding texts poetically (instead of treating them as muddled prose) proceed according to the principle of self-organization from noise? Yes, insofar as the reader is forced to move on to a new level of understanding in order to integrate features which at a simplistic level seemed merely interference in a message. No, if by self-organization from noise is understood the appearance of the new, the unexpected, as a result of an ordered system's encounter with something not connected to it by any relations of causality. There may be very definite links between the first-order message coded in ordinary language in a text and the kinds of second- and third-order structures that will be constructed to accommodate what does not fit into the first level. (The relations of meaning suggested by, say, the use of rhyme may be complementary or antithetical to, but not likely irrelevant to, the relations implied at the level of syntax.) More important, the second- or third-order signifying systems, although not immediately apparent to the reader, may be themselves perfectly coherent and unambiguous, so that rather than an autonomous creation of meaning out of noise, we have a process that moves inevitably toward the reconstruction of a meaning that was already clearly indicated by the message, even if this reconstitution requires the agility of a reader capable of using what at first may seem like disorder to construct new codes and thereby encounter hierarchically superior forms of order. In other words, the ambiguities may not be real ambiguities but simply temporary uncertainties which could in theory by unambiguously integrated into a final structure of meaning. If this is the case, then the meaning of a text is not something organized contextually between reader, text, and textual disorder; it depends entirely on the text and is reconstituted by the reader in a process where the appearance of organization out of chaos is produced by the reader's relative and temporary ignorance of specific textual codes. In this view, the reader could consider self-organization from noise to be a valid model for describing the process in which he is caught up while reading, but to an outside observer, one who knows something of the history of readings of the text in question, the reader would seem to be merely approaching a universally accepted meaning determined by the text and eventually shared by all readers.

The subtle and empirical description of what I have just been describing schematically is in fact the project of a considerable body of criticism known as reader-response theory. This theory is already quite advanced on its own terms, without recourse to disciplines such as cybernetics or theoretical biology, and presumably in cases where the different levels of signifying systems in a text function in an ultimately unambiguous manner, theories of self-organization from noise have little or nothing to add to reception theory per se. I write "per se" because it may be that drawing attention to the similarity between theories of reader response and those of self-organization could be of considerable cultural and intellectual import, even if it does not add anything to either theory in itself. In particular, it may be possible to see in this light both the resemblances and differences between reader-response theory and theories of nondirected learning, to which the formalism of self-organization from noise has significant connections.[43]

The possible implications of self-organization as a reading model do not stop, however, with reception theory: in fact, when the notion of *reception* theory fails or becomes problematic, recourse to the concepts of self-organizing systems becomes particularly pertinent. De Man argues that precisely such theories as reader response are engaging in the most subtle and effective resistance to literary theory, because they imply that the ambiguity and undecidability of texts could be reduced by transgrammatical means, by the postulation and discovery of unambiguous rules for decoding beyond the sentence, analogous to those rules of grammar that users of a language employ to process its sentences.[44] For de Man, the most profound literariness of language lies in the resistance of texts to this kind of transgrammatical decoding, a resistance that makes of literary theory a theory that theorizes its own theoretical impossibility. De Man's brilliantly rigorous readings thus lead time and again to aporias, to the failure of meanings that would claim to transcend the rhetoricity of language. For him, these aporias become the very "meaning" of literary texts, the most profound mode of understanding such texts being to assume the aporia in its most devastating implications. It is in the context of de Man's and Derrida's deconstructions of literary language, not that of the reception theorists, that the concept of self-organization is potentially most relevant to literary studies, for deconstruction is our strongest theory of textual noise.

What the theorists of textual undecidability and dissemination seem to be saying, in informational terms, is this: the message is not always received, intact, as it was sent, and the very concept or possibility of "message" is simultaneously structured and undone by the possibility of its dispersion. Because of internal and external noise, and particularly the noise produced by language as a rhetorical system never fully

---

[43]See Jean-Claude Tabary, "Auto-organisation à partir du bruit et système nerveux," in *L'Auto-organisation: De la physique au politique*, ed. P. Dumouchel and J.-P. Dupuy (Paris, 1983), 238–256.

[44]"The resistance to theory which, as we saw, is a resistance to reading, appears in its most rigorous and theoretically elaborated form among the theoreticians of reading who dominate the contemporary theoretical scene" (de Man, "The Resistance to Theory," 18).

present to itself, what "arrives" is less clear and orderly (but more complex) than what was "sent." *Une lettre n'arrive pas toujours à destination*, as Derrida wrote in his article on Lacan's analysis of Poe.[45] Serres has suggested that the passage from nineteenth-century to twentieth-century French philosophy, from Bergson to Derrida, can be understood as a displacement of the second law of thermodynamics from physical to informational systems—the shift, one might say, from Boltzmann to Shannon. Bergson's philosophical system, for Serres, is one of heat engines, of reservoirs, differences, circulation of energy. If one replaces energy reservoirs by informational reservoirs, this system can be translated into one of textual dissemination: "It immediately became obvious, or was taken as such, that a store of information transcribed on any given memory, a painting or a page, should drift by itself from difference to disorder. . . . By an act of simultaneous translation, one can derive with relative ease the philosophical terms in use today."[46] This is an oversimplified account of deconstruction, but perhaps the impact of deconstruction in American literary criticism has less to do with the subtlety of Derrida's readings of Heidegger than with the kind of simple schema to which Serres seems to be referring in his lapidary remarks. In other words, what has been arguably most influential in Derrida's work is not its place in the history of philosophy but its easily if abusively abstractable antiphilosophy of text and meaning, "anti-" in that it effectively undoes the traditional methodological and ideological presuppositions of the literary disciplines.

These disciplines have traditionally assumed that their task is to recover an authorial message or to reach as objective an understanding

---

[45]In Derrida's *La Carte postale*, Freud's *Principe de Plaisir* and *Principe de Réalité*, themselves avatars of thermodynamics (the stocking and dissipation of energy), are transformed (perhaps whimsically, perhaps seriously) into PP and PR—Postal Principle and *Poste Restante* (general delivery), but also grandpa and father (*PéPé* and *PéRe*). The divisibility, the mortality, the sent-ness of posted letters precedes and conditions the possibility of their actually communicating meaning. But this sent-ness or postality is not only a feature of the age of postal technology or even of language; it is an avatar of Derridean *différance*, the originary movement of difference and deferral: "In short (this is what I would like to articulate more rigorously if one day I write it in another form), as soon as there is, there is difference (and it doesn't wait for language, especially human language, and the language of being, just the mark and the divisible line), and there is postal organization, relay, delay, anticipation, destination, telecommunicating set-up, possibility and therefore fatal necessity of diversion, etc." (Derrida, *La Carte postale*, 74).

[46]Serres, *Hermes: Literature, Science, Philosophy*, 73.

as possible of autonomous textual structure. Practitioners of the discipline position themselves as receivers of a message assumed to be sent by the author (or perhaps his culture or milieu, or his unconscious) or by the text itself considered as object of observation. Now if we consider only a closed system consisting of sender, channel, and receiver, the unreliability of message transmission inevitably brings loss of communicated information. This is why the radical assumption of language's rhetoricity poses such a strong challenge to literary studies *as they have been traditionally constituted.* If language is a noisy channel, and it is, then humanism in its more or less authoritarian avatars and formalism in its more or less scientific avatars are irrevocably compromised—not broken beyond use, but cracked beyond repair. These stances, however, which depend ultimately on a claim of successful, reliable, even superior communication, are not the only ones available to the reader or critic of literature.

As I noted much earlier, any use of information theory in complex systems makes sense only if the level of communication to be considered is specified. To discern the ambiguities of natural language, it is heuristically useful to assume as a model of unambiguous communication a computer language or a metalanguage suitable for treatment by a computer. In discussing the seeming ambiguities or undecidables that occur at the intersection of different levels of literary coding, it was similarly expedient to take natural language in turn as a noiseless channel, a vehicle of transmission without error. Of course these levels, and these perspectives, coexist in any verbal text. But even though we know that, let us suppose for a moment a complex system of linguistic and literary communication, functioning on many levels but susceptible to unambiguous decoding at all but a final level at which we find the textual undecidables of de Man and Derrida. In other words, we are considering as complete and well analyzed a system of literary communication as possible—and also the residue that falls outside of it, that part which inevitably appears to the most sophisticated observer as noise, as an ultimate ambiguity inherent in the literary channel. De Man would argue that the reader is at this point forced to remain before an aporia, or on the horns of a dilemma: since there is no way of recovering an unambiguous meaning, the very impossibility of doing so becomes the only "meaning" literally recoverable. Whence, in the hands of readers and critics less rigorous and original than de Man, a series of readings—often, but not always, of modernist works—designed to show that the true subject of these works is the impossibility of their attaining a stable meaning, of producing anything that could be called a theme or subject other than this impossibility itself. But what sort of meaning is declared impossible by this kind of aporia? The answer can only be: a *communicated* meaning of which the author or the text itself would be the master.

The theory of self-organization from noise suggests that this ambiguity as well can be converted into information by a change in site of the observer, by a reader who can take into account the ensemble of what has been communicated *and* the noise that inevitably accompanies that communication. It is not hard to show that in deconstructive reading, for example, the production of meaning—considered as an autonomous, self-organizing process—does not come to a halt. What is undermined is only meaning as the literary historian or New Critic conceived it. Suppose a text declares itself to mean one thing but describes another, and then assume that a very subtle reading of this text has been produced. Now the good deconstructive reader, like de Man, will not claim to have imposed *his* reading on the text but will argue that he has simply "teased out warring forces from within the text," in Barbara Johnson's phrase; he has made explicit an ambiguity or aporia that was already there. The deconstructive reading is thus an enactment of what can be considered noise in the textual channel. But for anyone who now observes the ensemble formed by the text and its deconstructive reading, the text's meaning has been considerably complicated: to what it declares and describes must now be added the relation of undecidability between the two. "Rousseau" plus "Derrida's Rousseau" is culturally a more informative text than "Rousseau" alone, a fortiori more informative than "Rousseau minus the Rousseauian undecidables that would someday become Derrida's Rousseau." The deconstructive reading functions as the point of exchange, of change in observational site, that makes ambiguity a positive factor in an unforeseen organizational complexity, rather than simply a negative factor inhibiting the transmission of preestablished information. And lest one think that this is something arbitrarily or externally added to the text by the critic, de Man is there to contend that the deconstructive reading finds nothing that was not already within the text.[47] Such a reading makes explicit the moment in which a text's

---

[47]See de Man's essay "The Rhetoric of Blindness: Jacques Derrida's Reading of Rousseau," in *Blindness and Insight* (New York, 1971), 102–141, in which de Man argues that Rousseau's *Essai sur l'origine des langues* was already as aware of its own

meaning differs from itself, in which one cannot assume that there is a meaning received that could coincide with a meaning sent. The text's meaning must thus become one of two things: an insufficient or imperfect version of the message assumed to have been sent, or a new kind of message constructed by the reader using both the message and its ambiguity. This construction of a new kind of message implies, of course, that we renounce the intention or authority of "original" meaning, and recognize the role and responsibility of critics as cocreators of the meanings of the texts that they summon from the archive.

It may very well be objected that in the transfer of Atlan's formalism of organization from noise to the reception (or more properly—to use the terminology of nondirected learning—the assimilation) of literary texts, we have forgotten an important condition that was present in the biological system: that of an "extremely highly complicated system." In such a system any receiving instance is connected to any emitting instance by a number of different paths, so that the information "lost" due to noise in a given transmission channel is rarely altogether lost, because it is probably available to the receiver by other paths. This type of system redundancy makes it possible for "autonomy-ambiguity" to outweigh "destructive ambiguity": noise can function as supplemental information leading to an increase in complexity, because it can be added to the message as received nearly intact by other paths.

If one assumes the critical confrontation with the text to be as the New Critics imagined it, as the encounter of a reader with an isolated, self-contained, and self-sufficient verbal structure, then the preceding objection does indeed ruin any possibility of gaining information from ambiguity or undecidability. For in this situation, the message-as-sent has but one channel by which to reach the receiver, so that the noise in this channel will diminish its information, however fascinating or exquisite the contemplation of that noise may be to the reader. In this case the undecidables, the profoundly unresolvable aporias of rhetoric that de Man was so good at identifying, are indeed irrecuperable and cannot be said to produce any gain in information, any new meaning, since by definition meaning is supposed to be produced only from what is received through this channel, through the given text. The context given by the New Critical model of interpretation accounts for much of

---

rhetorical strategies as Derrida would be in his reading of the text in *De la grammatologie.*

the difference between deconstruction in America and deconstruction in France; it explains why on these shores the work of critics like Derrida and de Man has been at once so influential, so unsettling, and yet so functionally compatible with the academic status quo. As Culler astutely pointed out, American deconstructors, by pointing to the deconstructive operation as already working within the text, make deconstruction into a kind of interpretation of the text and thus into a critical act acceptable in the American academic community. But by this same restriction to the text itself, they make it an interpretation that seems nihilistic, an interpretation about the impossibility of meaning, and thereby shake the faith of those who cannot help but admit that the deconstructive critics are playing according to the rules of the academic game, but in whom adherence to New Critical methods is combined with a faith in the meaningfulness of literature. Whence the arbitrary and theological character of so many antideconstruction essays, whether for academic or popular consumption.

There is an alternative to the New Critical stance and it is in the context of this alternative that the model of self-organizing systems may help us move away from the impasse of deconstruction-as-nihilism or the humanistic denial of deconstruction's insights. That alternative is quite simply what we call culture: the circulation of language, texts, and concepts, thanks to which we never confront a text in a vacuum, as an isolated structure of sounds heard or words perceived on the page, and into which we cast our critical productions. Of course, the New Critics were men of culture and would certainly have admitted that were they not so their readings would have been poorer. Yet their methods tend to isolate the literary text as an object of study rather than integrate it into culture, into the life not just of the individual mind but of the cognitive community in which minds participate.

Why should the notion of culture be so important in this context? If a single organism, or the brain of a single organism, qualifies as an "extremely highly complicated system," then the same can be said a fortiori of culture, considered as the circulation and storage of languages and concepts in many millions of human brains (and external storage devices, such as books) over thousands of years. Literary messages are much less unique than the theologians of the individual and autonomous work would have us believe. If we transgress their edicts for a moment and allow ourselves the heresy of paraphrase, if we try to pull out of a text what is not specific to its uniquely individual, transgrammatical articulation of language, then we will encounter commonplaces and repetition far more often than uniqueness and originality—a fact that few critics, and doubtless few New Critics, would deny. In other words, since we are part of an extremely highly complicated cultural system, we can be fairly sure that the nonpoetic part of the message is something that we already know. Culture provides, indeed consists of, the alternative transmission circuits, the redundancy in the system of texts and minds that enables us to make up for the surprises and ambiguities of literary texts, convert into meaning what is in some sense an obstacle to the clear communication of meaning.

We can describe how this process works for a famous deconstructive reading to which I have already alluded. Derrida, in *De la grammatologie*, discerns in Rousseau's *Essai sur l'origine des langues* an opposition between what the text declares (the priority of speech) and what its rhetorical structures describe (the anteriority of something like writing). Derrida chose this text, and read it, as a particular moment in a Western tradition that valorizes speech over writing, a tradition that is part of what he calls the metaphysics of presence. Given this tradition, he can be quite confident of what Rousseau's text declares: he does not need every scrap of information provided by the *Essai* in order to constitute the schema by which the Western philosophical tradition valorizes speech and presence over writing and deferral. If some parts of this schema are not intact in Rousseau's text, no matter: he has them from Plato, or Condillac, or Husserl. If Derrida were reading the *Essai* as an idealized New Critic might and were relying solely on it to produce an interpretation concerning speech and writing, he could hardly arrive at such a schema, precisely because of the rhetorical effects that he ferrets out with such tenacity and skill. These rhetorical moments, by going against Rousseau's declared thesis, would have modified this hypothetical message before it could ever have been received, so that the *Essai* could be read as an ambiguous theory of the priority of speech or writing, or as a text about the impossibility of communicating precisely about the origins of language. There is of course something of this in Derrida's reading, but there is more as well: Rousseau's moments of rhetorical blindness are shown to be indexes of particular kinds of aporias that beset the valorization of speech and the metaphysics of presence. Derrida does not simply point to a failure of unambiguous meaning in a minor work by Rousseau; he uses that failure to construct his own philosophical position vis-à-vis the speech/ writing problem, vis-à-vis the metaphysics of presence, and this position has elements of originality with respect to the tradition. The deconstructive encounter with the text of Rousseau creates meaning, and can do so because of the cultural context in which it takes place.

To put it another way: we do not need all of the paraphrasable information contained in the literature we read, because for the most part literary texts restate things that we already know. We have read other works of literature and other forms of discourse concerning ourselves and the world. What we seek in a literary text is something unique to that text's verbal arrangement, unique to its way of not exactly communicating what we might think it means to say. By saying differently, by producing meaning through systems that are not those of everyday language, not even those of everyday literature, but that belong to a particular verbal text, where we must discover them, the text solicits our entry into a learning process, it incites us to learn to become its reader. Moreover, because it does not express a message exactly, because it brings us some specific verbal material unlike anything we know, which is thus incapable of being completely integrated into *the schemas we already had for knowing*, the text leads us to modify ourselves, to shift position, to change and adapt our ways of mind a little so that it can become a part of them. The disorder, the noise of literary language can become information for us, can bring us to more subtle forms of understanding, because it is the unexpected, the radically different to which we can respond only because we are already complex beings capable of yet more complexity.

The noise in literature is no disaster for culture, no stumbling block for education. The critical decision to assume noise ruins only a limited stance toward literature and its study, a peculiarly modern approach that makes of literature an object of knowledge, a thing to be understood rationally in and for itself. In other words, assuming rather than excluding noise is a disaster only for the study of literature considered in what we might call its disciplinary dimension: a pseudoscience trying to gain knowledge of a kind of object, to receive and retransmit a particular set of messages. The study of information theory or self-organizing systems, in other words, will not stabilize an already unsettled discipline. The literary text is neither an object fit for formal study nor a reliable vehicle for communicating truths or values. It is a precommunicative utterance, a message that exceeds our capacity to receive it and thus invites us to learn its codes and to construct its meanings. This makes of literature not the object of an academic discipline as traditionally understood but rather a point of departure for contextual and inventive thought.

4 Strange Objects: Complexity, Autonomy, and Literary Texts

> In physics, we try to say things that no one knew before in a way that everyone can understand, whereas in poetry . . .
>
> Attributed to Paul Dirac

In the last chapter I argued that literary language, by its very failure as a system for the communication of preexistent information, becomes a vehicle for the creation of new information. For this to be the case, literature must be, to a degree, both obscure and repetitive; were it perfectly clear, nothing new could arise in the transaction between author and reader, and were each of its utterances original, its relative obscurity would destroy information faster than it could create it. Self-organization depends on both noise and redundancy. But Paul Dirac, in his understated reproach to his friend Robert Oppenheimer, who had been writing poems, reminds us of the high cultural price that must be paid for embracing repetitiveness and obscurity.[1] Modern science owes much of its prestige to the creation of new bodies of stable knowledge, unsuspected by two thousand years of literary culture originating with the ancient Greeks. What accomplishments does poetry have to set beside the theory of general relativity, the understanding of the genetic code? And yet the charge of obscurity is perhaps graver, when one considers the use of literature in education. It would seem both more rational and more egalitarian to teach subjects that, though they might be difficult, nevertheless attempt to be as transparent as possible, as accessible to one mind as to another, rather than a

[1]Quoted in the *New Yorker*, November 26, 1984, p. 38.

subject that, by the admission of its most profound theorists, makes its own inscrutability its very center. Viewed from the heights of twentieth-century physics, the cultural project of poetry may seem retrograde or irrational. To argue that literature must stick around to "humanize" a world otherwise given over to "cold and calculating scientists" is a very poor position, one that concedes from the outset literature's exclusion from serious forms of knowledge and then opposes science with a critique made in the name of emotion, or morality, or perhaps spontaneity. Literature becomes either a substitute religion or a marginal counterculture, a haven for would-be sermonizers or flower children of the mind.

If our hypothesis—that literary understanding can be seen as a self-organizing process, as a creation of meaning out of the placing of meaning in jeopardy—is to have any real bearing on literary studies, it will do so through its cultural implications and not because it furnishes technical innovations in that arcane subdiscipline known as literary theory. In the last chapter, I moved from science to literature so as to suggest a new conceptual framework for problems of textual communication, indeterminacy, undecidability. The movement of this chapter will be the inverse, an attempt to suggest the larger cultural implications of literature in the context of this informational approach.

In an ars poetica written in 1944, "The Creations of Sound," Wallace Stevens inveighed against a poet, X, "a man / Too exactly himself" who attempts to make poetry the direct communication of something he understands, feels, or is. Stevens indicts the would-be bard of transparency in a peremptory and far from obvious apostrophe to his listener or reader:

> Tell X that speech is not dirty silence
> Clarified. It is silence made still dirtier.

As literary readers, we may thrill to this enigmatic and lapidary defense of the murky powers of poetic language, but it should not surprise us if many responsible thinkers see in the cultural mission of the word something other than "silence made still dirtier." We are defending a strange mode of speech. A few lines later, we read that the poems of X

> do not make the visible a little hard

> To see, nor, reverberating, eke out the mind
> On peculiar horns, themselves eked out
> By the spontaneous particulars of sound.

In making the visible a little hard to see, the poem functions as an instrument not of communication but of complication, supplementing and stretching the mind, drawing it into new spaces, new relations, new dilemmas. The earlier lines concerning silence and dirt amount to just such a set of "peculiar horns." Stevens seems to be trying to make a specific point, and it could have been made more clearly, but instead he pushes the reader to construct a meaning located between and around the usual meanings of the words he uses. We start with the false notion, attributed by negation to the naive poet of transparency, that "speech is . . . dirty silence clarified." X himself would not have put it that way, for what is made clearer by calling silence dirty or saying that it can be clarified? Silence, here, must be something other than silence: it opposes speech not as the void opposes being but as inarticulate and confused thought or feeling would oppose their pristine expression. Silence for X, according to Stevens, would be the semiarticulate magma of self upon which speech can confer unambiguous clarity. Stevens then uses this conception of silence to make his own statement and "eke out the mind" even further: "speech . . . is silence made still dirtier." Again, if silence were silence, and dirt dirt, the phrase would be nonsensical. But we already know, from the false assumption attributed to X, that we must read silence as a kind of raw material of speech, dirtiness as the confusion of this material before speech comes to clarify it. So if speech is silence made still dirtier, then speech adds ambiguity and complexity, makes what was not yet clarified even less clear. And yet Stevens has not put it this way: he wrote of "silence made still dirtier," forcing us, if we wish to construct meaning, to allow his words to come together in new ways, to make them mean something other than what we thought they meant. We must experience words in the act of differing from themselves, encounter language as it introduces a confusion that silence cannot contain.

This language less clear than silence comes as if from "a different poet, / An accretion from ourselves": the otherness of language, its failure to communicate precisely ourselves, makes of it the bearer of something new. We can read Stevens's little poem as an evocation of certain properties of poetry, properties that we can now describe as the creation of meaning in a system with a noisy channel. But many other poems, or statements about poems, could be read in the same way; the poem does not, in the usual sense, say anything hitherto unsaid. Nor has it been written so as to be uniformly intelligible to all. Dirac's unfinished phrase is still waiting: do poets attempt to say things that everyone knew before in ways that not everyone can understand?

The type of response that we are able to give to such questions has implications that go beyond the study of poetry. Our understanding of the cultural and epistemological status of literature concerns not only literature itself but also nonliterature and the relation between the two. Debates on literature and its study cannot be spearated from debates on the cosmos and human community, and their study in the natural and social sciences. Disciplines form a system: one does not change independently of the others. In suggesting that scientific concepts can and should be made a part of our thinking about literature, I am calling into question a romantic tradition of literature as a domain of protest against science's manipulative disenchantment of the world; I do so with the awareness that the scientific project itself has undergone profound change and redefinition since the era of Laplace. And just as those in literary disciplines may react with some concern and anger if someone imports scientific models into their territory, scientists do not always take kindly to proposed displacements of the status of their disciplines. Change in the most basic or global categories of one's thought and institutional affiliation is seldom a comforting thing, but it cannot be avoided, at least as long as we remain finite beings exploring a world that is itself in the process of becoming.

Complexity and Interdisciplinarity

In 1977 the Russian-born Belgian scientist Ilya Prigogine received the Nobel Prize in chemistry for his work on phenomena of nonequilibrium thermodynamics known as dissipative structures. As was noted in Chapter 2, closed systems move over time toward thermodynamic equilibrium, and the nature and rate of this irreversible movement can be described in general laws. But in open systems, where external constraints can maintain a state far from equilibrium, such general laws do not apply, and seemingly strange things can happen. Thus when a cylinder of liquid is subjected to an appropriate temperature gradient—that is, when one end of the cylinder is maintained at a high temperature and the other end at a low one—there appears a highly regular pattern of hexagonal cells in the liquid, known as Bénard cells. To an observer, this cellular pattern appears to be far more complex, implying far greater specificity and differentiation, than the simple application of a temperature difference that produced it. The Bénard cells provide a simple physical example of a self-organizing system. They are what Prigogine calls a dissipative structure, a structure whose existence depends on the continual expenditure or dissipation of energy that keeps it away from thermodynamic equilibrium. Prigogine and his group have studied many such structures and see in them one of the building blocks of a scientific understanding of how the new and the unpredictable come into being in the natural world:

> The thermodynamics of irreversible processes have discovered that the flows of energy that move through certain physico-chemical systems, and distance them from equilibrium, can nourish phenomena of spontaneous self-organization, ruptures of symmetry, evolutions towards growing complexity and diversity. Where general laws of thermodynamics stop, the constructive role of irreversibility can be revealed; this is the domain in which things are born and die, or are transformed in a singular history woven by the chance of fluctuations and the necessity of laws.[2]

In Prigogine's view, this kind of discovery implies more than the addition of some new laws or principles, however subtle they might be, by which scientists can predict and/or manipulate natural phenomena. Dissipative structures point instead to a new conception of scientific work and of the place of the scientist in the universe, a conception in which the pursuit of general operational laws is complemented by an attentiveness to the ways in which laws and circumstances combine to give rise to phenomena that are local and unique. The "noise" of microscopic fluctuations, in open systems far from equilibrium, cannot simply be excluded as insignificant.[3] Thus if new alliances between the sciences of nature and those of man can be developed, this opportunity stems from the new role of the scientist, no longer the external observer seeking to predict and dominate his object by universal laws: "Within a rich and diverse population of cognitive practices, our science occupies the singular position of a poetic listening to nature—in the etymological sense in which the poet is a maker—an active, manipulating and calculating exploration, but henceforth capable of respecting the

---

[2]Prigogine and Stengers, *La Nouvelle Alliance*, 271.

[3]Isabelle Stengers writes, "What does the study of certain physico-chemical systems far from equilibrium . . . teach us? It teaches us that the separation between what is significant (*signifiant*) and what is merely noise is not absolute, but depends on the situation." ("Découvrir la complexité?" in *Cognition et complexité*, Cahiers du C.R.E.A., 9 [Paris, 1986], 239).

nature whose voice it brings forth."[4] It has long been known that there are microscopic, random fluctuations in matter, such as the Brownian movement of molecules; what is new in the theory of dissipative structures is the notion that these fluctuations, absolutely unpredictable and unspecifiable by any system of measurement, can under certain circumstances give rise to significant and equally unpredictable changes of state at the macroscopic level. This implies that our own existence in the world as observers—the fact that we cannot make infinitely precise measurements—becomes a fundamental limit to science's capacity to predict or manipulate nature according to general laws. In classical physics it was assumed that observation could approach, as a limit, a perfection corresponding to an observer external to the universe and therefore not subject to finitude, and that to this limit of observation corresponded a limit in predictability, which could likewise be approached arbitrarily closely.[5] But in the systems studied by Prigogine and his colleagues, the approach to limits of observability does not entail an approach to limits of predictability. This forces the scientist to confront the unpredictable and local appearance of the radically new: arbitrarily precise knowledge of a system's initial conditions does not make possible arbitrarily accurate prediction of its evolution.

Prigogine and Stengers thus emphasize both a new awareness of our place within the universe and a new appreciation of the random and the unpredictable, as they argue that natural science can now forge new alliances with the sciences of human history and language. Their vision of a science less unlike poetry than previously supposed, however enticing it may seem to readers of poetry, has not failed to draw criticism from scientists. René Thom, the mathematician best known for his work on catastrophe theory, has attacked Prigogine, Atlan, and other theorists of self-organization from noise as betrayers of the scientific ideal of deterministic, reproducible, and thereby universally consensual knowledge. "A random process," writes Thom, "is one which cannot be simulated by any mechanism, nor described by any formalism. To affirm that 'chance exists' is therefore to take the ontological position which consists in affirming that there are natural phenomena which we shall never be able to describe, therefore never under-

[4]Prigogine and Stengers, *La Nouvelle Alliance*, 281.
[5]This classical assumption was already invalidated by quantum mechanics, specifically by the Heisenberg Uncertainty Relation.

stand."[6] Thom's own position, he claims, does not depend on the postulation of an absolutely deterministic universe but on the recognition that the task of science is to reveal determinisms at work in whatever kind of universe we inhabit: "Determinism in Science is not something given, it is a conquest. In that sense, the zealots of chance are the apostles of desertion."[7] The local, the aleatory, the nonrepeatable are thus simply not a part of science.

Atlan and Prigogine vigorously reject Thom's indictment of the concepts of self-organization, turning against him the charge of making a metaphysical postulation, namely, that deterministic laws are the only things to discover. It would be inappropriate to attempt to resolve such a debate, or even intervene seriously in it, in a literary essay; my goal is simply to situate the discussion and consider some of its implications. The debate appears to hinge on the problem of the scientific observer, on the assertion that there are microsopic phenomena that are intrinsically unobservable and that must inevitably enter into any scientific formulation as random fluctuations or noise. Thom propounds essentially the classical scientific position: rather than supposing in advance that chance exists, and thus accepting that knowledge will be a transaction with noise and fluctuation, we should pursue the task of connecting what appears to be noise and fluctuation to something that we can formalize and thus work on deterministically. Prigogine argues rather that such determinism will always remain impossible at some level—since we are finite and not perfect observers—and thus that science's task is to accept this limitation and thereby gain an understanding into how new things come into being. Whether theories of self-organization are or are not strictly speaking scientific thus depends on one's definition of science, on whether science can be said to be at work in situations concerning which we possess only partial, statistical knowledge, not deterministic operational explanation. What is clear, however, and is not put into doubt by Thom's objections, is that when the observer does not have complete knowledge of a system, then apparent self-organization, at least, is possible. In other words, self-organizing phenomena exist for observers who must remain in a state of partial ignorance concerning the systems

---

[6]Thom, "Stop Chance! Silence Noise!" trans. R. Chumbley, *SubStance*, no. 40 (1983), 11. This issue also contains responses to Thom from Atlan, Prigogine, and others. The articles originally appeared in French in *Le Débat* in 1980.
[7]Thom, "Stop Chance!" 20.

they observe, an ignorance implicit in the use of the term *noise*, whether or not this observational condition be that of the scientist.

Consequently, if we set aside debates on chance and determinism in the universe and on whether science is identical to the search for deterministic general laws, we are left with self-organization as a formalism for describing cognitive situations in which knowledge is but partial, ignorance bound up with information. Such situations arise with respect to *complex systems*, the word *complex* being used in a specific sense given by the theorists of self-organization.[8] It is not hard to conceive of simple systems: a pendulum, a piston, a single logical operation at the level of bits in a microprocessor. We can understand fully the operation of such systems. *Complicated* systems, such as a clock, a car engine, or a home computer, can be fully understood as the interaction of their component parts, so that whereas knowing them requires much more of one's time and patience, in principle nothing prevents us from explaining their operation just as fully as we can explain that of the simple systems of which they are made up. What distinguishes the *complex* system, on the other hand, is a discontinuity in knowledge between the parts and the whole. This is the case, for instance, for the human brain: between what is known about the electrochemical properties of neurons and what is known about cognition there is a considerable zone of uncertainty. Complexity can be identified with information in the Shannonian sense of a quantitative measure of the observer's uncertainty (see above, pp. 54–56). According to Atlan, the notion of complexity

> expresses the fact that we do not know, or do not understand a system, despite a background of global knowledge which enables us to recognize and name this system. A system that can be explicitly specified, when detailed structure is known, is not really complex. Let's say that it can be more or less complicated. Complexity implies that we have a global perception of it, together with the perception that we do not master it in its details. That's why [complexity] is measured by the information that we do not possess, and would need in order to specify the system in its details.[9]

When we do not know precisely how a system operates, how to describe the actual causal connections between components that produce its overall behavior, or when for reasons of observational convenience

---

[8]On the implications of complexity, see Isabelle Stengers, "Découvrir la complexité?" 223–254, and see Jean-Pierre Dupuy, "La Simplicité de la complexité," in *Ordres et désordres: Enquête sur un nouveau paradigme* (Paris, 1982), 211–251.

[9]Atlan, *Entre le cristal et la fumée*, 76.

or economy we choose not to investigate the details of its operation, then we are in the presence of a complex system. Such a system can be differentiated from its environment, described globally with respect to that environment, but the mechanisms of its operation remain at least in part unknown. In particular, this situation arises when we attempt to understand the articulation of two levels in a hierarchically organized system, each one of which is understood operationally, but whose interaction cannot be described in terms of unambiguous laws and simple or complicated processes. To take an example familiar to students of literature: linguistic science can make quite precise statements about formation rules of sentences, and readers of literature have little trouble talking about poems and novels in thematic terms at the level of their overall effect. Yet despite a conviction that texts are made up of language, the passage from linguistic structure to textual effect cannot be described with anything like the regularity or predictability to be found in the grammatical explanation of the sentence.

This passage between levels, only partially understood, corresponds to the passage between two disciplines, here linguistics and literary criticism, which define themselves precisely by choosing to describe one kind or level of phenomena and not another. Atlan has argued that in this sense the passage from one discipline to another always implies a cognitive encounter with complexity, since it implies stepping outside the domain of the operational explanations that each discipline generates.[10] The complexity inherent in the passages between disciplines thus accounts for the fact that "the frontiers of knowledge are found not only, as is often believed, in the very small or the infinitely large, but in the articulations between levels of organization of the real that correspond to different fields of knowledge whose techniques and discourses do not overlap."[11] It is not a priori obvious whether or not the probabilistic knowledge that can be obtained of such complex situations can one day be replaced by an operational knowledge of deterministic laws. The notion of complexity thus does not by itself provide a new rapport with knowledge or an intellectual revolution, writes Stengers, but it does force us to consider "what the type of disciplinary formation invented for the so-called hard sciences in the course of the nineteenth century makes of knowledge."[12]

[10]Atlan, "L'Emergence du nouveau et du sens," in *L'Auto-organisation*, ed. Dumouchel and Dupuy, 122–130.
[11]Atlan, "L'Emergence du nouveau et du sens," 129.
[12]Stengers, "Découvrir la complexité?" 249.

Far from constituting what Kuhn calls a disciplinary matrix, the cognitive approach to complexity is in effect a version of the principle of self-organization from noise. The complicated operational specificity of a given systemic level obviously constitutes information, and not noise, for that level itself, but for an observer who does not understand what is going on at that level, this information, if observed, amounts to noise: the observer, in effect, does not possess the code that would enable him to interpret variety and differentiation as information rather than as noise. And yet this noise, this uninterpretable diversity, must function as input to the observer's construction of a global explanation of how this first level fits into the larger system. It is not simply a matter of the observer figuring out the code of the lower-level system: what the observer (or the higher level itself) must do is to construct an autonomous explanation of how the lower level is integrated into the overall system.

Let's try to make this discussion more concrete by adapting it, tentatively and without any presupposition as to its efficacy, to a problem of understanding in literature. We suppose that a poem presents itself to the reader as a complex system of relations. These include the usual relational structures of language considered as a system of signification; the relations between sounds established by rhyme, rhythm, meter, assonance; the thematic relations between the signifieds of the poem's signs; most important, the relations between these categories themselves: between meter and syntax, rhythm and theme, and so forth. The reader brings to her assimilation of the poem a knowledge of linguistic codes, and if she is an experienced reader of poetry, some general knowledge of the ways in which the other relations that make up the poem may operate; she may, for instance, in a general sense be prepared to find semantic relations of synonymy or antonymy obtaining between elements placed in opposition by rhyme or meter. But unless she is rereading a poem with which she is already intimately familiar, she does not begin with a precise, operational knowledge of how all these different phenomena will interact and thereby contribute to the poem's effect, exactly how they will combine to produce what she may call the poem's meaning—something she will be able to describe in the metalanguages of criticism or commentary. In other words, the reader does not initially possess all of the codes needed to understand the poem, to convert its complexity into information, and it should be added that this situation arises not from the individual

reader's incompetence but from the fact that the specifics of the relations between elements of a poem are generally unique to that poem
and hence cannot have been learned anywhere else.

This amounts to a way of defining the difference between poetry
and communicative prose: the latter is deemed effective if the reader
possesses in advance as much as possible of the necessary codes, so that
he can immediately receive *as information* as high a percentage as possible of the information that the prose is capable of transmitting. The
literary utterance, by contrast, is precommunicative, in that it takes
place in a situation that has not yet become fully communicative, for
whereas writer and reader share the natural language in which the text
is written, the reader does not yet possess the specifically literary language peculiar to that text. Thus to the reader of a poem who starts out
as a reader of prose, whatever "prosaic" information is transmitted by
the poem will initially be accompanied by, and very likely obscured by,
"poetic" complexity that at first, in the absence of understanding of
how it is articulated, can be experienced only as noise. Of course, such
an experience is more obvious in the case of a student confronting serious poetry for the first time than in that of an experienced reader who
has at least some general expectations regarding the relational structure of poems. The specific relational structures of a given poem, however, will not be known in advance even by the experienced reader. But
in either case, the reader's construction of a meaning for the poem proceeds by a process of self-organization from noise: complexity not
explainable in and of itself becomes an ingredient of a new level of
explanation.

It may seem perverse to insist on a "new level of explanation": isn't
the poem itself what the reader comes to explain (operationally, not te-
leologically) and thereby understand? That is of course the way we ordinarily describe the process, and yet other things we ordinarily say
about reading and interpreting poetry imply that "understanding the
poem" may be a somewhat illusory phrase. It is generally accepted that
critical statements made about a poem *are not the poem*, that the commentary never becomes the equivalent, or even the representation, of
the text. But the concept of an operational description, one that would
render unambiguous all of a system's articulation, implies precisely this
kind of equivalent. It is true that for many, the irreducible difference
between text and commentary is a matter of aesthetics, and while such
a position is perfectly reasonable, it amounts to saying that poetry is

plain prose made prettier; what I am attempting to define in this book are cognitive, rather than aesthetic, grounds for understanding how poetry (and literature generally) are able to say what prose (and non-literary language) are incapable of saying. What the reader constructs is the reader's reading of the poem, which may then be given written form as a commentary. This reading or commentary may of course make use of detailed explanations of the poem's relational articulations, and it will in general become richer and more informative the more it uses and takes into acount the specificity of the poem's construction, but it will never become informationally equivalent to the poem, will never operate on the same level as the poem itself.

We have been considering two related cognitive situations in which the acquisition of new information proceeds along the lines of a self-organization from noise: the problem of understanding relations between different levels of a system, each one described by the language of a discipline, and the assimilation of the radically new, the exceptional. Not only are both at work in the reader's assimilation of a text, but both have a particularly close relationship to essential characteristics of literary discourse. We may recall, in this context, what Lotman wrote about the artistic text's capacity to transform what might seem an extrasystemic fact into what he called a polysystemic one. A reader begins to confront a text with certain linguistic and cultural codes and begins to identify coherent relations within the text: we might call this the reader's first-order approximation of what he encounters. In the nonartistic text, Lotman would argue, once an initial apprehension of meaning has been made, it will not be much disturbed by the remainder of the text, which will seem progressively more predictable and less informative as the reader simply refines his initial understanding, filling in the more or less complicated details. Not so, however, for the literary text, which by its nature continues to surprise the reader (and thus goes on bombarding him with a high level of information) by means of elements that seem incompatible with the initial construction of a meaning, features that are situated outside of what have thus far appeared to be the text's categories. At this point the reader of an artistic text makes a crucial assumption, namely that a new feature, rather than being simply a chance variation or an isolated event better ignored than worried about, indicates the presence of a new or additional systemic level at work within the text. What falls outside level A must indicate the presence of level A': the reader therefore goes about identifying a new level of coherence, a new signifying structure within the text.

This conduct of the reader's is inextricably linked to his distinction of an artistic text from a nonartistic one or from some other kind of object. The reader makes a postulate concerning the text, that of its internal, autonomous coherence, its subjugation to its own laws. In other words the reader excludes the possibility that something in the literary text just fell in there by chance, in accordance with an external causal series independent of the text's organization. Confronted by successive disruptions of already elaborated levels of coherence, the reader constructs new levels, produces interpretive contexts not identical to the already existing ones. These levels of description can be hierarchical (e.g., lexical, syntactic, metrical, thematic), or they may be overlapping and intersecting (simultaneous presence of different thematic unities). What matters most is that the reader does not produce a *single* description of the text, does not integrate all its features in one uniform level of coherence—even if the reader, as critic, may subsequently write up all of his descriptions in a single interpretive article and signal the coherence between them. To say that the reader produces different descriptions, identifies different levels of coherence, does not imply that texts themselves are incoherent but only that their coherence must be described at a number of distinct levels. It is perfectly possible for the reader who has identified several intersecting or nested structures within a text to produce what might be called a metareading, in which the relations between these levels themselves become the objects of interpretation, but the reader cannot arrive at this stage without first having confronted the text as the locus of its subsystems' intersections.

This process so closely resembles the production of information from noise, for Lotman, that it can even extend to cases in which "real" noise, actually external to the artistic work, interferes with its reception: the toppled statue and the misprinted poem can be taken as themselves artistic texts, their final level of disorder or complexity in effect internalized and converted to information. The notion of self-organization from noise can thus describe literary reading whether we consider textual noise to be internal or external, reducible or irreducible. In many cases what first may appear (to the reader) as unassimilable disorder may prove to be quite unambiguously determined as to its effects by the text's internal laws; in other words, its status as noise or indeterminism may be transitory, a negative moment in an unambiguous construction of meaning guided ultimately, if indirectly, by the laws of the text. But it may also be that the text is undecidable, forcing the reader either to abandon the game or to construct meaning where several alternative, even incompatible constructions are possible. What the humblest deviation and the most baffling undecidable have in common, however, is the structure of the cognitive demand they make on the reader. The intersection of different levels, different features of language, or different mimetic projections within a text is not fully disciplined by preestablished rules; it must be found out and ultimately constructed by the reader, who possesses considerable knowledge of linguistic and cultural codes to aid her in her task but who must literally discover the autonomous codes by which a given text is itself organized.

Viewed from this perspective, the defining feature of literary studies would be what we might call its *interdisciplinarity from within*. I use this phrase in the context of Atlan's identification of a discipline with a level of operational description, of interdisciplinarity with the forging of a language with which to speak of the passages between the phenomena that our several descriptive languages enable us to describe. The literary text cannot be described at a single level; it can be reduced neither to linguistic phenomena nor to rhetorical figures nor to global structures of poetic or narrative form nor to psychological categories. Attempts to make such reductions, to account for the whole in terms of a single set of parts or a single procedure for organizing the parts, have never obtained general assent, precisely because they are always incomplete. Nor is such a reductive understanding what we really want out of literature.[13] A mode of interdisciplinary understanding must necessarily be present within the single empirical discipline of literary studies. At present, this can be seen in the proliferation of theoretical schools, which often have very little to say to one another. By viewing each other as members of different tribes, many critics avoid confronting the necessity of interdisciplinarity in the study of literature and thereby maintain the fiction that theirs is an object suitable for disciplinary study—and that their own tribe is working in the true matrix of that discipline.

---

[13]Richard Rorty writes: "The reason 'literary criticism' is 'unscientific' is just that whenever somebody tries to work up [a constant] vocabulary he makes a fool of himself. We don't *want* works of literature to be criticizable within a terminology we already know; we want both those works and criticism of them to give us *new* terminologies" (*Consequences of Pragmatism*, 142).

Thus the literary is not a single level of linguistic or psychological or cultural reality, to be described and then fitted into a larger schema of things, as though we literary scholars were producing some part of a larger work, say, a general history and explanation of human culture. Rather, the literary already brings together problematically within itself features that can be approached only as different levels, different discourses necessitating different descriptions. The literary text demands of us that we approach it as a totality, yet it simultaneously reveals itself to belong to no totality that we can conceive. It is, we may safely say, a strange object.

Romanticism

This formal sense of a totality incapable of being seized by any single cognitive procedure is perhaps what still binds us to that grandiose project for literature known as romanticism. Prior to the advent of romanticism, as noted in Chapter 1, "literature" designated all culturally valued writings, all writings that were deemed of general or lasting importance. The imaginative genres were defined not by the fact of imagination but by the kind of mimesis or imitation they involved. By the middle of the eighteenth century, however, harmony had come to rival mimesis as a principle for explaining beauty. In his *Encyclopédie* article "Beau," Diderot argued that beauty depends on "the idea of relations [*rapports*] . . . the perception of relations." This was not in itself an original position, but peculiar to Diderot's argument was his contention that the perception of relations is a fundamental human experience because we live in a culture of machines and devices, of made things:

> We are born with needs which oblige us to have recourse to different expedients. . . . Most of these expedients were tools, machines, or some other invention of this kind, but every machine supposes combination, arrangement of parts tending towards the same goal, etc. Here then . . . are ideas of order, arrangement, symmetry, mechanism, proportion, unity; all these ideas come from the senses and are artificial; and we have passed from the notion of a multitude of artificial and natural beings—arranged, proportioned, combined, and made symmetrical— to the positive and abstract notion of order, arrangement, proportion, comparison, relations, symmetry, and to the negative notion of disproportion, disorder and chaos.[14]

[14]Diderot, *Oeuvres esthétiques*, ed. P. Vernière (Paris, 1968), pp. 415–416.

Only secondarily, according to Diderot, do we find these characteristics in natural beings; they originate with artificial, utilitarian objects. Accustomed as we are to the organic metaphors of romanticism, we find the priority assigned by Diderot to the device or tool to be at once refreshing and disconcerting, much as we can be intrigued and skeptical concerning the circulation of concepts between communications engineers, biologists, and literary scholars. For Diderot, the aesthetic is the relational but not the organic.

The romantic formulation of the idea that beauty consists in the harmony of parts of a work can be found in perhaps its earliest manifestation in the essays of Karl Phillip Moritz. Writing in the 1780s, Moritz associated the primacy of relations with the idea that the work of art is a totality that constitutes its own finality, and that in this it is like nature, a created and self-creating being. For Moritz, the beauty of internal organization appears when it is recognized that there is no external finality: "where an object lacks an external use or end, this must be sought in the object itself, if it should awaken pleasure in me; or, I must *find so much finality in the isolated parts of this object, that I forget to ask, what exactly is the whole thing for?*"[15] Although here Moritz emphasizes the parts rather than the whole, the lack of external finality identifies the aesthetic object with the organon, the natural being or nature itself. This kind of identification enabled the romantics to redefine the imitation of nature as a mimesis of process rather than of objects or forms. The proposition that "art should imitate nature," wrote A. W. Schlegel in his *Lessons on Art and Literature*, "means in effect that art should create like nature in an autonomous manner, being organized and organizing, to form living works that are not moved by a foreign mechanism, something like a pendulum clock, but by a force residing in themselves, like the solar system, and that return to themselves in a completed manner."[16] The relational character of art is no longer likened to artifice or device, as it had been for Diderot, but to the autonomy of natural systems.

With these changes in the notions of finality and imitation, the or-

[15]Moritz, "Versuch einer Vereinigung aller schönen Künste und Wissenschaften unter dem Begriff des *in sich selbst Vollendeten,*" *Schriften zur Ästhetik und Poetik*, ed. H. J. Schrimpf (Tübingen, 1962), 3–9. On the position of Moritz, see Tzvetan Todorov, *Théories du symbole* (Paris, 1977), 179–197.

[16]Schlegel, *Die Kunstlehre*, in *Kritische Schriften und Briefe*, (Stuttgart, 1963), II, 91.

ganism replaced the machine as a positive conceptual model of complexity and organization. The valorization of the organism by the early German romantics cannot be separated from their rejection of that great Enlightenment conceptual model, the machine. In the eighteenth century (and still in the early nineteenth century in France) machines and in particular clocks had served as ideal figures of organization, rationality, complexity, but the romantic machine was to be, in Judith Schlanger's words, "oppressive, sterile, artificial, and dead."[17] The new organic comparisons of the romantics reflected an ideal of freedom, of life, of self-contained and self-producing finality. Philosophy, language, religion, and art could henceforth be theorized on the organic model, understood either as individual organisms or as the organically productive totality of nature itself. A. W. Schlegel's reference to the solar system shows that the romantic concept of organicity was by no means limited to or dependent on the biological as such. Sometimes the living organism is directly invoked, sometimes not. More important than a specific disciplinary or scientific reference are the aspirations and formal intuitions embodied in the concept of organicity.

Schelling's statement from the introduction to his *Philosophy of Art* is in this respect characteristic: "If it interests us to investigate as far as possible the structure, the internal dispositions, the relations and the intrications of a plant or of an organic being in general, how much more should we be tempted to know these same intrications and relations in these plants, considerably more organized and intertwined with themselves, that we call works of Art."[18] Here the organicity of the work of art motivates and justifies an interest in the complexity of its harmonies and relations. This is more than a heuristic comparison, for the work of art is said to be in fact more organic than the organism itself. The study of art would thus lead us into a space of autonomous and infinite "relationality." A similar interdependence of autonomy and inner relation is evoked by a political comparison in one of Friedrich Schlegel's fragments: "Poetry is republican speech: a speech which is its own law and end unto itself, and in which all the parts are free citizens and have the right to vote [*mitstimmen dürfen*]."[19] Poetry is simply speech in its autonomous and self-legislating mode, and this mode realizes to a maximum the possible relations between the elements of

---

[17]Schlanger, *Les Métaphores de l'organisme* (Paris, 1971), p. 59; cf. p. 121.
[18]Schelling, *Sämmtliche Werke* (Stuttgart, 1859), part I, vol. v, p. 358.
[19]*Friedrich Schlegel's* Lucinde *and the Fragments*, 150 (Critical Fragment 65).

speech. Rather than being defined by its seriousness, its contents, the prestige of its practitioners, or by anything other than itself, literature could henceforth be specified by its relation to its own process of production, by its privileged link to creation itself. The justly famous *Athenaeum* Fragment 116 outlines for romantic poetry a theoretical mission of creation beyond all finite theory:

> The romantic kind of poetry is still in the state of becoming; that, in fact, is its real essence: that it should forever be becoming and never be perfected. It can be exhausted by no theory and only a divinatory criticism would dare try to characterize its ideal. It alone is infinite, just as it alone is free; and it recognizes as its first commandment that the will of the poet can tolerate no law above itself. The romantic kind of poetry is the only one that is more than a kind, that is, as it were, poetry itself: for in a certain sense all poetry is or should be romantic.[20]

In the words of Lacoue-Labarthe and Nancy, "romanticism is . . . *theory itself as literature* or, what is really the same thing, literature producing itself as it produces its own theory."[21] Romantic poetry was to be the genre of genres, the poetry of poiesis itself.

The concept of the organic work of art, still invoked complacently by many a critic and student of literature, has a major disadvantage: no arguments can justify the assimilation of a class of objects produced by living organisms to the status of organisms themselves. Theories of the organic text confuse and mystify those who accept them uncritically, because they attribute to the literary work faculties of organization so absolute as to be already questionable with respect to biological objects and simply inapplicable to cultural ones. Nonetheless, as was noted in Chapter 3, our modern literary formalisms spring from the romantic concept of literary autonomy, which was inseparable from the organic metaphor. The Russian formalists, in emphasizing the systemic and organized character of literary language, were pursuing the linguistic consequences of the romantic doctrine that the work produces and contains its own finality. Jakobson, for one, openly acknowledged the influence of Novalis and Mallarmé on his own early aesthetic thought. Doubtless more important than direct intellectual influences, however, was the fact that the literary situation that the formalists set out to describe rigorously was itself a part and product of romanticism: in defining "literature," they were setting out to redefine an

---

[20]*Friedrich Schlegel's* Lucinde *and the Fragments*, 175–176.
[21]Lacoue-Labarthe and Nancy, *L'Absolu littéraire*, 22.

object already defined implicitly by the doctrines and practices of romanticism in the large sense. This does not of course imply that literary formalism is the same thing as romanticism, but simply that the cultural space defined by the latter gives rise to and provides the point of departure for the former. *Literary formalists attempt to make the organization of the autonomous text into an object of inquiry on its own terms*, rather than considering this organization to be synonymous with an ineffable, undefinable organicity. As Todorov has recently written, "the somewhat abstract and hollow formula of the Romantics according to which the work of art should be perceived in itself, and not in view of anything else, will become not a doctrinal affirmation but a practical reason that will push the Formalists . . . to perceive the work itself, to discover that it has a rhythm, which one must learn to describe; narrators, whom one must know how to differentiate; narrative devices, universal and yet infinitely varied."[22] In trying to specify the organizational principles of something whose organicity was, previously, merely asserted, the formalists were not alone: the history of modern biology is in a sense the history of attempts to give specific content to the early nineteenth-century assertions concerning the organized character of living beings. For literary formalism and modern biology, organization must cease to be a transcendental and become a terrain in which operational explanations are produced.

There is an undeniable relation between the literary interpretation of the biocybernetic schema of organization from noise and the romantic postulate of the organicity of a work of art, although this relation cannot be reduced to an identity. The critical filiation from romantic doctrine to formalist method and practice implies that modern theorization of literary autonomy and self-organization exists only within the cultural configuration put in place by its romantic, organicist precursors. Lotman's formal conjectures concerning the reader's approach to the disorderly and the nonunderstood in a literary work are themselves a formalistic elaboration of the consequences of treating literature as an autonomous organon. If, for the reader, there can be no extrasystemic facts in the literary text, it is because the systematicity of the text has already been postulated as a limitless process of organizational concatenation. In other words the organicity of the text has become not a property of its verbal architecture as such but a convention

[22]Todorov, *Critique de la critique*, 33.

governing its reading and thereby determining its function as a dynamic system. Lotman's use of information-theoretic concepts should not mask the fact that he is producing a formalist projection of the romantic divinization of literature as literary form, that he is describing how this cultural concept of the work of art actually operates as an organizational principle of reading. The same must be said a fortiori for my own argument in this book, at least insofar as I have proposed the formalism of self-organization from noise as an explanation for the production of meaning out of the polysystemic complexity of a text. As a literary explanation, the process of self-organization from noise belongs to the closure of romanticism, at once a revalorization and a demystification of the romantic project of a singular and creative status for literature. A revalorization: the idea that noise and the incomprehensible can in literature become a springboard to meaning at once depends on and modernizes the ideal of poetry's autonomous creative power. And, at the same time, a demystification: the informational approach locates the creative potential of literature not in lifelike properties of the work itself but rather in a formal mechanism that, although perhaps privileged by the conventions of literature and the study of organisms, cannot be limited to or even identified with the poetic, the organic, or even the autonomous.

Todorov has suggested that criticism is now emerging from the era of romanticism, precisely because the doctrine of literary autonomy is being discredited and abandoned. Poststructuralist criticism, in this view, has moved away from a focus on literariness to a consideration of literature in the contexts of other kinds of discourse: "It would thus seem that it is already possible to see the end of the romantic episode, during which the autonomy of literature has been postulated, and the return of the previous conception, according to which the characteristics of literature are part of the objects of various theoretical disciplines without *constituting* that of any one."[23] It is perhaps attractive to think that literary autonomy, and with it romanticism, can be left behind this easily, through a change in critical understanding. But the downfall of an autonomous *discipline* of literary study does not imply that we cease to identify literary texts as distinct and autonomous. As long as we give cultural status to literature as a particular mode of dis-

[23]Tzvetan Todorov, "Evolution de la théorie littéraire," *Encyclopédie Universalis* 17 (1980), 139.

course, as long, in other words, as we can write phrases like "the characteristics of literature," we remain to a degree within the conventions according to which we identify the literary text as a unity and react to it by treating it at least to a degree as an autonomous object. The peculiarity of literature's status in our late romantic era is that while we cannot give up the convention of autonomy—that is, the fact that as observers we identify the text as a unity—we no longer believe that autonomy suffices as an explanation of the text's existence and form. Our understanding no longer coincides with the conventions to which the object we try to understand owes its existence. We cannot get along with or without literary autonomy. As critics and readers, we move from moments when we must treat the literary text as autonomous to moments when we must not.

Autopoiesis and Autonomy

The supposition of self-organization from noise in literature depends to a degree on the romantic notion of literary autonomy, even as it undermines that notion in its traditional form. But romantic autonomy inself can now be reread in the context of contemporary, nonvitalistic and nonteleological approaches to the autonomy of organisms. The problem of autonomy is at the center of the Santiago school of theoretical biology, notably in the work of Humberto Maturana and Francisco Varela.[24] Strongly influenced at the outset by the work of Heinz Von Foerster and the Biological Computer Laboratory at the University of Illinois, Maturana and Varela have since the late 1960s elaborated a formal theory of living organization as *autopoiesis*, self-production or self-creation. Their starting point is the autonomy of the organism, and their project is the description of living organization in strictly formal, logical terms that imply neither the reduction of biology to physics or chemistry nor the postulation of vital properties unique to living matter. They locate the specificity of the living in a kind of *organization* that can be realized in physicochemical *structures* but that is not reducible to them.

[24]See Maturana and Varela, *The Tree of Knowledge: The Biological Roots of Human Understanding* (Boston, 1987), published too recently to be included in my discussion. Varela's major work, on which I rely most heavily here, is *Principles of Biological Autonomy* (New York, 1979). Two important early papers can be found in Maturana and Varela, *Autopoiesis and Cognition: The Realization of the Living*, Boston Studies in the Philosophy of Science, 42 (Dordrecht, Holland, 1980).

Maturana and Varela do not view their work as a theory that would endeavor to transcend the perspective of ordinary scientific work, but as an exercise in experimental epistemology, a particular kind of cognitive and conceptual shift that can be used in the design of experiments, notably in perception, cognition, and immunology. In all of these fields, the traditional approach has been representational: the organism has been assumed to acquire a picture or map of its surroundings, an adequate representation of bacterial or viral invaders. The nervous system and the immune system, in this view, can be defined by the way in which they process and transform inputs. But for an autonomous organism, Varela argues, there are no inputs and outputs, only the structural changes of a system modifying itself in the face of perturbations from its environment in such a way as to maintain its organizational identity. Thinking in terms of representation, of inputs and outputs, is appropriate for the design and control of artificial systems but inappropriate for the investigation of autonomous systems, where information must be redefined in terms of autonomy.

Students or observers of systems, Varela argues, must make an epistemological choice. Do we consider a given system as a "black box" to be defined by the relations between its inputs and its outputs? Or do we consider it as an organization having its own relational properties, changing in conformity with its own laws in the face of environmental perturbations that cannot be considered instructions to the system? There are, of course, systems for which one or the other approach seems preferable, and many systems for which both are possible. But the former approach, in effect that of the designer or control engineer, has long been culturally dominant in the West and has become more so with the development of computers and the sciences of information. Varela even refers to this stance as the "gestalt of the computer."

Varela notes that in many cases it may be desirable or necessary to shift from the control to the autonomy perspective, and argues that this change of epistemological stance has far-reaching implications:

> The effect of considering a system's environment as a source of perturbations and compensations, rather than inputs and outputs, is far from trivial. In the latter, control-based formulation, interactions from the environment are instructive, constitute part of the definition of the system's organization, and determine the course of transformation. In the autonomy interpretation, the environment is seen as a source of perturbations independent of the definition of the system's organization, and

hence intrinsically noninstructive; they can trigger, but not determine, the course of transformation. . . . In one case an input (partly) specifies the system's organization and structure: in the other case a perturbation participates in the transformation of an independently specified system.[25]

To consider a system as having inputs and outputs is to identify it as organizationally open, since its organization is defined by something outside itself. The autonomous system, for which environmental activity constitutes perturbations and not instructions, can be considered organizationally closed.[26] The shift from an input/output perspective to organizational closure thus implies a redefinition of what is information with respect to a given system.

Information, in the representationist perspective, is defined independently of the system; consequently, the system's own state, its own informational configuration, is considered as a representation of its environment, as a map of its input. "Information, for the computer gestalt, becomes unequivocally what is *represented*, and what is represented is a *correspondence* between symbolic units in one structure and symbolic units in another structure."[27] Varela's own biological research concerning the immune and nervous systems suggested to him that the representationist model of input/process/output is limiting and unworkable when applied to these highly developed instances of biological cognition. The immune and nervous systems are better understood, for him, as mechanisms of structural plasticity for maintaining organization and autonomy in the face of perturbations than as mechanisms for representing something outside the organism.[28] The need to take the autonomy of natural systems into account thus implies not that we abandon in all cases the representationist perspective but that we recognize that the autonomy perspective exists as well. The epistemological stances of representation and autonomy must complement one another. In the autonomy perspective, the interpretation of infor-

[25]Varela, *Principles of Biological Autonomy*, 261–262.

[26]An organizationally closed system, it should be noted, may be thermodynamically open, receiving energy from and increasing the entropy of its environment without being organizationally specified by anything outside itself. For Varela, this kind of organizational closure is characteristic of living systems.

[27]Varela, *Principles of Biological Autonomy*, xiv.

[28]For a clear and nontechnical discussion of the advantages of the autonomy perspective in understanding the perception of color, see Francisco Varela, "Living Ways of Sense-Making," in *Disorder and Order*, ed. Livingston, 208–224.

mation changes; no longer dependent on correspondence with something outside a system, it becomes a matter of internal complexity and consistency: "by discussing autonomy, we are led to a reexamination of the notion of information itself: away from instruction, to the way in which information is constructed; away from representation, to the way in which adequate behavior reflects viability in the system's functioning rather than a correspondence with a given state of affairs."[29] The meaning of the concept "information" changes because in shifting from a control to an autonomy perspective we are shifting our attention, and our definition of "system," from one phenomenal domain to another. In studying vision in frogs, for example, one can define the system as the frog, or as the frog plus environment. Since the experimenter can observe the frog's environment just as he can observe the frog, it is quite natural to adopt the representationist perspective and see the frog's vision as establishing correspondences between its environment and the animal's internal state. But the frog does not share the experimenter's perspective; its concern is the maintenance of its own viability in a complex and changing world, not the construction of representations. The representationist approach to perception sees the frog as a machine for receiving and responding to instructions from its environment, not as a machine for being a frog.

It is not hard to see that most literary critical stances can be situated with respect to the alternative between control and autonomy perspectives. Literary historical, biographical, psychological, or sociological approaches take the text to be in some sense a vehicle of transmission, something to be described as a representation of a reality external to it. New Critical and structural approaches, on the other hand, consider the text as referring ultimately to itself, as an autonomous entity whose organizational principles must be sought within it and not in some external, referential domain. Each critical theory in effect defines a different phenomenal domain, interprets literature as a different kind of system.

It is worth noting this parallel between the issues of system definition and perspective that divide literary scholars and those that divide cognitive scientists and biologists. But the implications of Varela's and Maturana's work for literary studies, and especially for our understanding of the romantic notion of the literary text's autonomous

---

[29]Varela, *Principles of Biological Autonomy*, xii.

organicity, go far deeper. The problems of phenomenal domain, of autonomy versus control, are the starting points of their theory of living organization, not its substance. In *Principles of Biological Autonomy* (1979), Varela puts forward not an empirically based characterization of living organisms but an axiomatic theory of *autopoietic systems*, systems that are both autonomous and continuously self-producing or self-creating. Autopoietic systems, for Varela, "produce their own identity: they distinguish themselves from their background. Hence the name *autopoietic*: from the Greek αὐτός = self, and ποιειν = to produce."[30] Varela's concept of the autopoietic system makes possible a distinction between the autopoietic and the autonomous, or between, on the one hand, living systems, and on the other hand, systems that share some organizational characteristics with living systems. An autopoietic system consists of a network of processes that produce a set of components. The relation of components and processes is recursive: the network of processes produces the components, which constitute the system's topological identity in some space and realize or maintain the network of processes.

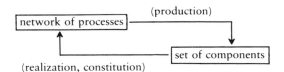

The system's real, topological existence as an identity in some space depends on its components, while the existence and transformation of the components depends on the network of productive processes realized by, but never reducible to, the components.

Varela claims that autopoiesis in physical systems is necessary and sufficient to characterize living systems. Living systems are physical autopoietic systems, and physical autopoietic systems are living systems. In point of fact, the only known physical referent for the formal definition of component production in autopoiesis is the chemical production that takes place in living systems: one cannot say that animal or human societies, or particular human institutions, are autopoietic and thus living. But as a definition of the living, the importance of the autopoiesis definition lies in its lack of dependence on empirical or in-

---

[30]Varela, *Principles of Biological Autonomy*, 13.

tuitive characterizations of life. If living systems can be defined formally, then it should be possible, without recourse to inadequately
understood and often misleading metaphors or analogies, to speak
meaningfully of other systems that share certain of their formal characteristics.

In particular, Varela proposes that autopoietic systems are a specific instance of a more general class: autonomous systems. Autonomous systems need not be self-producing, but they are, like autopoietic
systems, self-defining. The autonomous system's unity as properly defined by the observer must coincide with the system's unity as defined
by its own form and processes. Autonomous systems define their own
organizational unity, but this unity need not imply a topological bound-
ary, and autonomous systems do not necessarily produce the components of which they are made up, as autopoietic systems must.

The formal distinction between autopoiesis and autonomy offers a
framework for considering organizational and structural parallels between living and nonliving systems without confusing or amalgamat-
ing the two. "I am saying," writes Varela, "that we can take the lessons
offered by the autonomy of living systems and convert them into an
operational characterization of *autonomy in general*, living or otherwise."[31] This program differs fundamentally from that of biologizing
the study of society or culture, for it locates the conceptual interest of
biological objects for these other fields of inquiry neither in their naturalness or vitality nor in a potential reduction of other phenomena to
their properties, but rather in their status as compelling examples of
autonomy, of a set of organizational characteristics found in, but not
unique to, living systems. Of course the organic metaphor likewise implied that living beings were compelling examples of autonomy, but
the metaphor did not contain the means of distinguishing between the
living and the nonliving, and was generally founded on a transcendental rather than an operational understanding of organic autonomy.
The autonomy of living systems (autopoiesis) can be seen in Varela's
theory as a particular kind of autonomy, noteworthy as an example
but not to be confused with the characteristics of autonomous systems
in general.

The phenomenal domain in which we recognize an autonomous
system is identical to the domain constituted by the system's own mu-

---

[31]Varela, *Principles of Biological Autonomy*, 55.

tually dependent processes. In other words, what we say such a system is corresponds to what the system itself says it is. Because of the circular and interdependent relation of processes in its networks, the system "attains coherence through its own operation, and not through the intervention of contingencies from the environment."[32] This is what is meant by "organizational closure." An organizationally closed system subordinates its changes, in the face of external events, to the maintenance of its own identity. Like a thermostat controlling a heating system, it is a homeostatic system, but whereas the thermostat seeks to maintain a condition defined by external reference (the user's temperature setting), the autonomous system has no external source of reference: the invariant that it seeks to maintain is its own organizational identity.

If a human institution such as a university exhibits organizational closure, then its changes in the face of events outside it will be determined by the imperative of maintaining the institution's identity within the limits of coherence compatible with its organization. It will not respond, as such, to external events: for an organizationally closed system there are no inputs or outputs but, rather, perturbations and changes of state or structure compatible with the system's organizational identity. Of course, nothing prevents an autonomous system from functioning, within a context larger than itself and to which it has become coupled by recursive interactions, as an *allonomous* system, that is, as an instrument or component definable within a larger system by its inputs and outputs. For example, the hypothesis of a university's organizational closure does not rule out the possibility that the same university provides educational services to a sector of society. But to the extent that the university defines itself as an organizational unity, the autonomy perspective will be necessary to describe its phenomenology completely—to explain, for instance, why what the university does to maintain its identity may not always coincide with what the users of the university would have it do to maximize its usefulness to them. These two kinds of description of the institution—as autonomous or as allonomous system—are not incompatible; they simply pertain to different phenomenal domains, one of which is identical with the system as it defines and maintains itself through its operation, the other amounting to a larger system such as the society within which

[32]Varela, *Principles of Biological Autonomy*, 55.

the autonomous institution exists and functions as an allonomous institution.

Similarly, as was noted above, literary texts are sometimes treated as autonomous, sometimes as allonomous components of a larger system that may in general be characterized as a literary text plus a particular kind of context. The alternative, however, is far from exclusive in practice; most literary criticism actually written adopts both the control and autonomy perspectives at different moments. This should be no surprise, given Varela's observation that an autonomous system can function, in some larger context, as an allonomous one. There is no consensus in literary studies as to whether the proper object of study is the text itself or the text in some given context, so it is quite naturally treated as sometimes autonomous, sometimes not. It may also be that literary texts are objects or systems exhibiting some features of organizational closure without being fully autonomous; in this case the recourse to different perspectives in the study of literature would be one of its essential features, determined by the nature of its object. To the extent that a literary text is organizationally closed, that is, defines itself as a unity through its internal relations, then this self-definition should coincide with our identification of it as a unity. We may of course choose to place this unity in the context of larger systems, but without the autonomy perspective our understanding of it will be incomplete.

How does the theory of autonomous and autopoietic systems account for the function of an autonomous system as an allonomous part of a larger system? In other words, how do systems whose intrinsic behavior is to maintain their own organization in the face of perturbations come to function in ways that can be described by inputs and outputs? Obviously there are observable regularities between autonomous systems and their environments, regularities that give rise to and confirm the representationist perspective. An observer can describe the correspondence between what goes on inside a frog's brain and the frog's visual environment; the sounds emitted by two biologically autonomous human individuals can be understood as communication and conversation.

For Varela and Maturana, these phenomena are best described as instances of *structural coupling*. Structure, in their terminology, is the changeable form in which autonomous systems realize their invariant organization. Autonomous organization, in other words, permits a variety of structures and thus a variety of possible developmental paths for the organism. The actual realization of one path as opposed to others—ontogeny—is codetermined by the system and its surroundings; it is simply the way in which organization is preserved in a manner consistent with the environment. And most environments are not pure noise or random perturbation: they present regularities and redundancies. Two autonomous systems may be parts of each other's environment. In this case, as Maturana writes, "the structurally plastic changes of state of one system become perturbations for the other, and vice versa, in a manner that establishes an interlocked, mutually structuring, mutually triggering domain" of states and behavior.[33] Relations of input/output, of representation, between autonomous systems and their environments, and in particular between more than one autonomous system, are not essential or eternal; rather they are the outcome of histories of mutual interactions. An observer can, of course, describe them synchronically, as relations of representation or communication, but this kind of description belongs to the observer's phenomenal domain, not to that of the individual autonomous system.

Language, in this view, is the product of a particular kind of structural coupling.[34] An established linguistic domain can be viewed synchronically by an observer as a system of communication, a means of exchanging information. But this communicative function is attained only as the end product of a history of behavior, a conversation, by which individuals participate in the emergence of a higher-level autonomous system. The entire tradition of which language is the current state is such a conversation or autonomous system. Any natural language can be considered an autonomous system: one that has defined and continues to define itself in the course of the recursive interactions that are its use by those who speak it. But language can also be taken, at any given moment, to be an allonomous system, serving a purpose

---

[33]Humberto Maturana, "Biology of Language: The Epistemology of Reality," in *Psychology and Biology of Language and Thought*, ed. G. Miller and E. Lenneberg (New York, 1978), 35–36. Cf. Varela, *Principles of Biological Autonomy*, 32–33.

[34]Varela writes: "[when] two (or more) living systems become sources of mutual perturbations for each other . . . they can recurrently generate a domain of stabilized interactions which an observer can describe in semantic terms. Such linguistic domains occur in multifarious ways in nature (e.g., bee dance, group role in primates, courtship sequences). A language proper arises when (and only when) the linguistic domain can make distinctions within the linguistic domain itself, i.e., when a recursive capacity appears" ("Experimental Epistemology," *Cognition et complexité*, 114).

outside itself: this occurs whenever its speaking subjects attempt to use it as an instrument for transmitting, receiving, exchanging information.[35] A language is far more complex than what any of its individual users can do with it, far more complex than any communication system that someone might set out to *design*.[36]

It is precisely this autonomous complexity of language, never fully present to any of its users, always excessive or lacking with respect to the communicative use they try to make of it, that makes it possible (and necessary) to speak of noise in verbal texts, and a fortiori in literary texts. The uncertainties of literary language arise out of the properties of language itself as system. Language's unreliability as a communicative instrument is due to ambiguities, overlappings, and uncertainties that occur because it has its own, internal, self-referential laws, its own features, which are not those of the message one seeks to send through it. They are rather the features of an autonomous system that is the accretion of all the other messages that have been sent within it. These internal, codependent relations within language are exploited in the literary text, whose author, as Julien Gracq has observed, always derives some part of his inspiration from, or is guided in his choices by, the language itself.[37]

The Artificial Autonomy of Literature

But can we call the literary text itself autonomous? Major components of our critical tradition already do so, most often identifying autonomy and organicity. If our excursion into the theoretical biology of the Santiago school is to yield insight into this question, we must consider the distinction between autonomy and autopoiesis, the dynamic or systemic interpretation of autonomy, and the autonomous character of the conversation(s) that make up language.

The distinction between autonomy and autopoiesis enables us to distinguish autonomous systems that produce the components through

[35]Varela, *Principles of Biological Autonomy*, 268–270; Maturana, "Biology of Language," 54–55.

[36]The lack of deep complexity is precisely what makes computer languages seem "unnatural" and unfit for a wide range of human uses; conversely, computer languages are designed because natural languages are far too difficult for our machines to handle.

[37]See Gracq's reflexions on writing and language in *En lisant, en écrivant* (Paris, 1981), 157–167.

which they are realized and those that do not. Autonomy is a necessary but not sufficient condition for autopoiesis; component production is not necessary for autonomy. The understanding of autonomy as a formal property characteristic of living systems but insufficient to define them can contribute to a reevaluation of the cultural use of organic metaphors in such phrases as "the organic unity of the text." Poems are relational structures realized in words, but poems do not make the words. Nothing really justifies calling the literary text a living organism, though perhaps Varela's very choice of the term *autopoiesis* gives us an idea of why the metaphor has been so seductive and powerful: it seemed intuitively fitting to the romantics to identify the *autonomy* of literary works with their production or creation, their *poiesis*. But to call the text an organism on this basis is a category mistake, and indeed one aspect of romantic theorization points to the error: the identification of literary poiesis not with the completed work but with the fragment. The fragmentary text points to infinite imperfection, to an incommensurability between the creative process and the self-sufficient work.

By separating the organizational properties of autonomy from the component-producing properties of autopoiesis, we can pursue the idea that the literary text may have formal characteristics in some way comparable to those of living organisms and yet not be organic. Similarly, the text may exhibit some characteristics of organizational closure and not be fully autonomous. We need to consider not so much the stark alternative of literature as autonomous or allonomous but, rather, the nature of its apparent organizational closure, the ways in which it exhibits properties of autonomous systems.

The literary text would appear to be an autonomous object whose specificity arises out of the use it makes of its medium, language, insofar as the latter is also an autonomous system. And yet what in the literary text can legitimately be considered autonomous? This question has no easy answer, for the notion of the autonomy of a verbal artifact quickly reveals itself to be a nebulous ideal or intuition and not an operational description. It is not clear exactly what system should be taken as a candidate for autonomy. A first possible answer would be roughly that of the New Criticism: the text itself, as "verbal icon," would be the autonomous thing. This conception of autonomy appeals to our representations of the book as a work of art, of the text as words against the whiteness of pages. It satisfies the intuitive notions we may harbor of a parallel between literature and the plastic arts, since it confers on the text an existential uniqueness and independence similar to that of the artwork as self-contained object of contemplation. Still, in the context of Varela's definition of an autonomous system, the literary text as such turns out to be an inappropriate object, because by itself it is static, a fixed structure and not an organization of processes. To be considered as a possible autonomous system, the text must be understood dynamically and not statically. This is possible, but it implies a choice of moments: obviously excluded are those moments when the text lies unread, inert, in some new or dusty tome, but there remain the only moments that really matter, those of writing and reading. When it is coming into being in a dynamic interaction of author, language, and tradition, when it is being assimilated by the mind of its reader or the collective mind of its culture, then the literary text is a possible autonomous system. In these two cases, the boundaries of the system that might be considered autonomous are different, and in neither case are they identical to those of the verbal text as a static arrangement of words or a performed sequence of sounds.

When the text is written, an autonomous system arises as the organization of what has already begun to be written becomes an input to the processes that determine what will be written next. In other words, whatever initial impulsion or project there may have been of "something to say" becomes complicated by the internal laws of the form in which something is now being said, so that the text's composition, the ongoing decisions as to what shall be part of it and what shall not, begins to be determined not by external factors (such as what the author "had to say") but by the internal features of what is already being said. Obviously the author's mind, language, and literary and nonliterary cultural traditions are all systems from which the autonomous process of self-definition and composition draws material, even once it is under way, but the determination of which elements of these sources become part of the emerging verbal structure depends increasingly on that structure's own organization, on its properties, potentialities, and exclusions. At some point, can the composition of a verbal text be said to be entirely self-determined, turned back upon itself so as to take up and assume within its autonomous organization any initial, allonomous intention of meaning? The finitude of minds and works suggests that it cannot. The process never becomes completely autonomous. In works such as Balzac's *Le Chef-d'oeuvre inconnu*, the romantics pointed to this incomplete autonomy by opposing creative genius to finished work, an opposition implied as well in the promotion of the fragment to the status of a genre. Although literary creation doubtless involves a concatenation of processes similar to what is at work in autonomous systems, it is most unlikely that this process ever attains organizational closure, unlikely that the composition of a text can ever be determined entirely by the laws arising within its own composition.

Quite different is the question of the text's possible autonomy as it is being read. The determination of the text's limits, of what is and is not the text, is given to the reader by virtue of the fact that she experiences it as a text; it arrives, as it were, as an allonomous object, as something to be made use of by the reader. Nonetheless, as the reader reads, or in other words as she makes the text part of a process or processes in her own mind, she must in effect elaborate the relations of its organization, must have some working knowledge, explicit or not, of how elements of the text are related, of how they operate to produce meaning. This means that the reader will reach a position from which she may experience the text as either autonomous, subject to its own laws, or allonomous, bearing the mark of some external principle—or simply of incomplete or imperfect autonomy—in its organization. Perhaps the reader makes no decision as to which of these possibilities best describes the text at hand but simply assumes, in accordance with romantic expectations, that since it is a poetic text it is autonomous and thus that its features should be read as such, as manifestations or consequences of its own organization. In this case the text's autonomy functions as an interpretive convention, operative whether the autonomy in question is fictive or real. It is this type of "autonomy convention," as has been noted, that leads the reader to consider what appears to be disorderly and unintegrable as part of the not yet fully understood organization of meaning within a text. The likelihood remains, however, that at some point this process of organization of meaning from noise will come to a halt, falsifying the autonomy hypothesis: contrary to expectation, something incomprehensible in the text is there for reasons irreducible to any internal principles of textual organization, and thus cannot lead to the discovery of a new level of coherence or meaning that could be said to belong to the text.

One may very well ask how the consideration of the literary text as a locus of self-organization from noise fits into the autonomy-control distinction. It appears that the perspective initially adopted is one of control, since the literary text is treated as a transmission channel, as a process having inputs and outputs. When so considered, the literary text inevitably appears to be a faulty transmission system, a black box whose input can never be recovered from its output. This amounts to saying that what is asserted by deconstructive critics concerning the literary text as an impossible vehicle of representation, or of transmission of a theme or of a state of consciousness, pertains specifically to a representationist context in which information is defined as something external that the system transmits. It is in this context alone that the insights of deconstruction, often wrongly assumed to be some sort of general critical nihilism, can be said to have negative implications for literary studies.

But if we introduce the idea of organization from noise, we introduce at the same time a shift in context. The initial shift, as explained in Chapter 3, was not directly toward consideration of the text as autonomous object but rather toward our taking the text, with its unreliable transmission of information, to be a component of a larger system, that of cultural circulation, in which what seemed like a dysfunction at a first level of communication would turn out to be a positive element contributing to the complexity of the larger system. In this sense we are still considering literature as a transmission channel and thus as an allonomous system, but we have shifted its context from one of simple transmission to one of cultural circulation and creation in general; we have moved, in other words, from a context in which literature is a faulty component to one in which it is, at least potentially, an optimally effective one. We are considering literature as part of a cultural conversation that may itself be autonomous, for which literature is perturbation and not input. This shift would be the only one implied by the self-organization perspective, if we were to restrict the term *noise* to what is ultimately ambiguous or indeterminate in the literary text after all the rational resources of reading have been exhausted. But as we have seen, it is also possible to invoke the concept of organization from noise at a level internal to the text and its reading: the reader of literature encounters elements that cannot initially be decoded or integrated and that thus appear as noise—as differences that don't make a difference, to negate Gregory Bateson's famous definition of information. But rather than dismissing them as noise, that is, as being external to an allonomous, communicative system, the reader makes a particular kind of assumption about them, namely that they indicate the presence of as yet unknown codes or levels of meaning at work *within* the text. As we saw in Chapter 3, this assumption amounts to a postulate of textual autonomy: what cannot be integrated under a known law of the text is presumed to be operating under another law, as yet unknown, of the same text. In other words, what is in the text is assumed to be there in conformity to an organization that belongs to the text and not for reasons externally caused or defined. This assumption, which for Lotman characterizes the reading of the artistic text, does not in and of itself prove that such a text is truly an autonomous object, but simply asserts that part of its culturally defined role is to persuade its reader to treat it as autonomous and experience it accordingly. The implications for the question of literature's place in the autonomy-control perspectives are nevertheless considerable: the text appears to be an object that solicits its treatment as autonomous by the reader.

The literary text, at the moments of its production and assimilation, is thus an *artificially autonomous object*, conceptually comprehensible only if one remembers both the project of autonomy with which it is invested and the fact that its putative autonomy remains the effect of precisely this external project. An artificially autonomous object cannot be an absolute, cannot become the object of a theology of autonomy, and yet it can be said to exhibit properties of autonomy and, more important, to contain the fiction of its own autonomy as one of its central organizational principles. In its production, the literary text is formed by the intersecting action of several systems, which may themselves be autonomous: its author's mind, its language, its society, cultural and genre traditions. But it cannot be assumed that the creative process out of which the text arises ever attains complete autonomy. The work may become part of an autonomous system at a very general level, say, a given culture, but nothing in the theory of autonomous systems authorizes us to take the individual work as itself wholly defined or delimited by the interactions of its own laws and processes. In its assimilation, the literary text presents itself to the reader as an allonomous object, defined by its place within a larger cultural totality and not by its own features. Yet at the same time, it is an object from which the reader may well derive the most information by treating it as autonomous, by understanding it and interpreting it insofar as possible in accordance with its own unique internal characteristics. Literature's effective function as an allonomous object, in other words, would depend on the convention according to which it is treated, provisionally at least, as autonomous.

The artificiality of textual autonomy should not be taken as a defect, as a mark of falsehood or imperfection, but simply as an aspect of how literary texts can be understood in the context of informational systems. Only if one subscribes to the poem-as-organism fallacy will the artificiality of textual autonomy appear to be a failing. The romantic, organic metaphor has long masked the fact that whereas the literary text may have *some* of the formal features of biological systems, it cannot have all of them, and it cannot in any case escape being created and used as an allonomous object by systems not itself. The organic comparison also leads us to isolate texts as objects of study, to cut them off from their sociopolitical and historical contexts. It was the romantics' defensive response to the dominant ideology of their day, but is itself ideological as well, for with it the romantics and their followers attempted to pass of as natural and universal what was actually their own conception of literature: an ineffable, independent, infinite cultural totality, a domain of absolute creativity. That doctrine remains powerful and functional: far from being a descriptive discourse that could simply be refuted and replaced by another, it remains an essential factor in the way the institutions of literature continue to operate. To recognize the artificial status of the text's autonomy is not to topple literature from its romantic pedestal but simply to call into question the naturalness of its lofty position. We still live in the era of "the literary absolute": our task is not to reject or abandon the bases of this era but to understand them from within, to shake ourselves from the habit of either taking them for granted or revering them as museum pieces. Of course, this process of defamiliarizing romantic literary ideology is a part of cultural change, part of a displacement that will doubtless one day make romantic assumptions about literature as inoperative as neoclassical ones have been in our own time. Our theoretical modernity is both directed against the naiveties of romanticism and situated within a conceptual space that cannot yet exist apart from notions that we would question; nonetheless, our acts of translating and debunking participate in the unpredictable processes of change that will rearrange our conceptual horizons and one day make romanticism as much a thing of the past as neoclassicism is today.

It is perhaps inevitable that my use of concepts from the theory of information, and in particular my characterization of textual autonomy as incomplete and artificial, will trouble and even offend many who are devoted to the enjoyment and study of literature. Familiar notions are hard to revise, all the more so if they are broad in scope and generally implicit. In a very limited sense, the theory of literature outlined in the last two chapters is a move outside of deconstruction, insofar as it provides a way of describing processes by which what is disseminated may be taken up in a new bringing together, in a new production of meaning. One might expect such a theory to enrage deconstructionists and delight their tradition-minded detractors. But the latter possibility, at least, is unlikely, for the hypothesis of self-organization from noise in literature does not deny but, rather, assumes the most discomforting truths of deconstruction. The information-theoretic approach I am proposing suggests that the theory of literature advanced implicitly or explicitly under the rubric of deconstruction is not false, but is only part of the story. Deconstruction has thus far emphasized the negative moment, the destructive ambiguity of noise in communications channels. In suggesting that the literary text contains noise, that its autonomy is at best artificial and imperfect, I am asserting—in a different conceptual language—propositions that are equivalent to some of the ideas of deconstruction that have met the most resistance. Since at least the polemics surrounding deconstruction are well known, it is probably useful to comment briefly on this equivalence, on the conceptual relations between noise, autonomy, and deconstruction.

No one seriously denies that the literary text, considered as a vehicle of communication, is less than completely reliable. Those who defend, polemically, literature's fullness of meaning do so not on the grounds that literary language is a noiseless transmission channel but because of the organizational richness and unity of the text. The absolutely organized, autonomous nature of the text is taken to be capable of bringing together and unifying whatever may be dispersed or confused by the devices of literary language, considered individually. Since Moritz, literary mimesis has been associated with the organicity of the work, with the formal capacity to bring together what may seem disparate in a harmony unique to the artistic text. Romantic theorists and New Critics are thus in agreement with structuralist or deconstructionist critics in rejecting a positivist, literary historical approach that would identify mimesis with transcription of the real or that would claim that the literary text simply expresses or illustrates a meaning that precedes it, that is totally exterior to its own laws. The romantics and New Critics locate the authority of the text not in its mastery by an author considered as simply an external creator, but in the autonomous process of creation in which the author is not so much an empirical individual as an agent in a unique process of absolute organization and production. In preaching that critics must *submit themselves* to the text, must *serve* the text and above all not claim with respect to it a position of intellectual superiority, the opponents of deconstruction enthrone not the doctrines or extraliterary opinions of authors, but the authority of the autonomous process in which the author becomes the text's creator. Above all, they reinforce the ideological injunctions to treat knowledge as objective and to serve authority.

The deconstructive insight amounts to an unmasking of autonomy's incompleteness, a denial of the infinite self-coherence of the text. If the autonomy of the text were complete, then the only noise in it would be temporary, an epiphenomenon brought about by the reader's provisional ignorance of the text's higher-level codes: whatever instability or dispersion of meaning would arise from figural language, that is, from the *communicative* unreliability within literature, would be recovered, brought together by the marvelously complex organization of the text, necessarily adequate to the task of assuring its own coherence and ultimately a vehicle of superior communication. But at some point, there will be a fracture in the text's seamless, organic unity, a blind spot of the text to itself, and something will remain that is a contradiction or that cannot be decided. What is dispersed and disseminated in the recourse to language, and especially to figural language, cannot be completely retrieved. In our still-romantic age, this is perhaps the most troubling insight of deconstruction: the recognition of irreducible allonomy, heterogeneity, a mark of limitation or finitude, in the supposedly organic and absolute text.[38]

Common opinion identifies deconstruction with the dethroning of the author, with arrogant graduate students who imply that they know more about Henry James than did Henry James. Yet it is precisely because literary works are *artificial* autonomous objects, authored by fi-

---

[38]There is perhaps an analogy here to Gödel's theorem on the undecidability of propositions in certain formal, logicomathematical systems, an analogy that resides not in a formal equivalence but in the cultural import of deconstruction and of Gödel's theorem. The text, according to deconstruction, cannot be a closed, consistent, complete system; it cannot coincide perfectly with the development of its own axiomatic.

nite beings and not created by completely impersonal combinatory processes, that their autonomy is incomplete, that they are incapable of mastering their dissemination. To characterize texts as artificially and imperfectly autonomous is not to eliminate the role of the author but to deny the reader's or critic's submission to any instance of authority. This perspective leaves room neither for the authorial mastery of a communicative object nor for the authority of a textual coherence so complete that the reader's (infinite) task would be merely to receive its rich and multilayered meaning. If in literary communication there is an irreducible element of noise, then the reader's task does not end with reception, for reception is inherently flawed. What literature solicits of the reader is not simply reception but the active, independent, autonomous construction of meaning. Such a construction is situated not at the level of communication, not at a level at which it might still make sense to speak of authorial mastery or textual authority, but at a new level, no longer coinciding with the text as intention or as object of knowledge. This construction of meaning is surely a form of knowledge, but a form that is not identical with knowledge *of* the text. It exists in the irreversible time of reading and of the reader, not in the abolished time of convergence toward a text's unchanging truth. Constructed meaning is not a representation of what has already occurred but an elaboration of newly significant material that participates in the unforeseeability of what is coming into being.

We can now turn to the problem of literature's strangeness. The text appears to us as a kind of singularity, as an object that undermines but does not abolish its own status as object. We may reject considering it as either determined by or independent of what is outside it, and yet we may be unable to describe its form and function without invoking representation and autonomy. Are literary texts formal objects to be analyzed or are they subjective messages to be received? They are both and neither. Attempts to define or classify them lead to paradoxes, to apparent contradictions between what turn out to be different but interlocking levels of description: to the realization, in short, that they are strange objects. I borrow the phrase from a chapter of Jacques Monod's *Chance and Necessity*, in which the French biologist asked where the living organism fits into the distinction between natural objects and artifacts. He imagined a probe from the Martian equivalent of NASA landing on earth and subjecting things it found to an unambiguous, step-by-step test for naturalness and artificiality. Crystals, organisms, and such organic productions as beehives appear in this context to be strange objects whose existence would force the probe's designers to abandon the postulate of objectivity as a criterion for identifying the natural. The categories of Monod's discussion are not strictly relevant to literature, but a moment's reflection on the metaphor of the organic work should convince us that if organisms are epistemologically strange, literary texts—artifacts created to accomplish the project of being creations without a project external to themselves—are stranger still. In this definition the literary text can exist as object only in the ambiguities of context that allow a logical contradiction to be realized: not at a single level, where it would be contradictory, but in a tangled hierarchy of levels. The definition itself is what Douglas Hofstadter calls a "strange loop" in which two propositions seem to abolish or engulf one another.[39] The domains of allonomy ("artifacts created to accomplish the project of . . .") and autonomy ("being creations without a project external to themselves") do not coincide, and this difference makes literature possible. In the biological case, it is possible to denounce the "teleonomic" character of living systems as an illusion of the observer, as Varela has done, but it is as impossible to reduce the literary object to the status of a natural one as it is to deny it all characteristics of autonomy.

The efforts of twentieth-century formalism to characterize the literary text, although they do not depend on organic comparisons, nonetheless cannot escape the consequences of the literary object's strangeness. To consider the linguistic and semiotic dimensions of a text implies taking it to be a communicative object, one that serves as a vehicle of information and meaning: these approaches, however, have led to a criticism concerned with the text as such in its autonomy, to what Todorov calls "immanent criticism." In other words, the epistemological problems of such disciplines as linguistics and semiotics do not remain the same when they are used with respect to literary texts, with their peculiar mimicry of the autonomous, as when they are applied to more general cases of the use of language and signs. If the literary text, on the one hand, seems to embody a highly specific project in its use of language, the strange nature of this project, on the other hand, is to aspire to the status of an autonomous object, whose "project" can only be found in or identified with itself. To those who would investigate it,

---

[39]Hofstadter, *Gödel, Escher, Bach* (New York, 1979).

the literary text implicitly says: "Consider me as an autonomous, natural object. Try to discover my laws of organization, of operation, laws which you must assume to be specified only by what you find within me. To do so, of course, you will have to study the communicative components of which I am made, the signs of language, even though if you assume from the outset that I am a vehicle of communication, you risk missing what is most specific to me. And yet, for all this, my autonomy or organicity is in the end a fiction. I am not a natural object but an artifact, and my meaning is a function of my communicative participation in a larger system."

It is therefore most doubtful whether, or in what sense, the literary text can be an object of knowledge, something that one can appropriately set out to know objectively. The literary text in effect demands of us that we figure it out, that we attempt to understand fully what it is and how it operates—but at the same time it instills in us a doubt, a reservation, as to whether this is really the right question, whether this kind of inquiry is really the response that it solicits from us. A similar paradox confronts us if we begin from another direction, say, with the hypothesis that the real function of the text is to provide pleasure, or to communicate some particular, most likely affective, kind of meaning: we quickly realize that the fact of pleasure or the creation of a certain kind of meaning can best be apprehended or appreciated if we delve into the text's individual and (pseudo)autonomous properties. The poem communicates the most to the reader willing to set aside immediate communication in favor of a deeper inquiry into the specificity of the poem.

The literary text thus appears as *something like an object of knowledge* but certainly not an object of knowledge in the scientific sense. Its real interest lies in the "something like," the "pseudo-." There is no reason to assume that we can know it fully, and the cultural interest of a definitive understanding of a literary work is questionable, to say the least. If we could "explain" fully a single text, once and for all, that text would in effect lose all its potential cultural interest. Imagine the day when the English department solves Shakespeare—and must therefore remove him from the curriculum! Literature is a complex artifact, one which we are never in a position to understand when we begin to understand it. As such, literature provides the cognitive experience of a confrontation with complexity—whence the applicability to literary understanding of the principle of self-organization from noise.

While Prigogine and Thom debate the validity of this kind of principle as a tool of scientific inquiry, a similar debate takes place in literary studies between those who, like Paul de Man, believe that the rhetoricity of language always produces undecidable features, irreducible to grammatical or semiotic determination, and those who, like Michael Riffaterre, consider the recourse to undecidability to be an intellectual abdication.[40] For René Thom, the only valid scientific task is the revealing of determinisms, but whatever the merits of this position for science, the situation of literature is quite different. Linguistic and literary form, both in the production and reading of texts, depend on the workings of the human mind and brain; in other words, on processes to which we will never have anything like objective access. Moreover, as we have argued in this chapter, the fact that literary texts are artificial autonomous systems implies that their internal laws of organization are inevitably incomplete or imperfectly coherent. The biologist can assume that the phenomenon of self-organization from noise depends on his observational ignorance of the system's operation: the autopoiesis of the organism implies that within it a complete set of operational rules do in fact exist. The biologist thus has every reason to proceed in the identification of these rules, even if for the time being he finds it expedient to make use of a probabilistic approach. The student of literature, on the other hand, has every reason to assume that at some point the internal laws of coherence break down or are incomplete, that the pseudoautonomous structure must bear the mark of its finite, allonomous creation. The rigor of literature's (pseudo)autonomous systematicity intensifies the already unreliable system that is language. What is communicatively unreliable must necessarily be complex, since we lack the information that would specify it fully. If literature assumes its noise, and consequently its unreliability, as a constitutive factor of itself (see above pp. 83–91), then as readers and critics we are called to construct a kind of knowledge radically different from that of any discipline, one that may be described as the creation of meaning out of noise and disorder. Prigogine and Atlan argue that at the microscopic level where measurement fails, and at high levels of biological organization where we approach the complexity of our own brain, this kind of negotiation with disorder—with our ignor-

---

[40]Riffaterre, "Interpretation and Undecidability," *New Literary History* 12 (1980), 227–242.

ance—is the only kind of knowledge accessible to us, because we are not the disincarnated observers postulated by early modern science but beings belonging to the world that we try to understand. And this world, unlike the disenchanted, predictable universe postulated by scientific determinism, is an open world, one in which the unpredictable appearance of the new is not irrational. Knowledge, in this context, entails risk and dialogue, not mechanisms for ensuring maximal certainty and professional consensus. In the words of Isabelle Stengers, "the professionally occulted problem of pertinence and risk becomes an intrinsic theoretical problem in the situations we have called 'complex.' "[41]

If all human communication were reliable, completely specifiable by determinisms, the cultural world would be as unchangeable, as predictable, as the Laplacian universe: it would be impossible to understand how new and unexpected ideas or works arise, how cultural history would be anything but the unfolding of a process governed by eternal laws. Fortunately, language is neither a transparent nor a perfected system. The imperfection of our language, and thus of our knowledge of such things as literature, is the necessary condition of invention and unpredictability in culture.

We should therefore have no regrets if the experience of "knowing" a literary text remains an encounter with complexity. Literature, with its exploitation of language's ambiguity, its strange bringing together of the sensuous and intellectual aspects of language in a synthesis that cannot be fully explained or predicted, places us in immediate contact with a complex system of relations, a system that we can neither reduce to something simpler nor account for by adding together simple things. To read as fully as possible the literary text, we need codes that we do not at the outset possess, because only by experiencing the text's complexity can we begin to construct them. Literature, and to an even greater extent its study, can thus constitute the cultural apprenticeship of a science or knowledge of the complex. This experience of complexity, of knowledge irreducible to universal, predictive laws, is one that classical modern science, and the disciplines modeled on it, have to a large extent occluded or denounced as unscientific: the successes of science, at least until recently, have been won by progressively reducing the complex to the complicated, to the unmysterious articulation of the simple. Much disciplinary study of literature, whether positivist or

[41]Stengers, "Découvrir la complexité?" 251.

formalist, has served to repress this encounter with complexity, to reduce literary knowledge to the objectified, reified modes dominant in science and society. Yet if the study of literature now appears particularly fitted to the cognitive encounter with complexity, this capacity derives in part from the fact that, as the residue of an earlier, avowedly textual mode of knowing, literary studies have not had to found themselves as modern disciplines only by imitating the natural sciences: their own prehistory has never been completely excluded and has functioned as an alternative model. Prigogine and Stengers evoke a "metamorphosis of science": the importance of "order from fluctuations" makes science into something that no longer needs to be isolated from history and culture. But if the chance of a "new alliance" between disciplines is to be preserved, it is important that cultural studies retain their specificity, that they not imitate the science of universality and predictability.

Literature has become the experience of complexity to the extent that the literary text has become an artificial autonomous object, one that appears to generate its own domain of description, reducible neither to language nor to thought as representation. By giving itself characteristics of autonomy, the literary text constitutes a phenomenal domain that is never, a priori, a familiar one to the reader, one for which he already possesses an adequate description in language. Whence the experience of complexity, equivalent to the cognitive encounter with an autonomous system or an unfamiliar discipline, highly organized along operational principles unknown to the observer. Undecidably pseudocommunicative or pseudo–self-referential, the literary text seems to embody a strange project: in it, things that have been known before are said in ways that not everyone can understand, and from this intersection of redundancy and confusion, there arises—not always, not everywhere, but sometimes—the new.

5 Texts and Their Study: Intellectual Invention in an Open World

> We learn to prefer imperfect theories, and sentences,
> which contain glimpses of truth, to digested systems
> which have no one valuable suggestion. A wise writer
> will feel that the ends of study and composition are
> best answered by announcing undiscovered regions
> of thought, and so communicating, through hope,
> new activity to the torpid spirit.
>
> EMERSON, *Nature*

Before we have read a work of literature, we do not know how to read what is most literary in it. We may be fluent in the language in which it is written, familiar with the codes particular to its genre, its era, or its author, but nothing can fully prepare us for the text's most secret strangeness. Only by reading it can we become its reader, because it creates its own codes beyond all other codes. In its aritifical autonomy is its difference from what is outside itself: in its autonomy is its noise. And in its noise is its potential to create new and unforeseen meaning in the mind of every reader.

This means that literature is both more and less than an act of communication: more because it is less, and less because it is more. Autonomous verbal complexity produces noise that impedes communication; noise in turn gives rise to new meaning beyond whatever could be said to have been communicated. It has long been a commonplace to note that literature, and poetry in particular, is language that endures after communicating, rather than vanishing once its meaning has been transmitted. It has been less well noted that the literary text is a precommunicative utterance, cast out into a system that is not yet structured in a way that guarantees its arrival. This latter characteristic, however, is crucial to literature's role in the cultural processes of intellectual invention.

Communication poses a special problem in the theory of autonomous and autopoietic systems discussed in the last chapter. The information-theoretic model of communication fits systems designed to communicate, to receive inputs and transmit outputs, but its pertinence to autonomous systems is questionable. By definition, autonomous systems do not have inputs or outputs; they do not engage in "instructive interactions," that is, receive and respond to external commands. Instead they change in accordance with their own organization, such change being triggered by, but not specified by, external perturbations. An observer may describe the interactions between an autonomous system and its environment as instances of communication or instruction, but this is a symbolic explanation, valid for the observer's cognitive domain, and not an operational explanation directly applicable to the autonomous system. What the observer perceives as communication is the outcome of structural coupling between the autonomous system and its environment, or in particular between two or more autonomous systems. The term *structural coupling* refers to the process of recursive interactions by which recurrent or redundant perturbations from system A give rise to recurrent or redundant changes in system B that in turn form recurrent perturbations for system A and so on. It is the process by which systems come to "learn" each other's behavior and "respond" in predictable ways.

Autonomous systems, in other words, do not intrinsically communicate, but they may, through a history of mutual interactions, come to behave in ways that can be described as communicative or instructive. Such a description belongs to the cognitive domain of an observer — but that observer may be one of the systems itself. We can describe our own behavior as communication because we can observe ourselves interacting with those with whom we communicate.[1] To call human language communication is to explain it at this symbolic, observational

[1]The capacity for self-observation in consensual behavior is not a feature of all autopoietic systems but depends on "the occurrence of distinct relations of relative neuronal activity that operate as *internal structural perturbations*. When this takes place, even in the slightest manner, within the confines of a consensual domain, so that the relations of neuronal activity generated under consensual behavior become perturbations and components for further consensual behavior, an observer is operationally generated" (Maturana, "Biology of Language," 49, emphasis added.)

level; the concept of communication cannot account for what goes on operationally as we speak, for the changes in neurons and vocal chords and facial muscles as we utter words. Most important, what we can call communication must be the outcome of a history of interactions, a process of mutual structural coupling. Before there can be communication, there must have been precommunicative utterances, perturbing signals to which there was not yet a stable or recognizable response. There must have been noise out of which coded regularities would eventually be constructed. The changes of one autonomous system are noise for another such system, but such changes may become meaningful in the higher-order autonomous system formed through structural coupling by the two systems together.

To treat an utterance as communicative is to assume that such a history of structural coupling has already taken place, so that sender and receiver together form a system in which both possess the codes needed to make of the utterance a fully decodable message. Such an assumption is valid for many linguistic utterances, because language itself is the outcome of a historical process of structural coupling. As such, a language and its speakers form a system in which a great many interactions can properly be treated as communicative.

But even as we communicate at the linguistic level, we can use language in novel, precommunicative ways. In a conversation, we can not only transmit and receive information but also seek to establish interlocking patterns of behavior and understanding with our interlocutor—private or semiprivate codes that are the possible outcome, and not the precondition, of the conversation. We make use of an already shared language, but our utterances are also novel moves in a game out of which higher-order communicative domains may emerge. Such utterances must at first be partially indecipherable to their receivers, not fully resolvable in their implications. They must contain, in other words, an element of noise if they are to contribute to the production of not yet shared codes and meanings. When we begin to exchange letters with someone, for example, the not-quite-decipherability of the letters for their receivers is a precommunicative feature that leads to the mutual construction of a particular and novel form of communication and thus to the semiotic uniqueness of every correspondence.

Literary texts, similarly, are novel moves in the open-ended game of cultural conversation. If the authentically literary text does something with language that has never been done before, then it does not so much communicate to the reader as it tries to make of her the reader with whom communication would be possible. Imitative works that break no new ground in language or form, conversely, are far more likely to be received unproblematically by their readers as communications *about* some subject or other. Perhaps after reading fifty Balzac novels one becomes the more or less fully competent reader of *La Comédie humaine* and can simply take each new novel as a message about nineteenth-century France, its Nucingens and Bianchons: this may explain why specialists who read all of such enormous works as Balzac's often go in for referential, extrinsic criticism. The new and "noisy" work refuses us this complacency. Its author is sending a pseudomessage that could only be a message in a channel that does not yet exist, that may come into being through the process of reading but that does not precede it. Of course literature is not exactly a conversation, for the readers do not respond on anything like equal terms: a certain "response" comes back in the form of reviews and letters and sales figures, but the real responses are themselves new literary works, sent forward in time to their virtual audience and not back in a circle to their author's predecessors. Literature is a conversation that never catches up to itself, that never stabilizes in a single mode of communication.

That, at any rate, is what literature has become with romanticism. Before that, the potential for open-ended inventive games in language surely existed but was not considered synonymous with literature or privileged by aesthetics. Neoclassicism, for example, was an attempt to organize the structure and function of literary discourse along more communicative lines by supposing a homogeneous community of language and expectations that united writer and reader. The aesthetic conventions of neoclassicism increased the readability of works and limited the degree to which they could surprise or make interpretive demands on their readers. The status accorded to masterpieces of antiquity as universal models of distinct mimetic forms meant that the literary could not be defined by formal innovation or self-transcendence, as it would be by romantic theorists. The neoclassical aesthetic may have represented as close to an ideal of communication as literature has ever come. As such, neoclassicism as aesthetic doctrine cannot be taken as typical of all literature before romanticism or even of neoclassical literature itself. Stendhal certainly thought not when he claimed that

Sophocles and Euripides were romantics, that "all great writers were romantic in their time."[2] The normal practice of literature, in this view, would be to invent its forms in the present, to innovate in ways appropriate to the historical situation. Neoclassicism would be an attempt—only partially "successful," of course—to restrict the innovative potential of literature by placing a priori constraints on the development of its forms.

Formal innovation may not always have been a defining characteristic of literature, yet it can be said that an inventive strain runs throughout the history of singing, telling stories, and writing. Italo Calvino suggested that what the storytellers of oral cultures do can best be described as a combinatory game in which familiar elements of language are put together in unexpected and hitherto unheard ways. In some of these playfully or accidentally produced combinations, listeners come to "recognize" myths, statements that could not have been made consciously or intentionally but which, once uttered, seem to express unconscious feelings, problems, and fears.[3] Nothing appears further removed from the romantic ideology of the creative genius, yet the romantic or modern writer is likewise an explorer of disorder and of the inarticulate, one who attempts to say what has been left unsaid by consciousness and rationality. The possibility of pushing language to its limits to create new patterns and ideas is probably as old as language, though it has not always coincided with what has borne the name literature. With romanticism, literature became an intensified and self-conscious instance of what it had always in some sense been, something that moments such as neoclassicism had partially disqualified or constrained: an exploration of the disordered otherness at the limits of well-coded speech, an irreceivable pseudomessage that incites its audience to construct the conditions of its eventual reception.

It may be objected here that I am drawing far too sharp a distinction between romanticism and what preceded it, that, in particular, romantic writing, as opposed to modern writing, still participates in the neoclassical aesthetic of representation. This is a valid point but not really an objection to the kind of argument I am making. Obviously many an eighteenth-century writer was concerned with chaos, with the

---

[2]Stendhal, *Racine et Shakespeare* (Paris: Garnier-Flammarion, 1970), 71, 106.
[3]Calvino, "Cybernetics and Ghosts," *The Uses of Literature* (New York, 1986), 3–27.

problematic character of representation, with new and often mixed forms. And in much of the nineteenth century, representation remained a central textual strategy. What arrives with romanticism, at least in theoretical romanticism, is the notion that both the writing process and the work itself are, through their autonomy, the locus of the inventive interaction with disorder. But romantic theory for a time outran practice. Romantic writing often appears to be a heroic struggle with disorder, an effort to represent the unrepresentable, to encounter chaos but then communicate the outcome of that struggle in an orderly fashion. Modern works, turning away from representation as an aesthetic strategy, have increasingly cast aside the project of mastery and communication, and have attempted to bring the experience of disorder right to the reader. In short, where romanticism attempted to communicate to the reader about the not-yet-communicative, more recent writing presents to the reader a precommunicative utterance. Balzac describes and explains provincial stupidity and bad taste; Flaubert gives us a sentence whose structure mimics the layered incoherence of Charles Bovary's hat. Balzac writes *of* his childhood stammerings; Joyce writes, "O, the green wothe botheth." Increasingly, literature assumes the creative, autonomous, precommunicative role in which romantic theory had cast it.

It may appear, then, that the characterization of literary reading and study that I am advancing is pertinent only to romantic and modern literature. This is not the case for two distinct reasons. The first, already suggested in the discussion of neoclassicism above, is that no aesthetic of communication has ever completely eliminated what is literary in literature, its production of meaning out of noise. The second is that literarity is not the only feature by which literary texts can differ from existing cultural codes. Works from periods when literature was differently defined, emphasizing transparency rather than difficulty, now come to us with another kind of difference, one that they did not initially possess: they come from the past. The passage of time alters linguistic and, especially, cultural codes, takes away original contexts and intertexts, introduces noise in the "transmission" from author to modern reader. Literature from the past, even literature whose aesthetic was one of utterly limpid communication, now functions as a perturbation for present culture. In fact, the study of literature has throughout modern history been linked to the study of the past, and the two remain implicitly associated in our current critical and pedagogical practices. In the Middle Ages, the auctores were those who had already written, who had left writings that could be considered seriously as vehicles of knowledge. With the Renaissance, the texts deemed worthy of serious study were for the most part restricted to Greek and Roman antiquity, and the relation between the study of texts and the study of the past was thereby strengthened. In more recent times, as the study of imaginative literature has taken on disciplinary status, the study of contemporary literature has not always been accepted. Even when contemporary works do enter the academy, they are subjected to a discursive field essentially structured by its rapport with works of the past. By making the literary text into an object of study, the academy removes it from the contexts in which contemporaries normally react and respond to a new work.

The literary disciplines are in large part devoted to the study of cultural artifacts from the past: their difference in this respect from other, nonliterary disciplines lies in the otherness of the past itself, considered as a source of difference from the present. Of course, literary studies share this distinction with such disciplines as history, art history, the history of science, and the history of philosophy. But it is worth noting that all these fields are described by the word *history*, whereas literary studies do not coincide with literary history. In other words, there is in the study of literature a way of taking seriously the written words of the past that is not the same as that of the historian writing about the past or about the previous state of some discipline or art. The history of science corresponds to literary history or the history of criticism, not to the fact that we read seriously Shakespeare and Montaigne.

It must also be noted that the study of literature often coincides with the study of a foreign language. In fact, it is only in the study of literature, as a general rule, that one finds courses both devoted to a foreign culture and conducted in a foreign language. There are in the United States no departments of French sociology or German psychology or Russian mathematics, although works by speakers of these languages are read in those fields. Working in a foreign language implies yet another kind of difference from ordinary communication: it implies thinking, speaking, and writing in new categories, in a system of references that does not coincide with that of the culture in which one lives. In most nonliterary fields the difference that is a foreign language is treated essentially as an obstacle to be overcome, either by competence in the language or by use of translations: what matters is not the intellectual experience of working in a different language but simply the reception of the message written in that language. When language and literature departments offer courses in "civilization," as opposed to literature, they retain this third aspect of literary studies, an affinity with foreign languages, even if they give up altogether literarity itself. In some sense, any text studied in a foreign language functions as a literary text: it exhibits a "set toward the message" if for no other reason than that a foreign language appears less natural, less self-evident, and therefore less negligible than one's native tongue. At least for the student who has not mastered the language, a foreign text is inevitably a message for which he does not possess all the necessary codes, and his reading, his attempt to construct something of what he does not yet know, resembles in this sense the activity of a reader of literature. The resemblance is limited, because the puzzling text may turn out to be no more undecidable than "Défense de fumer." Nonetheless, when the presence of a foreign language coincides with that of a literary text, it adds a degree of otherness and unpredictability to what the reader must assimilate—and therefore serves as an additional source of complexity, of potential information.

When we use the term *literary studies*, we are not referring to a homogeneous unity that can be defined in a simple way. The literary, the past, and the foreign may all be present in a given activity of what we call the study of literature; in another such activity we may encounter only one or two of them. Similarly, other disciplines sometimes treat the literary, or the past, or material in a foreign language, although generally not all three. This characteristic of literary studies may best be described as a *tendency*, in certain disciplines, to take seriously that which is not of immediate, functional importance in the cultural here and now of a given civilization. Whenever verbal texts that are not instrumentally communicative, not contemporary, not indigenous, are taken seriously as objects of inquiry or sources of knowledge—and not simply as evidence for understanding an aspect or segment of the past—then we are to some extent in the presence of literary studies.

What is studied in literature appears, if placed in opposition to what is communicative and functional, as a *perturbation* of contemporary culture, as something at least partially unexpected that comes from the outside. It can be objected, of course, that what is studied in the literary disciplines is just as much a part of culture as anything else: that literary discourse has just as real a social or economic existence as any other form of discourse, that works of the past are an essential part of cultural memory, that given the current state of travel and communications, foreign texts can never be considered isolated. All these statements are true, and yet they do not overcome the impression that literary studies are devoted to marginal phenomena, to works that, while not external to culture or civilization, do seem to be outside the messages that are directly and immediately communicative in contemporary civilization's informational circuits.

What I am trying to propose in this final chapter is a way of understanding the reading and teaching of literature, *not* in a society in which such reading and teaching appears to be an essential aspect of society's continual self-production, but rather in a civilization where such teaching and reading are not essential or no longer appear to be. In Chapter 1 I suggested that the size and importance of literary studies in academic institutions and curricula, their continued prestige, might in effect be a holdover from the past—the result of a perpetuation by inertia of earlier attitudes and values—rather than a reflection of their current importance to society. If this is the case, then we may be in fact approaching a society that acts as if it can do without literary studies, at least as far as all practical tasks are concerned. Many official statements on the importance of the humanities sound hollow because they come straight from the past. It is as if the apologists of scholarship, haunted by the possibility of a society in which the activity they prize would be inessential, were unable to produce arguments that arise from or are applicable to the present context. If the study of literature is in fact essential to our civilization, it is something that present-day culture hides—or seems unable to articulate—so that we are invited to make do with archaic, quaint-sounding justifications for its existence. At this juncture our strongest move may be to suppose that literary studies *are* something marginal, to argue from the assumption that they are indeed no more than a source of perturbations on the edge of a cultural system that gives the appearance of being able to get along without them. Such a strategy is admittedly paradoxical. To see what importance literary studies might yet have, we may need to set aside the traditional idea that the study of the written, poetic past is an essential aspect of a civilization's continuity with itself and consider whether by starting from the very marginality and strangeness of literary studies we may not be in a better position to assess their value, not as defined in the past, but as it might be defined now and in the future.

To say that much of the material of literary studies appears to contemporary civilization as noise is to say that it does not fit into that civilization's communicative circuits, that it is not immediately receivable as a message. For many, the poetic, the archaic, and the foreign are simply unintelligible and are thus not treated cognitively at all or are at best treated as slightly frivolous aesthetic curiosities. The social and intellectual function of literature among the educated elite is simply less central than it was in the Renaissance, at the court of Louis XIV or even during that perhaps mythical early twentieth century when a British Petroleum executive was alleged to have said, "Just give me the best man in classics at Oxford, and I'll teach him the rest." There is no clear effect of the literary message on its contemporary receiver, no unambiguous procedure whereby the individual reader and the culture in which literature is read respond by becoming in any way different from what they had been without it. Of course, many people find the experience of literary reading to be highly significant, even to change their lives: the point is that this significance or change provoked by contact with literature is quite unpredictable, very different from the case of someone who reads a technical manual so as to be able to program a computer or who reads a work of popular psychology to try to cope better with coworkers or lovers. The person whose life is changed by reading a work of literature—or, perhaps, by reading any text in a literary manner—does not know prior to the actual reading experience how or even whether the reading will be significant. The reader is not, in advance, a system adapted to decoding a particular literary text and reacting to it in a certain way. Literary reading, as I have said before, is never a matter of simple reception, for its literarity is precisely what exceeds the model of communication, according to which the receiver is already equipped to decode the message and be affected by it.

To the extent that literature functions as noise, then it is not immediately informative, it does not supply direct answers to existing questions or uncertainties. "For poetry makes nothing happen," wrote Auden: it does not belong to the class of messages that function so as to cause events. This is why the identification of literature with informational noise is compatible with most of what has been written since romanticism about the nature or role of literature as opposed to utilitarian communication. And noise or perturbation, though not producing immediate or predictable effects, may lead to the complexification of the individuals or societies that assimilate them. This possibility has already been discussed, at the level of the individual reader, in Chapter 4. What I am suggesting now is that the function of literary studies may be to create knowledge and ideas out of that part of our verbal heritage that seems, at first, superfluous or irrelevant when set against the rationally defined questions and problems confronting society. On a utilitarian list of research or instructional needs, new interpretations of literary texts would occupy a very low position: it is not hard to understand why journalists can use a program of the MLA Convention to hold the scholarly profession up to public ridicule. If new interpretations of texts were nothing more than minuscule moves in the disciplinary project of reducing our uncertainties about the literary object, then we would neither need nor want them. It is not even clear whether we need the same old interpretations of these texts either. Conservative theorists such as E. D. Hirsch state that interpretation means finding authorial intention—but what are we to do with authorial intention, if and when we find it? We may have no cultural need to recover authorial intention, but collectively we need the diversity, the strangeness, the conceptual complexity of literary texts as a component of our culture, as an ingredient of our cognitive efforts. The value of studying literature lies not where our organization as a discipline would imply it does—in the knowledge we thereby acquire about literature—but rather in the transformations we and our students and readers undergo in the process. We need literary knowledge not so as to know literature, but so as to know the world and ourselves.

Intellectual Invention

It is all well and good to suggest that literary texts are sources of noise or fluctuations that account for the possibility and the unpredictability of cultural invention: one still has to explain how such invention actually comes about. As was noted in Chapter 3, any borrowing of concepts must be justified on the terms of the field doing the borrowing; the "application" of information theory to literary theory can be accepted only if the results are interesting in literary theory and not simply because the theory of information carries with it scientific prestige. The same criterion must be applied to the more general considerations in the present chapter concerning the cultural significance of literature and literary education. Whatever novelty value concepts from information theory or theoretical biology may have, they would in the end serve no purpose if they could not contribute to our ability to explain the circulation and production of ideas, concepts, theories, and explanations.

In the pages that follow I will discuss the theoretical work on intellectual invention of the Israeli philosopher Judith Schlanger; I will argue that her account of this process enables us to understand how the "noise" of literature can play a major role in it. Schlanger came to the problem of heuristics and inventive thought via studies of German idealism and organic metaphors. After a thesis on Schelling, she wrote a major work on the philosophic and political use of ogranic figures in the eighteenth and nineteenth centuries: *Les Métaphores de l'organisme*. In this study she chose to define her topic not lexically or rhetorically but in the context of cognition and argument: her approach to metaphor treats it not as a linguistic or aesthetic device but as an element in an argumentative or cognitive chain. In this view, metaphors cannot be treated adequately through typologies but must be investigated as they function in different contexts. One must examine why organic metaphors were taken up, how they fit into persuasive or speculative syntagmas, what possibilities for understanding or persuasion are opened up by their use. In a process of cognition, metaphors do not provide answers, but help open up new intellectual spaces, new elaborations and conceptual possibilities. Metaphoric language, Schlanger concludes, is a necessary condition for open-ended processes of both creation and destruction of meaning. Our inevitable use of a language's figurative dimension both prevents our cognitive efforts from claiming an immutable foundation and makes possible their creative change.

In her more recent works, notably *Penser la bouche pleine* (1975) and *L'Invention intellectuelle* (1983), Schlanger has moved from the specific problem of organic metaphor to the general problem of heuristics, of thinking the new. She excludes from her concern both noncognitive speech and nonverbal intuition, and focuses on "intelligence that uses words," "thought considered in its mass, the ensemble of thinking and of intellectual discourses in general."[4] This project necessarily implies a systemic approach to intellectual invention and to the cultural and verbal milieus in which invention can take place.

[4]Judith Schlanger, *L'Invention intellectuelle* (Paris, 1983), 217, and *Penser la bouche pleine* (The Hague, 1975), 19. Subsequent references to *L'Invention intellectuelle* given in parentheses.

Thought that is successfully inventive, in other words, cannot be isolated from thought that attempts to be inventive but fails; metaphors that contribute to new cognitive formulations cannot be considered apart from metaphors that contribute to formulations that turn out to be noncognitive or not pertinent. Imaginative or aesthetically oriented literature is not primarily an instance of what Schlanger calls intellectual invention, but it is definitely a part of the cultural and verbal context for the creation of new thought. Focusing on the intersection of *cultural* and *inventive* aspects of thought, Schlanger in effect defines for her speculation a domain that lies between the anthropological foundations of knowledge (the capabilities and limitations of humans as knowing beings) and applied, effective, or fully constituted knowledge (*savoir*). Intellectual invention needs to take place because our cognitive capabilities are finite ("an infinite mind would not invent" [259]) and can take place because the plurality of cultural and cognitive spaces and undertakings makes possible the displacements and recombinations of thought.

Finitude and plurality are for Schlanger necessary conditions of intellectual invention, but they do not explain the process itself. This process depends on the workings of metaphor and culture. The cultural stockpile and the figurality of language serve as elements of inventive thought because new ideas must be *relatively different*: they can be neither pure repetitions nor radically unimaginable utterances. If an intellectual statement is completely different from what has preceded it, if it seems altogether foreign to its context, it risks being labeled as deviant and rejected by the members of the relevant cognitive community. The assent of that community must be part of the process of intellectual invention; it is no less important than the production of the deviation, or écart, from what has already been formulated. In this sense a cognitive community constitutes a kind of self-regulating system, one that continues in its activity by producing differences and then integrating into its organization those differences that it finds acceptable. It is therefore necessary to account for how deviations from what has already been said can arise, and also how such deviations, while outside the system of knowledge as it existed before, are nonetheless often accepted, rather than excluded as being outside the bounds of rationality.

Schlanger attributes the possibility of producing and integrating deviations to the *plural* and *partial* character of participation in cultural fields. Within the global intellectual community, individuals or other subsystems (disciplines, schools, research groups) are in contact with more than one cultural or cognitive field, and their knowledge of any one field is never complete. "Each participates in a multiplicity of fields, can circulate among them, and can thus increase or modify scenes of representation and relational networks [*spectacles et circuits*]" (246). By moving between fields, effecting combinations with ideas from other domains, individuals and subgroups produce deviations that swerve away from what has been the norm in a given sector of inquiry. But deviation from a local norm, that is, from the accepted state of a problem in a given field, does not imply a move outside rationality itself. In other words, because different problems, fields, disciplines, and subdisciplines are only partially interconnected, it is possible to bring to them elements of exteriority that are not exterior to the rational enterprise as a whole. There are parallels here to the role of noise in self-organizing systems: what is noise for a given subsystem may be integrable in the context of the entire system. And what is already information for one system can become noise, and thus a source of invention, in another. Finitude and plurality thus give rise, for Schlanger, to a process of invention that includes both the production and subsequent reduction (or integration) of deviations: "If rational knowing were one and stable, then intellectual invention would be irrational. Besides, it would be impossible: invention implies plurality. Or inversely it is the visible manifestation of plurality. Since the rational space is such that it makes possible reasonable and meaningful [*sensé*] deviations, and since it feeds on them by reorganizing itself in function of them, invention and plurality are coextensive with thought" (254). In Schlanger's systemic perspective, then, invention arises from a deviation with respect to an existing state of a self-regulating system, followed by a self-adjustment of the system so as to integrate the new element into its organization.

Informationally speaking, the inventive deviation (*écart*) reduces redundancy: it is, by definition, what cannot be predicted. We have already encountered, in Chapter 3, the terminology of *écart* and *réduction d'écart*: these terms, as used by the Groupe μ, designate the successive effects of surprise and comprehension provoked by the rhetorical figure. As a departure from what is perceived as a norm, a figure decreases the predictability and thus increases the information of a text, but if redundancy still exists in the text, then the reader can perhaps make sense of the deviation, turn its complexity into significant information. To use a new figure, one that has not yet been deadened into a mere component of existing norms, is to initiate a process of invention; the figure, like the new conceptual idea, can then be either rejected as meaningless and deviant, or accepted into the systems of meaning and knowledge. It is therefore no surprise or accident that, for Schlanger, the figurality of language participates intimately in the process of intellectual invention, a process in which the displacement of concepts cannot be separated from the displacements of meanings and words.

Nonetheless, it would be foolish and shortsighted to give the impression that Schlanger's work is primarily literary, or, in other words, that metaphor or figure is the only form of deviation that functions in invention. The reality of invention can be both more complex and more banal than the model of metaphor would suggest. One of the most important sources of the inventive deviation is simply the internal transmission of what is already known within the cognitive community. Because that community is pluralistic, heterogeneous, and certainly not fully transparent to itself, its internal communications take many forms, have many functions, and perform with varying degrees of reliability. Results and theories are diffused in the form of textbooks as well as scholarly monographs, popularizing articles as well as papers at colloquia. Ideas are diffused in book reviews, passed on and deformed by word of mouth. More important, any individual participant in the act of knowing, whether she be at the stage of study or research, must to a large extent repeat what has already been said before, making it part of her own utterance. "It is clear," writes Schlanger, "that the very great majority of intellectual utterances are not original, and yet they are redundant and not tautological" (244). Intellectual statements are constantly being repeated, not verbatim but in different formulations and contexts, by persons of varying competence. This creates an inevitable process of deformation or displacement. Displacement does not by itself constitute invention, but it creates the space in which invention is possible: a space of multiple differences, of similar but not identical problems and formulations available in many contexts. In this space potentially significant deviations can be selected by the appropriate systems and placed in contexts where they can take on new meaning.

As an example, consider the work you are reading now: 90 percent of the time its author is making himself the spokesman of others, is retransmitting a part of the present-day cultural mass. Whatever originality there may be lies above all in the choice of what is repeated, in the connections drawn between elements that have perhaps hitherto remained separate and, not least, in slight deformations of what is being transmitted. As always, redundancy accompanies variety and is a necessary condition of intelligibility. The ideas set forth in *The Noise of Culture* are partly new and partly old. Concepts are being displaced from one part of the cultural field to another, where they are found to overlap with notions already present. Once integrated into their new domain, the "literary" versions of such concepts as self-organization from noise will in their turn serve as material for further intellectual invention.

We have used the term *noise* to characterize that part of a received message that was not part of the message as it was sent. Schlanger does not make explicit use of information theory as a conceptual framework, but she adopts the metaphor of noise to describe what arises when intellectual information is transmitted through imperfect channels: "As for the diffusion of information, the echoing of popularization, the repetitions of [intellectual] fashion, the jargon of sects, the problematic of the season, all that constitutes a speculative noise that also belongs to and marks the intellectual situation" (245). The word *noise* would not by itself authorize any assimilation of this statement to the theory of self-organization from noise, but the fact that Schlanger is describing the consequences of imperfect transmission suggests that the structural conditions of what we have been calling noise are present in her description and, indeed, would be there even if she had not used the word itself. We can thus read Schlanger's account of the production and integration of cognitive deviations as a special case of the organization-from-noise paradigm. The relevant self-organizing system is no more or less than the global cognitive community, where "faulty" transmission of intellectual information takes place in and between subsystems. As in the biological organism or the reader's response to an undecidable text, a gain in informational complexity can take place only if the imperfections of transmission are compensated elsewhere in the system by other channels of transmission, in other words, by the system's redundancy. The imperfect, inaccurate, deforming transmission of concepts, ideas, and observations would be ruinous for intellectual invention and for all prospects of knowing if it occurred in the only transmission channel available or if the same deformations occurred at once in all available channels. The cognitive community survives instances of imperfect communication because it contains within it so many channels that, one way or the other, messages that are sent can be retrieved with a high degree of accuracy. Like the ambiguities of a poetic text, the deformations of intellectual restatement can be a source of meaning rather than an obstacle to the construction of meaning, because those who receive (or, rather, assimilate) them have available in other forms the information that was being restated. Of course, literature is not the same as the transmission or diffusion of ideas produced in research: it is in fact an even more complex system of restatement and displacement. If the comparatively banal restatements of ordinary intellectual communication can produce displacements or instances of noise that may have a role in the invention of new meaning and knowledge, the same is true a fortiori of the deformations, both subtler and more overt, of poetic texts.

Self-organization from noise is more than a mechanism for explaining gains, as opposed to losses, of information: it implies the existence of a system that effectively organizes itself. It is the theory, in other words, of a continuous process of self-production and reorganization by which an autonomous system changes while maintaining its own identity.[5] Schlanger's theory of intellectual space as a domain continually reorganizing itself so as to integrate the deviations produced on the margins of its subsystems amounts to a theory of autonomous systemic organization, an affirmation that the global cognitive enterprise behaves like an autonomous system. Here is how she describes the systemic character of thought:

> Approached from the outside, through its historical-cultural body, the mass of thought presents itself as a system that authorizes differences and initiates deviations, so as to englobe them and displace itself in their direction. . . . The mass exists as thinking by the deviations that it sets up and founds. It regulates the deviations (it rejects them or integrates them), and they structure it by partially reorganizing it. Sometimes the reorganization can attain a magnitude that was not contained in the initial deviation. The reorganization can gain a consequence [*portée*] that was not included in the initiative of the deviation: and it is in this manner that the deviation is fertile. [248]

---

[5]If a system's organization is determined by information received from its environment, then it is not autonomous; the decision to treat what comes from the exterior as noise is an affirmation of the system's autonomy vis-à-vis this exterior.

The presence of deviations and their integration is what makes the system a thinking one, an active system and not an inert collection. The system determines its own limits, its future configurations, through the self-regulation of deviations; this process, however, can open onto developments of unexpected magnitude, since what seems at first a minor deviation can lead to a considerable reorganization, to significant gains in complexity. This means that the "mass of thought" not only regulates itself but founds itself in a continuous process:

> Intellectual invention is not only invention that takes place within the intellectual order, but, more fundamentally, the invention of that which is intellectual itself in its subsistence as an order. It is the intellectual order that is permanently invented, produced, regulated and legitimated by itself. So the heuristic question is the question of the self-constitution of meaning. . . . If meaning invents and founds meaning, the question of rationality is less the question of the foundation than that of the limit of the rational space. [250, 253]

Which utterances are accepted as rational, which are rejected as deviant is determined by a cognitive community whose tradition changes in continuity with itself. At any given moment in the history of such a system, there are utterances that are integrable and others that are not; there are, in other words, cognitive interactions of which the system is capable and others of which it is not.

The epistemological framework of Schlanger's systemic account of invention comes very close in this respect to the notion of *cognitive domain* advanced by Maturana and Varela. "The domain of interaction that an autonomous system can enter through structural plasticity without loss of closure," writes Varela, "constitutes its cognitive domain."[6] By "structural plasticity" is meant the capacity of the system to modify its form, its configuration, while remaining within the organizational constraints that constitute its identity. This is essentially what Schlanger calls "partial reorganization." Varela, in keeping with his insistence that the notion of representation does not do justice to the nature of information in autonomous systems, defines *cognition* as adequate and self-consistent behavior in the face of perturbations and not as the establishment of representations of a reality outside the knowing system. Schlanger, in the passage quoted above, likewise propounds a criterion of cognition located in self-regulation and self-

[6]Varela, *Principles of Biological Autonomy*, 263.

legitimation rather than in well-founded correspondence to an object. Since we have no direct access to our own cognitive domain, Varela argues, we cannot claim that it "represents" something existing independently of our experience or of our identity as knowing beings. Neither Varela nor Schlanger, however, are proposing solipsism or radical subjectivity, because as individuals we are linked by a world of shared regularities and by a consensual linguistic domain; moreover, the autonomous systems in which we participate, society and its subgroups, also function as units of cognition. Varela concludes, "Our knowledge, including science, can be accurately empirical and experimental, without requiring for it the claim of solidity or fixed reference."[7]

The resonances of Schlanger's work—the importance of the past, of metaphor, of verbal and cultural milieus, the schema of deviation and self-regulation within a knowing system—seem to be precisely those of our study of literary texts in an informational world, but the problematics of intellectual invention do not apply directly to literary study as we know it. Indeed, Schlanger specifically excludes noncognitive uses of language from her field of inquiry, just as she excludes nonverbal intuition. Literary studies are by no means absent from her work, but they can be recognized most often in Schlanger's countermodels, her examples of disciplines not centered on inventive thought. She describes two types of discourse on or around cultural texts that effectively deny their participation in intellectual invention. The first is "an exposition entirely conducted by what is cultural that speaks within it" (234), a discourse, in other words, that aims simply to reproduce or give voice to a part of culture without attempting to invent anything new. Here is how Schlanger describes one such disciplinary discourse: "the history of philosophy is led to seek its guarantees of seriousness in competence, technicity and the recognition of peers (erudition, punch cards, conferences). Where success has for its index the sentiment of seriousness, rather than fecundity, the history of philosophy is doomed to an essentially tautological conception of research. Serious research there cannot be anything but the opposite of innovation."[8] Here the researcher must fill in details and gather evidence without calling into question or modifying in the slightest the disciplinary practices of philosophy or historiography. This tautological temp-

[7]Varela, *Principles of Biological Autonomy*, 277.
[8]Schlanger, *Penser la bouche pleine*, 85.

tation stems from a situation in which the disciplinary matrix is not a paradigm that can itself enter into the dynamics of inquiry and innovation but a pseudoparadigm that remains locked into a relatively inflexible tradition, either because of academic inertia or because of lack of communication with genuine, contemporary intellectual problems.

This situation can certainly be found in literary studies in those places such as the old Sorbonne where the literary historical paradigm, epitomized in France by the *agrégation*, still reigns supreme. Jean Gaulmier, a recently retired literature professor from the Sorbonne, described his "annual metamorphosis" into the spokesman of one of the authors chosen for the year's examination as a "total abrogation" of the creative self: "the more allergic you are to the author who falls on you unexpectedly, the more you must strive to know him intimately so as to produce him in the profound truth of *his* being. He has all the rights, he does, and you, none. Nothing but the duty of placing yourself at his service."[9] This unquestioning defense of tautology is all the more remarkable in that its author, a novelist in his preprofessional youth, describes the cost of this severe discipline with bitter lucidity: "the teaching of literature, for whoever feels a creative gift, is a subtle form of suicide . . . here you are, transformed into a parrot (an erudite parrot, of course!) repeating in a docile voice lessons, clichés, banalities, platitudes." Gaulmier seems genuinely troubled by the cost in ruined creativity of tautological literary history, but at no point does he suggest changing the institution and the disciplinary configuration that are responsible. Like many of the critics who have inveighed publicly against what they call deconstructionist criticism, Gaulmier apparently considers the ideal of pure subservience to the author's message to be the only legitimate mission of the scholar. To the extent that such attitudes continue to prevail, the study of literature can certainly not be said to be a possible terrain of intellectual invention.

The second kind of discourse which for Schlanger keeps the cultural text at a distance from intellectual invention is textual formalism, which takes the text itself as its object of knowledge (234). Such is the project of the critics whom Rorty has called "weak textualists."[10]

[9]Jean Gaulmier, "Dépôt de bilan," *Le Monde*, March 8, 1985, p. 27.
[10]Rorty's weak textualists believe that literary works are autonomous, and that the critic's true task is the understanding of each text's unique formal codes. "The only textualists who . . . take seriously [the metaphysical-sounding claim that there are only texts] are the weak ones—the critics who think they have now found the true method for analyzing literary works because they have now found the fundamental problematic with which these works deal" (*Consequences of Pragmatism*, 153).

They may engage in inventive thought insofar as they refine their techniques of textual analysis, but in general they do not take seriously the cognitive aims or contents of the text in question. Whatever new information is gained concerning the noncognitive dimensions of texts comes at the price of setting aside their intellectual content. Such a sacrifice might well be of negligible importance, were the results of formal analyses themselves productive of new understanding. Unfortunately, the production of ever more sophisticated or simply different formal textual analyses does not necessarily participate in a cognitive project any more dynamic than that of resuscitating the thoughts of dead authors.

Literature and Knowledge

Literature and literary studies need not be consigned to a museum, far removed from the dynamics of intellectual invention: such at least is the major thesis of this book. The conjectures concerning literary and information theory, notably concerning the role of noise in the creation of meaning, amount to a secondary thesis, one which provides a context for arguing that literature participates in the process by which new ideas and new constructions of reality are formed. At the level of an individual reading, textual ambiguity and even undecidability oblige the reader to understand the text in a more complex manner and to participate actively and freely in a construction of meaning. Literary texts and their study thus provide what might be called a pedagogical service to the intellectual enterprise in that they constitute a cultural apprenticeship of complexity, of the approach to complex systems. Our aim in the present chapter, however, is to look beyond the intersection of literature and the individual mind toward an understanding of literature's place within the more extended cognitive systems formed by cultural groups or, ultimately, all of humanity. The individual mind, as Bateson, Varela, and others have taught, is not the only unit of cognition: one may quite reasonably dissociate literary studies from the primacy of the individual conscious subject, which has until so recently dominated them, without adopting the view that literature consists of meaningless free play.

Theories of intersubjective cognitive systems make the claim that knowledge advances in processes that have coherence of their own beyond any individual's mind or will. But these theories do not yet provide a full account of such processes or of how individual cognitive acts participate in them. I have taken Judith Schlanger's account of intellectual invention as a first approximation of this kind of process. The intellectual space of a cognitive community is itself a complex system, with many kinds of subsystems, each with its own organization, and varying degrees of communication between these. Within such a system, differences are produced which may be propagated, amplified, stored, or suppressed; through these transformations, the intellectual space is continually restructured but does not lose organizational identity. This intellectual space is homogeneous neither in space nor time; what passes for knowledge at one place or moment may not necessarily do so at others, and what has fallen into disuse somewhere, sometime, may later and elsewhere become significant.

Literary texts may not themselves be created with a cognitive aim or to advance knowledge, but they, their writing and reading, participate in the processes in which knowledge is created. When works *are* created with cognitive aims, these aims may have little relation to the works' eventual participation in the production of knowledge. Both individually and collectively, works of literature constitute a space of repetition and diffusion marked by difference and deviation. Cognitive statements are made in literature, although they may undergo a kind of transformation that gives them an internally referential or aesthetic function as well as a cognitive one. Literature thus restates and transforms utterances that are pertinent to the production of knowledge, although in the age of its own autonomization literature has been increasingly unconcerned with giving these utterances back to cognitive fields. But poems, novels, plays, and essays still belong to the cultural space in which deviations from existing norms of thought arise, and they can contribute no less, and perhaps more, to the invention of the new than do other forms of discourse in which the existing state of knowledge is explicitly circulated. In particular, the pseudoautonomy of the literary text necessitates a certain transformation of whatever semantic material enters it, a transformation in which a set of concepts, images, and linguistic elements become linked in a circuit of mutually implicating relations. What we call literary form, in other words, implies an internally oriented, pseudoautonomous context in which the elements of artistic text enter into a unique complex of relations. This new context differs, of course, from the much looser context within which these elements could have been situated in the general cultural circulation of ideas, images, and words. To be sure, the contextual and relational differences entailed by this process of literary textuality may often be of no cognitive bearing or importance whatsoever: the production of differences guarantees neither their pertinence nor their cultural survival and propagation. This amounts to another statement of the idea that literature can never be a reliable bearer of already fixed information; there is no use in making a dogma out of the proposition that "literature conveys knowledge," which would be better replaced by "sometimes literature 'conveys' knowledge in unpredictably interesting ways."

For those who identify knowledge with fixed, authoritative statements, and would consign other kinds of utterances to the domain of aesthetics or perhaps free play, the position I am arguing amounts to a paradox, the paradox of affirming that knowledge inhabits literature but does so in a way inimical to knowledge. My argument is addressed, rather, to those who would "make truth laugh," like Umberto Eco's William of Baskerville at the end of *The Name of the Rose*. Literary criticism in its most traditional form has too long been stern-faced and dogmatic, has too long been devoted to tautology and to the reproduction of fixed schemas from the past. As such it has been the necessary target of those who have sought liberation from the serious and heavy-handed truths supposedly guaranteed by representation, by fixed reference, by an unbroken link to origins. Their attack has quite naturally adopted formalistic stances that simply exclude the cognitive or knowledge-bearing character of texts. Can we now rehabilitate the "contents" of literary works, burning the quotation marks around that word so deeply in our minds as to keep us perpetually on guard against the dogmatism, the refusal to accept our immersion in language, that the notion of content implies?

The participation of literature in the elaboration of knowledge goes beyond the production of displacements or differences through pseudoautonomous textual organization. The operation of knowing appears in literature no less than in discursive forms that are overtly devoted to the production or diffusion of knowledge. No one can draw an unerasable line between aesthetically and cognitively oriented texts. Attempting to limit her own discussion to the latter, Schlanger observes that what we call literature, even in the modern age, includes much that is cognitive. "A profoundly intellectual meditation or diction is borne throughout cultural history by forms that are not abstract discursive forms" (216). The poetic project of combining elements of language in a way that has never been done before coincides partially with the inventive project of making hitherto unheard statements about the world. The inseparability of form and content, theorized since the romantics, has often been described by modern writers as a revelation of "content" through the act of writing. In 1985 the French daily *Libération* asked a large group of writers the question, "Why do you write?" John Ashbery answered: "if I did not write, I would have no idea of what I can write. I suppose that I write so as to find what I have to write."[11] If no "content" exists before "its" expression, then whatever "content" the work may be perceived to have depends, for its existence, on the process of writing as process of invention. Writers often describe this work of invention as cognitive rather than strictly aesthetic. Italo Calvino, in answer to the above-mentioned question, proposed: "To learn things that I didn't know . . . the written page [is a] trap in which I hope to capture some vestiges of the knowledge, the wisdom that in my life I have only brushed up against."[12] The composition of a verbal text seems to fulfill a heuristic function: it proves nothing, provides no guarantee of pertinence or truth, but aids in discovery. If one accepts the idea that there is no escape from language, no knowledge independent of codes and signs, then the finding of new formulations and the discovery of new ideas can never be fully separated. In this context, it is worth recalling Lotman's analysis of a language's potential for the conversion of aesthetic information into semantic information. The author may begin with something to say and choose between ways of saying it, but in so doing he invests "what he had to say" with increased informational specificity; for the reader, who cannot imagine the text "expressed differently," the fact of literary form has thus produced an increase in receivable information.

There are nonetheless two notable features of literature, or at least of much writing that passes for literary, that have been generally taken as incompatible with the discursive statements of knowledge. Poetic or fictional texts, as opposed to expository or speculative writings, seem to have a special rapport with the particular and with the affective. Since Plato and Aristotle, but even more strikingly since the great successes of early modern science, Western culture has identified knowledge with the general, the universal, specifically with the repeatable or

[11]"Pourquoi écrivez-vous?" *Libération*, special issue, March 1985, p. 47.
[12]"Pourquoi écrivez-vous?" p. 68.

reproducible. Scientific experiments, and their counterparts in the social sciences, must yield observations that are reproducible under like
conditions; otherwise they are judged invalid, not part of science.
Large sectors of our disciplinary landscape simply exclude from their
consideration phenomena that are singular, local, nonrepeatable. But
this is a cultural choice: it does not mean that concrete particulars or
unique experiences cannot become part of some other discourse of
knowledge. The debate concerning the status, in knowledge, of unpredictable, nonreproducible events does not divide science and literature,
for, as we have noted, it takes place within science itself. Commenting
on *La Nouvelle Alliance*, Serres wrote: "We are going to find science in
circumstances: they used to have no science. We are going to find circumstances in science: it used to have no circumstances."[13] If we were
now to exclude what is written in literature from the domain of knowledge, we would be doing so in accordance with a model of science past,
foreclosing what is at least recognized as a possibility in the science of
the present and the future. Ever since literature took on its romantic,
modern meaning, it has served in effect as the refuge of types of knowing and knowledge that fell outside the dominant categories of rationality or predictive efficacy. As the boundaries of disciplines, of what is
considered knowledge, shift ever more rapidly, there is no reason for
literary studies not to consider the types of knowledge that both reside
and mask themselves in literature.

There is, similarly, no need to maintain a radical opposition between the intellectual and the affective, to question literature's place in
the former because of its complicity with the latter. Rhetoric, for example, has traditionally been considered to contribute ornamentation or
persuasion, but the work of Derrida, de Man, and Schlanger (among
others) has shown it to be inseparable from intellectual content. More
important, perhaps, and still not fully assimilated by thinkers in the humanities, is the fact that physiology has long since done away with the
absolute opposition of the "head" and the "heart." What we call emo-
tions arise as a function of the nervous system; they may be distinguished, of course, from other neurological functions, but cannot simply be considered independent of and opposed to cognitive operations.
Literature's link to affectivity, far from disqualifying it as a source of
knowledge, suggests rather an enlarged concept of knowledge or ra-

[13]Michel Serres, "Commencements," *Le Monde*, January 4, 1980, p. 13.

tionality. I do not mean to offer a defense of feeling or irrationality or mysticism: the point here is not to affirm the fusion of intellect and emotion but simply to leave open the possibility that the two are not always radically opposed. By arguing that what is said in literature falls outside the field of knowledge, criticism has perpetuated what may be a reductive and archaic distinction between knowing and feeling.

If no generally valid opposition can be made between inventive thought and invention in language, if the two are at once distinct and intertwined, then the difference between cognitive and poetic acts should not be taken as natural or self-evident. Their difference belongs rather to our cultural practice of discursive genres; in other words, to historically established and defined rules concerning the legitimacy of different uses of language in different contexts. What is called cognitive, what poetic, has to do with relations of power. The criteria of evaluation and assent applied to a literary work differ from those applied to a work of philosophy or sociology, but this fact does not prevent each of them from being part of a process of cognitive invention. And these criteria of judgment, like other rules and practices governing the use of language, are themselves cultural products: they can be transgressed by individuals and eventually modified by collectivities. The division of knowledge is not eternal, nor is it simply a one-way process of division and exclusion: what has been separated can once again be brought together, what has been cast out can be reintegrated. Serres, in *Le Passage du nord-ouest*, argues that the split between literary and scientific culture, and the assumption that knowledge resides with the latter and not the former, cannot last forever:

> Where are the debris of the division of knowledge and of the sciences?
> . . . One day the epistemologists will go through the garbage cans. One day scientists, tired of a sterilized terrain where nothing will grow anymore, will go to look for a new fecundity on the very ground that they disdain today. Even among old wives tales, even among what they call babble, literature, imagination. We are, we literati and philosophers, more and more perceived as the residue of the division of knowledge. In fact, we are the reserve of knowledge. Yes, the fecundity of science to come. In the garbage cans of the division, we will find the world itself.[14]

The possibility of a role for literature in intellectual invention, in the creation of new meaning and eventually new knowledge, suggests the possibility of a double shift in the practice of what we call literary studies. In the first place, critical practice can perhaps better coincide

[14]Serres, *Hermes V: Le Passage du nord-ouest*, 109.

with what literature really is. We can move away from the idea that lit-erature is essentially representational (or, negatively, the scene of rep-resentation's impossibility); away, in other words, from the notion that reader, critic, and scholar are out to receive a message, submitting their work of reception to the primacy and authority of text or author. Such a conceptual shift need not be destructive: what emerges is not so much the loss of authorial meaning as the production of new meaning by readers. By this "production of new meaning" I do not refer to the solipsistic and arbitrary replacement of textual meaning by readerly creations but, rather, to the participation of reading in cultural systems of invention that cannot be reduced to transmission and reception. New meaning is produced not in a context of communication and re-ception but at a different level or moment within a system of which communication is but a part, a stage at which the work's position can-not be simply that of input to a transmission channel. The attempt to know a work as fully as possible, in other words, is not the only legiti-mate intellectual stance to adopt toward it.

The other aspect of the conceptual shift possible for literary studies would be a move away from the idea that literature is only really inter-esting for its form. The history of criticism shows that this idea has served as a refuge for those who refused the dogmatism of literary study considered as the passive reception and reproduction of a tradi-tion invested with authority. But if the rigidity of "dogmatic" criticism is definitely set aside, then the reductiveness of "immanent" criticism, which bracketed the question of content and meaning, may no longer be necessary.[15] Much has been learned by making literature into the object of a disciplinary inquiry with its own cognitive aims, but in the process the diverse cognitive aims dissimulated in literary texts have of-ten been set aside. It may now be possible to take such contents seri-ously, without investing them with an authority that would make them a source of dogma, that would make their cultural impact purely conservative.

We are now in a position to return to the speculations of Roland Barthes concerning science and literature. The latter, he argued, incor-porates within it all knowledge, in a unified, nonmutilated form. In encountering literature we moderns yearn to escape—temporarily —from the split, compartmentalized knowledge proposed by our sev-eral disciplines. Perhaps Barthes was too romantic in comparing litera-

---

[15]On "immanent" and "dogmatic" criticism, and their eventual *Aufhebung* in "dia-logical" criticism, see Todorov, *Critique de la critique*, 179–193.

ture to the "grand cosmogonic unity which so delighted the ancient Greeks."[16] The knowledge associated with literature may escape disciplinary categories, but this does not make it universal. In fact, Barthes's own preference for a literary knowledge, inseparable from language, implies a refusal of claims to universality. It is what he calls science, with its claim of getting outside language and of establishing truths independent of culture, that promotes its utterances to the status of universal explanations, its descriptions to the status of representations of what is natural. If, conversely, knowledge is taken to reside only in language (with language, of course, taken in its widest possible sense, as all possible cultural signifying systems), then knowledge must form a self-coherent system of the kind described by Varela and Schlanger. Cognitive statements in language form an autonomous system that undergoes structural change without loss of continuity. (A loss of continuity would, in this case, amount to the cessation of the collective cognitive efforts of *Homo sapiens*—a cessation that is not, of course, impossible.) In this view knowledge is not representational but coherent and effective. Barthes referred to knowledge in literature as *written*: there are of course other modes of being-in-language than that of writing, but this is a way of designating discourse that assumes fully the properties of language. It is no accident that Barthes notes the "regression of the autonomy of language" that accompanied the rise of rationalism and empiricism, for the notion of *written* knowledge precedes, and now follows, the Cartesian dream of knowledge produced in the unmediated rapport of the subject with ontological reality. To seek and find knowledge in literature—where the autonomy of language is made manifest—is to accept that the act of knowing resides in language and community, that it is part of an adaptive and self-coherent system and not a representation of reality.

Politics of Criticism?

> Dissent must be of a higher logical type
> than that with which it is in conflict.
> ANTHONY WILDEN,
> *System and Structure*

[16]Barthes, *The Rustle of Language*, trans. R. Howard (New York, 1986), 3–4.

Near the beginning of his masterpiece, *Hopscotch*, Julio Cortázar describes how erudition could serve as a refuge for the more intelligent members of the Argentine middle class by leading them to take seriously a field of knowledge totally removed from the fact that just down the street people are being taken away by the police and shot. The first problem for any "politics of criticism" is the question of what criticism does with the political potentialities of its practitioners. In the United States alone many thousands of intelligent, well-educated people busy themselves with academic literary research. The products of their work accumulate in scholarly journals and in monographs that owe their economic viability to the recommendation of these same scholars concerning the use of library budgets. As was noted earlier, there is no call for this production outside the academy. Anthony Wilden, in a book published in 1972, characterized this type of discourse as a "communication of worthless units of knowledge."[17]

Many would consider this situation harmless. But among the practitioners of literary studies are thousands of people expert in the analysis of sign systems and cultural artifacts, acutely sensitive to techniques of ideological manipulation and of psychic repression in texts. More important, perhaps, these few thousands of literary scholars and theorists are for the most part keenly dissatisfied with contemporary mass culture, with the words and images that are marketed to occupy the attention of so many. Literary studies provide for them the means of palliating an experience of aesthetic alienation from society. But in retreating into an all but closed world of cultural connoisseurship, they are fleeing political realities, the very realities that it is the function of most mass culture—but probably also of their elite culture—to obscure. Academic discourse, as Pierre Bourdieu and others have noted, typically serves to trivialize and thereby neutralize symbolic violence in society. It does so by channeling the potential for utterances that would disturb the social order into forms of pseudoknowledge, where Cortázar's imagined history of nail clippers would have more legitimacy than any challenge to the existing sociosymbolic order. I have already evoked the possibility of conceptual shifts in literary studies that would move away from the idea that we seek *knowledge* of either textual contents or forms. Here is the political question in light of which such shifts must be examined: *can we move away from a situation in*

---

[17]Wilden, *System and Structure* (London, 1972), xxiv.

*which literary studies function as a safety valve, an escape for those
who otherwise would be in intellectual revolt against the dominant ideological manipulations of our time?* What is at issue is the possibility of
any political role at all for literary studies and for the persons engaged
in them. I designate as *political* all significant interventions in those
real and symbolic relations that constitute society. In this sense the invention of new relations in the symbolic domain known as knowledge
can be political or not, depending on the social or economic significance of the invention. In other words, there are linguistic and conceptual inventions that have an impact on society, and there are others
that do not have such effect. In the present state of literary studies, with
texts taken (practically, if not always in theory) as objects of a specialized knowledge, the inventions of its practitioners seem to have almost
no informational value outside of a closed and marginal circle. The formulations of academic criticism, to paraphrase Bateson, are differences
that don't make much difference.

Traditionally, the "indifference" that characterizes relations between a portion of the academic world and the society around it has
been justified and even praised on the grounds that the pure search for
knowledge requires freedom from societal pressures and can never, in
any case, interest large masses of people. But aside from its elitist implications, this type of justification fails precisely because it begs the question of the search for knowledge that goes on in literary studies. Society
accepts—though it may be a terrible error to do so—that certain kinds
of scientific research are performed by a somewhat isolated elite. Presumably the results of such research, measured in economic or technical or social performativity, are supposed to justify its cost, and this exchange value of research effectively takes the place of an informational
exchange between the scientific community and society. But without
an exchange of either information or value, how do we justify, or legitimize, literary studies?

In 1979 the French philosopher Jean-François Lyotard published
La Condition postmoderne, a report on the status of knowledge in
postindustrial society. The dominant technological and infrastructural
feature of these societies, he assumed, is their computerization: their
increasing dependence on the electronic storage, retrieval, manipulation, and transmission of information. In a world whose organization
depends on data processing on a planetary scale, knowledge whose formulations cannot be translated into machine language will in all likeli-

hood become less and less viable and will be set aside or simply not produced. As the very definition of knowledge comes to be shaped by the new conditions of its storage and diffusion, the idea that knowledge resides in the unique competence of educated subjects will lose its traditional legitimacy:

> We can thus expect a thorough exteriorization of knowledge with respect to the "knower," at whatever point he or she may be situated in the knowledge process. The old principle that the acquisition of knowledge is indissociable from the training (*Bildung*) of minds, or even of individuals, is becoming obsolete and will become even more so. . . . Knowledge is and will be produced in order to be sold, and it will be consumed in order to be valorized in a new production: in both cases, the goal is exchange. Knowledge ceases to be an end in itself; it loses its "use value."[18]

Many would argue that to palliate the evils of such a dehumanized world of knowledge requires nothing less than a vigorous return to the most traditional aims of humanistic education. The study of literature, in this view, should shun contamination by other disciplines and concentrate on individual and social Bildung. Literary studies would oppose postmodern fragmentation by providing a common cultural foundation and fostering a human-centered mode of knowing. It is unlikely, however, that proclamations from the National Endowment of the Humanities or the Secretary of Education can do much to alter the structure of the information-based society. If we believe that literary education and research ought to continue as anything but comforting and prestigious anachronisms, we shall have to begin explaining why this is so in the idioms of postmodernism and information, and not simply by a nostalgic appeal to traditional grounds of legitimacy.

Lyotard's argument does not rely solely or even primarily on sociological speculation about computerization and its consequences. Instead he traces the cultural foundations of the contemporary crisis in the legitimacy of knowledge. Prescientific knowledge, he argues, is predominantly narrative, contained in the stories that people tell one another and legitimated in the rules and practices that govern their telling. Modern science separated knowledge from narration by providing new criteria for what constitutes knowledge and how it relates to the

---

[18]Lyotard, *The Postmodern Condition*, trans. G. Bennington and B. Massumi (Minneapolis, 1984), 4–5.

subject. As Kuhn noted, when science comes into its own and acquires paradigms, its practitioners cease to tell stories to each other; they begin to communicate in a more formal, synchronic language whose statements are supposed to have no dependence on the subjectivity or individuality of the person who utters them. The scientist's competence is ultimately professional and experimental, not something that can be founded on a story of individual development or Bildung. But science, while no longer locating knowledge in narrative, relied initially for its legitimacy on metanarratives, stories about the emergence and function of science. Throughout what Lyotard identifies as the modern period (which should not be confused with what we call modernism in literature), two master narratives, neither one too credible today, have legitimized the place of scientific knowledge in society. One tells the story of man's progressive political emancipation through the democratization of knowledge; the other, of man's intellectual progress and mastery over nature through the free pursuit of scientific and speculative knowledge. Primary and secondary education have traditionally sought legitimacy in the first narrative; the modern university in the second.

These heroic narratives of enlightenment and speculation, Lyotard argues, have long since lost their universality and thus their capacity to legitimize educational and scientific practices.[19] He doubts that conditions exist for restoring the narrative mode of legitimization, for "most people have lost the nostalgia for the lost narrative."[20] The changes in the structure of knowledge that characterize postmodern culture and the age of computerization are not in themselves ruinous for education, for research, or for society, but they appear so from the perspectives of the major narratives, which so many literary scholars still cling to or attack.

Among humanistic critics one can still find those who defend the cultural authority of traditional narrative knowledge, arguing, for example, that education should emphasize knowledge of Homer and the Bible. Somewhat more subtly, other humanists defend a position derived from the story of education as democratic liberation: they argue that literary culture must be perpetuated and shared by the many so as

---

[19]See Lyotard, *The Postmodern Condition*, 37–41, and his article "Histoire universelle et différences culturelles," *Critique* 41 (1985), 559–568.
[20]Lyotard, *The Postmodern Condition*, 41.

to produce a moral or enlightened citizenry. But this kind of knowledge or culture has always been that of an elite, and it could serve as the stuff of education only insofar as a certain individual mastery of the tradition was sufficient to ensure an individual's operational competence in society—his fitness to make decisions, for example. Today this competence depends primarily on expertise, on the ability to manipulate a precise sector of information contemporaneously defined as important. It is not very convincing to argue for the study of texts as an apprenticeship of human character, politics, and society when the student who swallows the argument then finds that society is willing to pay not for "humanity" but for the kind of expertise gained by studying, say, clinical psychology or business administration, not literature. As Barthes noted in "De la science à la littérature," the study of literature may immerse students in knowledge but does not lead to socially recognized competencies, except the teaching of literature. Literary education prepares less and less directly for any career outside the academy because society has, to a very large extent, substituted a contemporary and continually regenerated body of specialized information for the written works of the cultural past. In Lyotard's terms, the informed or informatized individual is taking over legitimacy from the formed or educated (*gebildet*) individual. Many of us in literary studies might like to live in a world in which this was not the case, but our nostalgia, even militant nostalgia, will change nothing. If we do not want the qualities we value in literary studies to fade slowly away, we must adapt our practices to reality and consider ways of promoting our sense of Bildung that are consistent with an informational world.

"Structuralist" and "deconstructionist" critical practices have so far had little success in providing new legitimation for literary studies. Like earlier critical formalisms, structuralism offered the hope of a literary study less dependent on the authority of traditional narratives or the cultural dilettantism of literary history. Formalisms have generally brought with them modern metanarratives of legitimation: stories of democratization, of demystification and intellectual mastery. Literature would finally be analyzed objectively as what it really was, a form of linguistic utterance, rather than as a traditional form of knowledge to be ingested. But the uniqueness of literary texts—which is of their essence, bound up with the uncertain nature of their autonomy and coherence—has kept literary semiology from attaining anything like the status of a science. Moreover, despite the intellectual excitement of the structuralist project, its potential cultural impact falls far short of that of the humanistic, authority-centered criticism it sought to supplant.

Into the breach opened between structuralism's program and its achievements stepped the several poststructuralisms—notably deconstruction—from which we have not heard the last. Post-structuralism appears to be the critical mode closest to Lyotard's "postmodern knowledge," a mode that has abandoned reference to both traditional narrative and scientific metanarrative. Deconstruction, because of the rigor, seriousness, and originality of its readings, possesses an intellectual legitimacy that only becomes more obvious when one considers the shallow anti-intellectualism with which it is attacked in both serious journals and the popular media. Deconstructive critics have produced a remarkably subtle and sophisticated work—yet one which has appeared to function as little more than a critical nihilism. This appearance cannot wholly be blamed on the bad faith of deconstruction's detractors. By agreeing to play the game of critical interpretation, by entering the space in which literary texts were assumed either to bear meaning or to be rationally analyzable, deconstructors were drawn into combat with humanists and formalists, and in this context their arguments typically functioned in a purely negative manner. In debunking the authority of the text, they were undermining no more than the former authority of a kind of culture no longer in power.[21] Jacques Derrida has always contended that deconstruction implies the questioning of institutional practices relating to knowledge, but most of his American disciples have used deconstruction as a technique for producing hair-raisingly unusual interpretations within business-as-usual interpretive institutions.[22] They have accordingly presented their many insights as being *about* the texts they are reading, and these insights have therefore seemed primarily negative,

[21]This may account for the defensive meanness of what we used to call in graduate school the "annual anti-deconstruction lecture": if traditional humanistic scholarship had not already lost cultural leadership, its apologists would hardly feel so threatened by deconstruction. Derrida discusses the antideconstruction campaign in a note to *Mémoires: for Paul de Man* (New York, 1986), 41–43.

[22]One important qualification must be made to this statement: deconstruction has had institutional and thus political consequences outside the study of literature per se by bringing in to the American academy philosophical traditions that had been excluded from it and thereby altering the "division of labor" between departments of literature, philosophy, and the social sciences.

sometimes trivial. Even while calling into question the foundations of interpretation, deconstructive critics have performed their readings within an academic institution where the interpretation of individual texts not only is the dominant form of discourse but passes for being a contribution to knowledge. Jonathan Culler, answering the charge of critical nihilism, wrote that "in fact, deconstructive readings draw far reaching lessons from the texts they study."[23] Granted, but they do so in the genre of the critical article or monograph, written ostensibly *about* literature and read effectively only by like-minded critics. Given this context, what might be far-reaching lessons have no more cultural impact than would the game playing of which deconstructive critics are often accused. As long as critics persist in writing *about* texts, their insights into the strangeness of texts as objects to be written about, no matter how powerful or brilliant, will remain moves within a small and unimportant game. Literary study in the era of poststructuralism is a discipline rich in complexity and intellectual effervescence, but unable or unwilling to articulate the conditions of its future legitimation.[24]

Lyotard echoes what is by now a commonplace when he states that since the fragmentation of traditional or enlightenment narratives, legitimation in both research and instruction has depended on *performativity*, on the ability to increase ratios of output to input. Politically, performativity implies the defense (through optimization) of the status quo, but that is not its only failing. An exclusive emphasis on performativity, as Lyotard notes, cannot long advance science or any other field of knowledge, for one necessary moment of that advance depends on finding the counterexample, the unintelligible, on identifying the point at which further input of resources to existing paradigms will yield almost no output. Performativity cannot ultimately legitimate research. Moreover, the contemporary transformation of science—the search for instabilities, the interest in noncontinuous, nonpredictable, self-organizing systems—takes us even further away from the linearities of input-output ratios.

In this changed situation, Lyotard argues that legitimation will depend on what he calls *paralogy*, the invention of new moves in the lin-

<hr/>

[23]Culler, *On Deconstruction* (Ithaca, 1982), 279.

[24]An even darker view is argued in a recent book by Michael Fischer, who writes, "deconstruction does make a difference: it reinforces established political and educational arrangements rather than damaging them or leaving them as they are" (*Does Deconstruction Make Any Difference?* [Bloomington, 1985], 125).

guistic and symbolic games that constitute knowledge and society. What will count as knowledge will be what permits new approaches, opens up new structures of relation, preserves systems from rigidity, and makes possible their transformation. Performativity implies the optimization of a homeostatic system, one whose goal is stability in sameness; paralogy implies the restructuring of a system changing in unpredictable ways. Paralogy is not limited to conceptual invention, for it includes innovations that are not purely cognitive but pragmatic, that intervene in society's symbolic transactions. It is reasonable, therefore, to seek in the study of literature not pure knowledge, not a means of dishing out a common cultural fare to the many, but a part of the process wherein new concepts, practices, and symbolic moves are invented and propagated.

Literature differs radically from the sort of communicative act likely to predominate in an information society, for what we regard as most significant in the experience of literary reading cannot be translated into machine language. Indeed were one to accept Lyotard's analysis fully, it would appear that literary practices in the strongest sense will simply disappear from the map of knowledge. This could happen. But Lyotard's own conclusions concerning the importance of paralogy suggest another alternative: forms of knowledge and discourse that appear irrelevant to an informational society might yet have a legitimate role if they can contribute to paralogical innovation, to the creation of new concepts in intellectual invention and moves in the pragmatic games of language.

There is a direct link between this kind of social speculation on the role of literary studies and the informational account of literature presented in this book. Literature is not and will not ever again be at the center of culture, if indeed it ever was. There is no use in either proclaiming or debunking its central position. Literature is the noise of culture, the rich and indeterminate margin into which messages are sent off, never to return the same, in which signals are received not quite like anything emitted. We do not live in the written culture of the past as in a splendid monument, wherein we might read, and bow down before, timeless inscriptions; we live rather on top of it as on a rubbish heap, and some of us are crazy enough to scrounge for treasures, or for bits and pieces from which we think we can invent something unique. Literary texts are imperfect vehicles of messages and imperfect autonomous structures: they do not reliably bear authoritative knowledge, and attempts to take them as objects of knowledge must confront both their elusiveness and the sheer irrelevance of such a task. By recognizing the irreducible presence of noise in literature, and in turn literature's function as the noise of culture, we can understand how literary meaning can be neither authoritative nor nonexistent, how literature's cultural function can be positive and yet not conservative. Out of old literature can come new meaning—but only if we cease to regard the question of certifying or debunking old meaning as the only valid one to ask. What might be called the innovative potential of literature remains inactive as long as the only system in which literature is taken seriously remains one whose only mission is to take literature seriously.

Literature is a residue of a no longer dominant mode of cultural organization. It can thus function as an internal perturbation of our cultural systems, not altogether foreign but marked by a trace of exteriority. Wilden has observed that "noise in the historical ecosystem is necessarily engendered by its being out of step with itself."[25] Literature is a discursive form and an archive that is out of step with technocratic modernity. It cannot therefore supply that modernity and its political institutions with reassuring narratives or metanarratives to live by; it can only perturb them as a kind of noise. Yet it is only because of internal perturbation, whether arising from memory or from the plurality of cognitive and discursive strategies, that we can be observers of ourselves (see note 1 above). Internal noise, in other words, keeps us from being so fully integrated into a silently functioning system that we would cease to be aware of it as system. In research and teaching, our most important task may be to preserve literature's potential as a source of noise and difference, to avoid containing its perturbations in reassuringly ordered theoretical and pedagogical constructions.

The theory of self-organization from noise is not a gadget for producing readings and interpretations: it is an attempt to describe what *can* happen, what sometimes but far from always does happen, when what is noise in one context enters another where it may become information. In the course of this book I have occasionally mentioned domains of opportunity for study using and involving literature that would not be limited to the study of literature. But these suggestions, spin-offs from the arguments pursued in these pages, are but a few inci-

---

[25]Wilden, *System and Structure*, 403.

dental possibilities, to which I wish to accord no privilege whatsoever. Above all, they are not methodological suggestions. With the exception of the simply illustrative discussion of *Le Cousin Pons* and Serres in Chapter 2, there are no "text interpretations" in *The Noise of Culture*, and their absence is both deliberate and essential. This book is not a work of practical criticism.

Any theory that can be "applied" to produce interpretations is of the same logical type as the theories that now proliferate in literary studies, and thus cannot be a form of dissent from those studies and the role that theories play within them. A critical theory that does not directly produce text readings has at least the potential of being more subversive than one that does, because it calls into question, if only for a moment, the whole context in which theory and practical criticism are carried out. What I am trying to suggest is that there could be serious intellectual uses of literature outside the limits of what is currently considered literary criticism. This is not a statement of literary theory but belongs, rather, to a metatheory about the possibility of cross-disciplinary writing involving literature and other discourses of knowledge. In suggesting this possibility, I claim no theoretical basis for privileging one kind of intellectual use for texts or excluding any others. Such choices must of course be made, but they are political choices, which cannot be made or avoided on the basis of a theory of literature.

Emphasis on the futility of taking literature itself as an object of disciplinary knowledge may sound like an indictment of literary studies, or perhaps their death warrant. But as the theorists of performative utterances remind us, indictments or death warrants can be enounced only by persons invested with the special competence and authority to do so. University departments and curricula devoted to the study of literature are a part of our culture and institutions, and an authority capable of pronouncing their dissolution would be quite properly terrifying. But practitioners of literary studies have considerable leeway in choosing their projects and intellectual preoccupations. They can, to an extent, move away from the dead center of their discipline, from the project of interpreting and describing texts as fully as possible.[26] They

[26]This freedom of individuals is constrained by institutions, so that what can be expected at most is a gradual structural transformation of the latter. Michael Polanyi's account of liberal institutions states the problem very clearly: "The recognition granted in a free society to the independent growth of science, art and morality, involves a dedication of society to the fostering of a specific tradition of thought, transmitted and culti-

can take forms of knowledge other than the strictly literary as components of their reflection, and this they have not infrequently done. More important, they can devote themselves to projects other than *knowing texts*. As disciplines literary studies offer the immense advantage of being defined (very loosely, at that) by large bodies of writings and not by any particular methodology—whence the leeway enjoyed by their practitioners in the choice and conduct of their endeavors. In this sense the presence of disciplinary centers in literature makes possible a considerable degree of autonomy in research vis-à-vis the more instrumental, competence-oriented disciplines. This potential for autonomy and variety, and thus for many different paths through fields of knowledge and discourse, nonetheless often remains either unrealized (because research lets itself be guided by transitory but powerful methodological doxas) or insignificant (because when literary research does not intersect with other areas of inquiry it remains a closed and isolated game). The discipline of literary studies per se can perhaps best be seen as a *fictive center*, forever differing from itself, constantly deviating from itself both in object and method so as to speak in many idioms, bring complexity out of the disorder of many crisscrossing series of messages.

Many will doubtless consider the emphasis on invention, paralogy, decentering, and shifts of interpretive context to be a manifesto for solipsism and anarchy, or perhaps for *relevance*. They have a point: nothing could damage literary studies more than a facile attitude according to which we should simply glean from poetic texts or works of the past whatever suits us for our own intellectual creations. The value of literature lies in its strangeness, its otherness, its capacity to surprise and confound, and these traits do not appear without serious study that re-

---

vated by a particular group of authoritative specialists, perpetuating themselves by co-option. To uphold the independence of thought implemented by such a society is to subscribe to a kind of orthodoxy which, though it specifies no fixed articles of faith, is virtually unassailable within the limits imposed on the process of innovation by the cultural leadership of a free society. . . . And we must also face the fact that this orthodoxy, and the cultural authorities which we respect, are backed by the coercive power of the state and financed by the beneficiaries of office and property" (*Personal Knowledge: Towards a Post-Critical Philosophy* [Chicago, 1958], 244). The extent to which literary studies have changed over the past twenty years, however, suggests that the "structural plasticity" of these disciplines may be greater than it once appeared to be. This probably reflects the degree to which they have lost much of their traditional function of legitimation.

spects, at least for a very long moment, the autonomy and integrity of the text. If the literary text fascinates us because of its irreducibility to any schema not itself, then we have everything to lose by reducing it from the outset to the status of a support for our own ideas. This is the essential tension of teaching literature: students should be encouraged to respond in original ways to texts, but without the discipline of rhetorical and historical training they will be unable to recognize what is most specifically strange and thus authentically provocative of originality in those texts. This kind of tension should be understood as being fundamental to research as well. Without a strong center of literary studies, without both historical scholarship and literary theory, what is potentially most unique in literature, from an informational standpoint, would probably go unnoticed. But the temptation is great to take this disciplinary center not as a supreme fiction but as an end in itself: to assume, in other words, that the ultimate goal of literary studies is more accurate literary scholarship and more precisely descriptive literary theory. Relevance has often been maligned, but its antonym is still irrelevance. And while the existence of an interpretive or cognitive community, capable of communication within itself, doubtless requires a certain degree of agreement, of redundancy in interpretation, there is no reason to regard the mission of literary education as the production of readers who will read in the same way, or who will read in conformity to an established tradition. Nor do we need teachers who will encourage sameness in reading.

Our freedom to create meaning out of texts implies intellectual responsibility within a community, not solipsism. Abdication of responsibility, on the contrary, lies in the attempt to make intention or tradition into guarantees of seriousness or even critical righteousness. We often treat texts as though they were messages in a transmission channel, as though our task was to recover as best we can what must have been the input to the channel. But in the way in which literary texts exist for us, this context of transmission has no particular privilege. To call a text a text asserts that it is now an informational structure cast into complex circuits of communication and dissemination; its meaning cannot henceforth be reduced to any authorial or even transpersonal intention, even if we recognize that some traces of a project to say something can always be recovered from it. Perhaps with every text there was once intention. There is now nothing but the text, no guarantee of being able to move behind or through it to a meaning not itself.

Once cast, the text becomes the stuff of dissemination, never again subject to the mastery of he or she who brought it forth in language. The responsibility to make the texts mean something, to use the texts, now belongs to us, who encounter them. Attempting to recover an original intention of meaning is but one way to proceed, a way that possesses to be sure a certain historical and cultural privilege but no absolute precedence. The responsibility for what kind of readings are made or fostered falls on the present-day community of readers. The choices are political and value-laden for us, not for the authors. If we encourage a purely aesthetic approach, then we are creating, perpetuating, and reinforcing a kind of society in which aesthetic practices and objects remain apart from "practical" or "serious" things. If we insist on the recovery of authorial intention, we are reinforcing the practice of controlled communication, of commands issued and obeyed. And so on. We have the choice of using texts from the past to invent the new, or of using them to inculcate what has been said before. We have, to be sure, a philological responsibility, that of preserving the texts as they were for the future, so that their strangeness does not erode into the familiar. But we have no obligation to make our own discourse an echo of what we preserve.

Literary texts, I have argued, organize and produce the noise of culture. They are a strange kind of object, both/neither autonomous and/nor intentional. In them we find an inextricable mixture of the unknown to be investigated and the intelligible to be decoded. Their study, taken as an autonomous activity, is a fairly recent cultural invention, one that has produced a rich and uneven body of knowledge. But, like other disciplines, it does not possess immortality. Its future, or the future of what is now part of it, lies in new cognitive groupings, as yet unrealized or even unsuspected ways of organizing and dividing knowledge. Tomorrow's disciplines will one day appear to have been situated across, between, interspersed among, the disciplines of today. By studying literature as an informational system, using a language that comes from science, we both theorize the necessity of interdisciplinarity for literary studies and begin to create the conditions for concrete interdisciplinary work. Out of a new dialogue between literature and science, out of interferences between disciplinary discourses, we may yet be able to arrange a graceful exit from the era of *Literaturwissenschaft*.

BIBLIOGRAPHY

Arac, Jonathan. Afterword to *The Yale Critics: Deconstruction in America*, ed. J. Arac, W. Godzich, and W. Martin. Minneapolis: University of Minnesota Press, 1983.

Arbib, Michael A., and Mary B. Hesse. *The Construction of Reality*. Cambridge: Cambridge University Press, 1986.

Atlan, Henri. *A tort et à raison*. Paris: Seuil, 1986.

———. "Créativité biologique et auto-création du sens." In *Cognition et complexité*, 145–189.

———. "Disorder, Complexity and Meaning." In *Disorder and Order*, ed. P. Livingston, 109–128.

———. "L'Emergence du nouveau et du sens." In *L'Auto-organisation*, ed. P. Dumouchel and J.-P. Dupuy, 115–130.

———. *Entre le cristal et la fumée: Essai sur l'organisation du vivant*. Paris: Seuil, 1979.

———. *L'Organisation biologique et la théorie de l'information*. Paris: Hermann, 1972.

Bar-Hillel, Yehoshua. *Language and Information: Selected Essays on Their Theory and Applications*. Reading, Mass.: Addison-Wesley, 1964.

Barthes, Roland. *Le Bruissement de la langue: Essais critiques, IV*. Paris: Seuil, 1984. Translated as *The Rustle of Language*. Trans. R. Howard. New York: Hill and Wang, 1986.

Bateson, Gregory. *Steps to an Ecology of Mind*. New York: Ballantine, 1972.

Blanchot, Maurice. *L'Entretien infini*. Paris: Gallimard, 1969.

———. *Le Livre à venir*. Paris: Gallimard, 1959.

Calvino, Italo. *The Uses of Literature*. Trans. P. Creagh. New York: Harcourt Brace Jovanovich, 1986.

Chambers, Ross. "Including the Excluded." Review of Michel Serres's
    Hermes: Literature, Science, Philosophy. Degré Second, no. 7 (July 1983),
    185–193.
Cognition et complexité. Cahiers du C.R.E.A., 9. Paris: Centre de recherche
    épistémologie et autonomie, 1986.
Cohen, Jean. *Structure du langage poétique.* Paris: Flammarion, 1966.
Culler, Jonathan. *On Deconstruction.* Ithaca: Cornell University Press, 1982.
———. *The Pursuit of Signs: Semiotics, Literature, Deconstruction.* Ithaca:
    Cornell University Press, 1981.
De Man, Paul. *Allegories of Reading.* New Haven: Yale University Press,
    1979.
———. *Blindness and Insight.* New York: Oxford University Press, 1971.
———. "The Resistance to Theory." *Yale French Studies* 63 (1982), 3–20.
Derrida, Jacques. *La Carte postale.* Paris: Aubier-Flammarion, 1980.
———. *Mémoires: for Paul de Man.* New York: Columbia University Press,
    1986.
Dumouchel, P., and J.-P. Dupuy, eds. *L'Auto-organisation: De la physique au
    politique.* Colloque de Cerisy. Paris: Seuil, 1983.
Dupuy, Jean-Pierre. *Ordres et désordres: Enquête sur un nouveau paradigme.*
    Paris: Seuil, 1982.
Eichner, Hans. "The Rise of Modern Science and the Genesis of
    Romanticism." *PMLA* 97 (1982), 8–30.
Gans, Eric. "Differences." *MLN* 96 (1981), 792–808.
Garin, Eugenio. *L'Education de l'homme moderne: La Pédagogie de la
    Renaissance (1400–1600).* Paris: Fayard, 1968.
Gaulmier, Jean, "Dépôt de bilan." *Le Monde*, March 8, 1985, p. 27.
Généalogies de l'auto-organisation. Cahiers du C.R.E.A., 8. Paris: Centre de
    recherche épistémologie et autonomie, 1985.
Gossman, Lionel. "Literature and Education." *New Literary History* 13
    (1982), 341–371.
Group µ. *A General Rhetoric.* Trans. P. Burrell and E. Slotkin. Baltimore:
    Johns Hopkins University Press, 1981.
Hassan, Ihab. *The Right Promethean Fire: Imagination, Science, and Cultural
    Change.* Urbana: University of Illinois Press, 1980.
Jakobson, Roman. "Linguistics and Communication Theory." In *Selected
    Writings*, vol. 2, 570–579. The Hague: Mouton, 1971.
Kuhn, Thomas S. *The Essential Tension: Selected Studies in Scientific
    Tradition and Change.* Chicago: University of Chicago Press, 1977.
———. *The Structure of Scientific Revolutions.* 2d edition. Chicago: University
    of Chicago Press, 1970.
Lacoue-Labarthe, Philippe, and Jean-Luc Nancy. *L'Absolu littéraire: Théorie
    de la littérature du romantisme allemand.* Paris: Seuil, 1978.
Livingston, P., ed. *Disorder and Order.* Proceedings of the Stanford
    International Symposium (Sept. 14–16, 1981). Stanford Literature Series,
    1. Stanford: Anma Libri, 1984.

Lotman, Jurij. *The Structure of the Artistic Text*. Trans. G. Lenhoff and R. Vroon. Michigan Slavic Contributions, 7. Ann Arbor: University of Michigan Department of Slavic Languages and Literature, 1977.

Lyotard, Jean-François. *The Postmodern Condition*. Trans. G. Bennington and B. Massumi. Minneapolis: University of Minnesota Press, 1984.

MacKay, Donald M. *Information, Mechanism and Meaning*. Cambridge: MIT Press, 1969.

Maturana, Humberto. "Biology of Language: The Epistemology of Reality." In *Psychology and Biology of Language and Thought: Essays in Honor of Eric Lenneberg*, ed. G. Miller and E. Lenneberg, 27–63. New York: Academic Press, 1978.

Maturana, Humberto R., and Francisco Varela. *Autopoiesis and Cognition: The Realization of the Living*. Boston Studies in the Philosophy of Science, 42. Dordrecht, Holland: D. Reidel, 1980.

———. *The Tree of Knowledge: The Biological Roots of Human Understanding*. Boston: New Science Library, 1987.

Moles, Abraham. *Information Theory and Esthetic Perception*. Trans. J. Cohen. Urbana: University of Illinois Press, 1966.

Monod, Jacques. *Le Hasard et la nécessité*. Paris: Seuil, 1970.

Morin, Edgar. *La Méthode*. Paris: Seuil. Vol. 1: *La Nature de la nature*, 1977. Vol 2: *La Vie de la vie*, 1980. Vol. 3: *La Connaissance de la connaissance/1*, 1986.

Polanyi, Michael. *Personal Knowledge: Towards a Post-Critical Philosophy*. Chicago: University of Chicago Press, 1958.

Prigogine, Ilya, and Isabelle Stengers. *La Nouvelle Alliance: Métamorphose de la science*. Paris: Gallimard, 1979. Revised and translated as *Order out of Chaos*. New York: Bantam Books, 1984.

Richards, I. A. *Science and Poetry*. New York: Norton, 1926.

Riffaterre, Michael. "Interpretation and Undecidability." *New Literary History* 12 (1980), 227–242.

Rorty, Richard. *Consequences of Pragmatism (Essays 1972–1980)*. Minneapolis: University of Minnesota Press, 1982.

———. "Deconstruction and Circumvention." *Critical Inquiry* 11 (1984), 1–24.

Saint-Amand, Pierre. *Diderot: Le Labyrinthe de la relation*. Paris: Vrin, 1984.

Schlanger, Jacques. *Une Théorie du savoir*. Paris: Vrin, 1978.

Schlanger, Judith. *L'Invention intellectuelle*. Paris: Fayard, 1983.

———. *Les Métaphores de l'organisme*. Paris: Vrin, 1971.

———. *Penser la bouche pleine*. The Hague: Mouton, 1975.

Serres, Michel. *Les Cinq Sens*. Paris: Grasset, 1985.

———. *Hermes: Literature, Science, Philosophy*. Ed. D. F. Bell and J. V. Harari. Baltimore: Johns Hopkins University Press, 1982.

———. *Hermès I: La Communication*. Paris: Minuit, 1968.

———. *Hermès III: La Traduction*. Paris: Minuit, 1974.

———. *Hermès IV: La Distribution*. Paris: Minuit, 1977.

——. *Hermès V: Le Passage du nord-ouest*. Paris: Minuit, 1980.

——. *Le Parasite*. Paris: Grasset, 1980. Translated as *The Parasite*. Trans. L. Schehr. Baltimore: Johns Hopkins University Press, 1982.

Servien, Pius. *Principes d'esthétique: Problèmes d'art et langage des sciences*. Paris: Boivin, 1935.

Shannon, Claude E., and Warren Weaver. *The Mathematical Theory of Communication*. Urbana: University of Illinois Press, 1949.

Snow, C. P. *The Two Cultures and the Scientific Revolution*. Cambridge: Cambridge University Press, 1959.

Stengers, Isabelle. "Découvrir la complexité?" In *Cognition et complexité*, 223–254.

——. "Les généalogies de l'auto-organisation." In *Généalogies de l'auto-organisation*, 7–104.

Thom, René. *Modèles mathématiques de la morphogenèse*. New ed. Paris: Christian Bourgois, 1980.

——. "Stop Chance! Silence Noise!" Trans. R. Chumbley. *SubStance*, no. 40 (1983), 11–21. With responses by Atlan, Morin, Prigogine, and others.

Thom, René, Claire Lejeune, and Jean-Pierre Duport. *Morphogenèse et imaginaire*. Circé: Cahiers de recherche sur l'imaginaire, 8–9. Paris: Lettres modernes, 1978.

Todorov, Tzvetan. *Critique de la critique: Un roman d'apprentissage*. Paris: Seuil, 1984.

——. *Théories du symbole*. Paris: Seuil, 1977.

Varela, Francisco. "Experimental Epistemology: Background and Future." In *Cognition et complexité*, 107–121.

——. *Principles of Biological Autonomy*. New York: Elsevier North-Holland, 1979.

Wiener, Norbert. *The Human Use of Human Beings: Cybernetics and Society*. Boston: Houghton Mifflin, 1950.

Wilden, Anthony. *System and Structure: Essays in Communication and Exchange*. London: Tavistock, 1972; 2d edition, 1980.

Index

Library of Congress Cataloging-in-Publication Data
Paulson, William R., 1955–
    The noise of culture.

    Bibliography: p.
    Includes index.
    1. Information theory in literature.   2. Criticism.
    3. Literature and science.   4. Knowledge, Theory of,
    in literature.   I. Title.
PN98.I54P38   1988   801   87-47822
ISBN 0-8014-2102-0 (alk. paper).